Jesus and the mystery of Christ

An extended Christology

Charles Hill

CollinsDove
A Division of HarperCollins*Publishers*

Published by Collins Dove
A Division of HarperCollins*Publishers* (Australia) Pty Ltd
22–24 Joseph Street
North Blackburn, Victoria 3130

First published 1993
Designed by William Hung
Cover design by William Hung

Typeset by Collins Dove Typesetting

The National Library of Australia
Cataloguing-in-Publication Data:

Hill, Charles, 1931–   .
   Jesus and the mystery of Christ.

   Includes bibliographies and index.
   ISBN 1 86371 162 7.

   1. Jesus Christ. 2. Jesus Christ — Person and offices.
   3. Mysteries, Religious. I. Title.

232

Acknowledgements
The Scripture quotations in this publication are from the New
Revised Standard Version of the Bible, copyrighted 1989 by the
Division of Christian Education of the National Council of the
Churches of Christ in the USA, and are used with permission.
All rights reserved.

Our thanks go to those who have given us permission to reproduce copyright material in
this book. Particular sources of print material
are acknowledged in the text.
Every effort has been made to contact the copyright holders of text material. The editor and
publisher apologise in those cases where
this had proved impossible.

Contents

Introduction

All good Christian theology is thoroughly traditional, as sound
Christian faith itself arises from solid contact with tradition. If my
faith is to be authentic, it must be a response to experience of God's
action in Jesus — not just my personal experience but as well the
community's experience mediated to me through forms of transmis-
sion, or tradition. Paul had his own special experience of the Lord, but
he still had to align that with the community's, as he admits (*Gal* 1.18).

Theology ponders the accents of the various traditional forms of
the community. In regard to God's action in Jesus that is the foundation of the community and its faith, *scriptural* tradition and other
forms present us with a double perspective: concentration on the
person, significance, life, ministry, Paschal Mystery of **Jesus**, and
on the whole divine plan, the mystery of **Christ**. What we may call
the Jesuological perspective occurs particularly in the Synoptic
Gospels, the more comprehensive Christological perspective in
Paul and also in John's Gospel. Outreach to the Gentiles in the early
Church found the Pauline perspective more helpful, while the
Gospels' later concentration on Jesus may be seen as some reaction
to this.

In succeeding ages both perspectives proved their usefulness.
Apologists seeking to uphold the reasonableness of Christian belief
alongside Jewish and pagan religions had recourse to the notion of
the divine Logos operating in people and things even before and
beyond their own community of Jesus. After Christianity's emer-
gence from persecution, theological debate and Council creeds
focused on the person of Jesus in all his uniqueness, an ontological emphasis different from the Scriptures' functional one. *Patristic* and *dogmatic* traditions thus exemplified the different perspectives available.

Throughout the ages of faith the narrower focus of the Jesuological perspective prevailed and determined the community's mission-

ary thrust. All who could were to be brought to faith in Jesus, no alternative Christology suggesting a different approach. The rise of Islam and the correlative prosecution of the Crusades lent a polemical character to mission and indiscriminate reference by either side to 'infidels'.

Only at Vatican II did the Catholic community come to acknowledge the validity of other religions and speak of their place in a divine plan in the manner of the Fathers. Since then, with developments in our postmodern world like Middle Eastern conflicts, the Gulf War and the reshaping of Europe and the USSR, we have come to a sharper awareness of those religions like Islam and Judaism, not to mention all the Asian religions, for whom salvation is not seen linked to the person of Jesus. Missioners have also reviewed their role within the wider Christological perspective.

As well, an ecological postmodern worldview has alerted us to our responsibility, as Christians and as citizens of the world, for planet Earth and all of the Universe (if not the whole of the universe beyond what we know). This responsibility comes to us not from the God of Abraham or even the Father of Jesus but from the God who created all things, and we share it with the Word, the Logos, through whom and for whom all things were made. Bhopal and Chernobyl, global warming and acid rain, famine and flood, AIDS and the Big C continue to demonstrate that our responsibility has to this point been imperfectly discharged. Where do we look for guidance — to that Christological perspective, the mystery and wisdom that is Christ?

These are questions that require an extended Christology for treatment, and life in the postmodern age demands a response. Our tradition in the community of those who follow Jesus as saviour provides us with the basis of a response as long as we take advantage of an adequate perspective that is available; unfortunately, many Christologies settle for being Jesuologies only, and the questions remain imperfectly answered. The fact that a growing two-thirds of the world's 5.4 billion people do not share our faith in Jesus urges us to try harder, as Paul and Justin had to break the mould in their day, without being false to faith.

A further incentive for a theologian living in the 'Southern Land of the Holy Spirit' (as early Portuguese explorers referred to Australia before ever reaching its shores) is the fact of Aboriginal presence here 45,000 years before Jesus came among the lost sheep of the house of Israel. The history of God's dealings with them, albeit unwritten, and their spiritual relationship with this Land suggest we do not ignore that wider canvas that escapes fuller treatment in our own community's scriptures, though hinted at there and in our other traditions.

Hence this book is written from that catholic perspective, seeking to take account of the religious traditions not just of the followers of Jesus but of other communities amongst whom the Logos has clearly been present. It is anticipated that its readers will largely be those who share with the author faith in Jesus as the Word of God coming and acting within the whole divine plan for all things that is the mystery of Christ. It endeavours to explore that relationship of person to mystery in the light both of faith and of our knowledge of the diversity and pluralism of the postmodern world, where the growing majority of people do not share that faith. Their situation cannot be a matter of no concern to us or to a proper Christology, nor can the welfare of the world that we do all share.

While the following chapters presume that readers have some acquaintance with Bible and theology, this is not a work for specialists. Its interest for the latter may lie in the perspectives adopted; scholarly detail has generally been kept out of sight. A glossary of traditional terms has been provided for those less familiar with the traditions. To render the material more user-friendly, each chapter begins with a brief summary of its general drift and closes with some points for discussion as well as suggestions for further reading. The biblical version employed, except where otherwise stated, is the New Revised Standard Version, of the Division of Christian Education of the National Council of the Churches of Christ in the United States of America, and is used with permission.

The book is dedicated to the students whom I have been fortunate enough to meet and work with over the years. Their faith, motivation and enquiring minds have stimulated me to ponder with them 'the boundless riches of Christ', a divine design for which the author of *Ephesians* understandably has to coin a neologism: *polypoikilos*, of a rich variety. May be all be graced to glimpse the many facets of the mystery of Christ.

Charles Hill

Abbreviations

AAS	*Acta Apostolicae Sedis*
ARCIC	Anglican-Roman Catholic International Commission
CCG	*Corpus Christianorum Graecorum*
CCL	*Corpus Christianorum Latinorum*
DS	Denzinger-Schoenmetzer, *Enchiridion Symbolorum*
Ep	*Epistula*
GCS	*Griechische Christliche Schriftsteller*
GS	*Gaudium et Spes* (Vatican II)
LG	*Lumen Gentium* (Vatican II)
(N)JBC	*(New) Jerome Biblical Commentary*
(N)RSV	(New) Revised Standard Version
NSW	New South Wales
NT	New Testament
OT	Old Testament
PG	*Patrologia Graeca*
PL	*Patrologia Latina*
SC	*Sources Chrétiennes*
WCC	World Council of Churches

1

Is it all a mystery?

Life in our postmodern age presents many new characteristics and poses many questions. It is an age of rapid change: globally aware, hi-tech, communications proficient, ecologically sensitive, egalitarian, pluralist in values and philosophies. There are recurring questions in this age about religion and religions, about history and its meaning, about the explanation the Bible offers, about my personal significance in it all. Can I relate Jesus to these changes and questions? Or is there a bigger picture in which all this makes sense?

A few years ago a friend of mine was accosted in a supermarket by a little old lady, like himself driving a shopping trolley. 'Young man,' she demanded unsmilingly, 'are you in favour of modern times?' My friend, naturally taken aback, felt that a negative response was expected of him. He felt equally that it would be un-appreciated if he were to offer any demur to the effect that there was little his preferences could do about it. It would likewise have been thought unhelpful if he had ventured the suggestion that, whatever of the shortcomings of modern times in which doubtless his aged interlocutor had lived, sociologists and historians assure us that now we are living in the postmodern age,[1] ushered in by the 'Great Wars' of this century and the changes they accelerated.

Irrespective of my friend's attitude to postmodernity or the little old lady's, the world of today gives rise in all of us to many questions that cry out for a solution. Those of us who are believers look to our faith for some of these solutions as an overall meaning system. God, our help in ages past, will be there to supply guidance in this postmodern age.

The postmodern age

It is certainly an age of rapid change; the little old lady was under-standably reeling under 'future shock', especially in that labyrinth of consumerism, the suburban supermarket, whose shelves speak eloquently of the superfluous appetites we have cultivated in our affluent First and Second Worlds. Conversely, and indeed consequently, our age knows also the poverty and starvation rife in underdeveloped countries, denuding their resources to keep our shelves full; the gap between their use of those resources and ours we admit is a scandal.

Their plight is not something we can ignore in this hi-tech, communications proficient, globally aware world of the late second millennium. We glimpse this and other inequities daily on our television screens, and are sensitive to privilege abused. The postmodern age is egalitarian in spirit, and rejoices to see walls crumble, boundaries disappear and unjust regimes fall to people power. It prizes pluralism above totalitarianism, if only through bitter experience; minorities — whether racial, sexual, religious — are increasingly allowed free expression, and the media ensure this exposure (at least where access is permitted, and this is not yet universal). East and West have come closer as former alliances weaken and new ones are formed; a rampant nationalism and introspective Europeanism could yet pose a new threat to world peace, not to mention the effect of rising trade barriers. The 'Third World' no longer exists if the Eastern bloc has disappeared; an impoverished 'South' may now receive less aid from the Haves of the 'North', who are diverting more of their surplus to needy eastern neighbours, the new poor.

Postmodern egalitarianism and pluralism extend beyond politics to values, religion, theology. For some, God may be dead, the secular city the norm, and materialism the prevailing ethic; certainly the world is predominantly non-Christian in religious allegiance and becoming more so. But the evidence is that, whatever of faith, religion is alive and well and increasingly ecumenical; representatives of world religions can meet in Assisi to pray together, and over three hundred Christian churches gather to discuss faith and witness, justice and service, education and renewal at the World Council of Churches (WCC) conference every few years. True, no longer can any one tradition legislate values and theologies; we have agreed to differ, at least within the limits of community faith. We know more of the positions and practices of other faith communities, in the post-Gulf War world particularly, so that the religious horizon of Christians can accommodate not only Judaism but now Islam, Hinduism, Buddhism and other Asian religions.

We know more also of our own planet and the Universe, even to the extent of discerning there 'the mind of God'.[2] We also know more of the planet's health and ours as the globe warms, forests fall, species disappear and resources dwindle. The atom bomb may not hang over us any longer, but we have yet to deal with plastic and spray can, not to mention drug abuse and diseases like cancer and AIDS. We are still pouring billions more into armaments than into aid for impoverished countries, whose life style suffers in the effort to meet repayments on their debts to us. The superpower of the day, after recent successes in space free of competition, plans to spend billions of dollars on a satellite city up there. We are learning more of the origins and future of the cosmos, and our own human origins; as Australians we appreciate the presence of aborigines on our continent perhaps 47,000 years ago,[3] even if we have yet to come to terms with their presence in our cities and towns in this millennium.

Yes, the ambiguous and kaleidoscopic developments in our lifetime can be confusing and give rise to questions about the meaning of it all. Faith tells us Providence is guiding the world created good and also redeemed, and guiding our own personal lives in particular; yet like Job in the Bible we can rail against the apparent injustice and inconsistency of this Providence, or in non-biblical terms demand like a modern psalmist, 'What's it all about, Alfie?' We look above all for meaning and the evidence of a guiding hand: can faith provide us with that?

Questions about religion

Our Christian religion should be able to enlighten us there — or what good is it? In the Catholic community expectations of an answer to life's problems have been heightened in the post-Vatican II church, which has had the benefit not only of that lengthy, in-depth review of Church life and teaching at the Council but also of periodic synodal statement from bishops meeting to discuss relevant topics. These statements as well a series of documents from recent popes and Roman curial bodies far outdid anything our forebears received by way of guidance from the Church's magisterium. For various reasons, however, particularly educational reasons, our ability to receive and assimilate all this teaching may not have improved; perhaps as a community we do not take advantage of the resources and instructional media that are normal for communication in other fields of postmodern life. As well as

3

that factor there is also the difficulty that some of these pronounce-
ments have apparently muddied the waters in the sense of bringing
division into the community, like the decisions on regulation of
birth and fertilisation, on liberation theology and on the
theologian's role generally.

Religion seems liable to that difficulty: where it should bring
clarity and peace, it can lead to division and hostility. In our age we
have witnessed and are witnessing wars and conflicts that at least
to some extent involve religious affiliation: in Yugoslavia, Northern
Ireland, India, Sudan, Israel, among the Arab states. Killing one
another in the name of God did not cease with the Crusades. How
could that be part of any divine design? One could be forgiven for
concluding that religion, far from having an uplifting effect on
people's lives, Christians included, encourages antipathy and bar-
barism. Dietrich Bonhoeffer, pastor in a Christian church during the
Second World War, reached this conclusion from his experiences in
prison in his own Germany:

> The thing that keeps coming back to me is, what *is* Christianity, and in-
> deed what *is* Christ for us today? ... We are proceeding towards a time
> of no religion at all: men as they are now cannot be religious any more.
> Even those who honestly describe themselves as 'religious' do not in
> the least act up to it, and so when they say 'religious' they evidently
> mean something quite different ...
>
> How can Christ become the Lord even of those with no religion? If
> religion is no more than the garment of Christianity — and even that
> garment has had very different aspects at different periods — then
> what is a religionless Christianity?[4]

Bonhoeffer's notion of a 'religionless Christianity' appeals to
many people for a variety of reasons, including those who conscien-
tiously wish to follow Christ but find Christianity gets in the way.
The division within Christianity between the churches is still a
notorious problem and scandal, despite the considerable recent efforts to repair it. Not only have the 'sister churches' (in Paul VI's
phrase to Patriarch Athenagoras) of East and West been at odds for
a millennium, but the Christendom we westerners know is
blemished with almost innumerable divisions and antipathies that
history has entrenched. How can we speak any longer of the Christian *Church*, the one body of Christ? What sort of understanding,
what theology of Church can accommodate all this division and
diversity? Should we look for a divine design operating here too?

4

Or should we Catholics just press on doing the Catholic thing, warts and all?

After all, 'outside the Church no salvation' — and that must mean at least the Catholic Church; it was St Cyprian in the third century who said so, and he must have been a Catholic, being a bishop. So if salvation is assured for good Catholics (though Cyprian doesn't quite say as much), what of all those others — is there no salvation for them? Or does the saying mean all Christian churches? In that case, what of all the non-Christians, who today constitute the vast majority of the world's population, a majority that is not diminishing — have they no way of salvation? The New Testament tells us God wants everyone to be saved (1 Tm 2.4): does that mean they all have to join the Christian church(es), to become followers of Jesus? Does that seem a realistic possibility for those three or four billion people who follow the way of Judaism, Islam, Buddhism, Hinduism, Confucianism and all those other religions? Is that the basis for operation of Catholic missionary endeavour — to bring these people a way of salvation because they have none as they are? If so, no wonder John Paul II sounds very concerned in his recent encyclical on Catholic missionary activity, *Redemptoris Missio*:

> As the end of the second millennium of the Redemption draws near, it is clear that the peoples which have not yet received the initial proclamation of Christ constitute the majority of mankind.[5]

And the Pope proceeds to urge further effort to found new churches. Is that the way to go? Can we hope to make a significant impact on that vast and growing mass of non-Christian people? Is there some other way to view this problem of their salvation in God's overall design? Do we have first to come to a decision about true and false religions, a risky judgment, or may we think of ways to salvation in all religions? Where does that leave St Cyprian: are these people within the Church if they find salvation?

In our multicultural, multifaith societies today this is a question that arises not only in the studies of theologians and pastors; our sons and daughters could be marrying into Jewish or Moslem families and raising our grandchildren in those traditions. Where can we turn to for the answer?

The meaning of history

Perhaps from time to time we have questions as well about the whole of human history, not simply the diversity of religions that have developed at different times. If we fought in a war or lost loved ones, for instance, the question must come: what's it all for? Again we search, sometimes in vain, for the evidence of that guiding hand of a Providence. Our multimedia postmodern society forces us to confront the large scale massacres of a Pol Pot, or the thousands of starving children in an African famine, or the huge loss of life in annual monsoonal floods, storms and volcanic eruptions. Is all this part of a pattern we should be able to read? Does life itself have any purpose?

The lifetime of many of us has included a Hiroshima and a Nagasaki, and more recently a Chernobyl, to convince us that Voltaire was right to discourage us from believing we live in the best of all possible worlds. We have difficulty perhaps in sharing the evolutionary optimism of a Teilhard de Chardin, who found evidence of the gradual divinisation of the world, and we wonder at the naivety of his positive evaluation of hydrogen bomb testing at the Bikini atoll: 'For all their military trappings, the recent explosions at Bikini herald the birth into the world of Mankind both inwardly and outwardly pacified. They proclaim the coming of the *Spirit of the Earth.*' [6] Since Teilhard's death in 1955 we have seen so many major conflicts, including the massive destruction of life and property in the Gulf War, that we have greater difficulty than he had in discerning a heartening pattern of world evolution.

For many of the Jewish people that pattern was shattered with the Holocaust, the *Shoah*, and for them faith in a provident God was lost beyond recall. How could Yahweh have so deserted them after all his promises to a chosen people? In his novel *The Gift of Asher Lev* Chaim Potok represents his central character discussing the movie *Au Revoir Les Enfants*, about Jewish children killed in the Holocaust, with his wife Devorah, who had barely escaped the same fate herself by being sealed up for two years in a Paris apartment. Distraught after this reminder of her ordeal, she asks Asher whatever he saw in her at their first meeting.

'That she let me draw her face after the interview.'
'That was a good drawing, and I did like it.'
'And I was able to see her as my wife and the mother of our children.'
'I would have been the mother of many more if there had not been the miscarriages.'
'That is God's will, my wife.'
'Is it? Is it? Why couldn't it have been God's will for at least one person in my family to survive? I would have someone of my own blood to

talk to about what happened.'

I held her. She was trembling.

'Isn't it strange that I can't remember what we ate? Two years of eating in that sealed apartment, and I can't remember a single meal. Asher, I am not sorry we saw the movie. It's a fine movie. Even though sometimes, sitting in a dark theater, I suddenly remember the dark apartment. If it's all God's will, my husband, there must be a plan. Don't you think there must be a plan?'

'Who knows? Maybe there's a plan.' [7]

Many people, without Devorah's personal ordeal, struggle through life's ups and downs to see a plan in human history without ever discerning it. What a pity.

Bible, help or hindrance?

The Jewish people and other believers, of course, have the advantage of a divine word revealing that plan to them in their scriptures — provided they can recognise it there. That proviso, unfortunately, affects many Jewish and Christian readers of their scriptures; there is what the biblical scholars call a hermeneutical problem, the difficulty of interpreting the writings correctly and seeing meaning there. Of course, we can all open the Hebrew Bible or the Christian Bible at any place and put our finger on a text — but that is not to find the total pattern: a classic case of not seeing the wood for the trees. We acknowledge this difficulty in the proverb, 'The devil himself can quote Scripture.' And people, theologians no less frequently than others, have often fallen short of the purpose of the revealing Word by listing a series of texts to support a point of their own making — 'prooftexts', we call them, as distinct from the overall, integral statement of biblical revelation, finding which takes rather more work and much more detachment. The scriptures of any religious tradition are open to this misinterpretation.

In the Christian tradition we should be able to turn to the Bible and find an account of God's dealings with the world and its people, composed though it has been through the very parochial vision of its human authors, who filter the message of the divine author. We expect this human, incarnational character in the case of the Bible, as we do with anything where the divine and human come together; but it makes the process of discernment that much more challenging. Jesus had occasion at least twice to lecture his lis-

teners on hermeneutics and upbraid them for failure to get behind
the text for the message — in *John* 5 in speaking to a Jerusalem
audience and in *Luke* 24 to the two disciples on the way to Emmaus,
disillusioned through failure to read the Scriptures aright. To both
audiences he gave the same advice: get behind the individual text
to the overall pattern, and you'll see my significance there. That
will dispel disillusionment — and God knows we can do with that.

As with so many human, incarnational realities like the Scriptures, however, following that advice is not so simple. We recall the
incident of the Ethiopian eunuch in *Acts* 8, lover of Judaism to the
extent not only of travelling to Jerusalem to worship but of endeavouring to read the text of *Isaiah* during the return journey,
'seated in his chariot' on the bumpy road to Gaza — surely an
index of devotion. When the deacon Philip at the instance of the
Spirit approached and asked how he was doing with the task of
grasping that difficult text, the eunuch replied, 'How can I understand unless someone shows me the way?' That reaction to the
biblical text must be true for most readers; they require mentors
who can guide them in finding the pattern that underlies the great
number and variety of biblical writings, affected by the ancient
manner of composition and the culture and purposes of the composers, not to mention later editors' adjustments.

At least the eunuch, already endowed with good will, had also
the good fortune to fall in with an informed and skilful guide who
could set the one song of the Suffering Servant being read by the
neophyte within the whole pattern of revelation; the result was
faith and baptism, so that the eunuch 'went on his way rejoicing.'
Not all of us in our questions and doubts about life's purpose feel
inclined to take up the revealed Word to find there an answer; and
if we do, not always do we meet the kind of guide that Philip was,
patient and informed. Unfortunately, in the Catholic community
the opportunity to find this kind of guidance in reading the Scriptures is not always ready to hand.[8] When we do come across reading or personal direction, it is not uncommon to find that our
mentors are content to settle for part of the whole — individual
texts (even Gospels or psalms or other texts) instead of the whole
picture that Jesus required his listeners to study. Even good
scholars can choose to read only 'a canon within the canon', a selection of favourite material instead of the whole Bible, and so we get
an unbalanced picture. Not only Catholic readers suffer this potential hazard in reading their sacred scriptures, of course, but also Or-

thodox, Protestants, Jews, and members of other religions of the book.

Here is an example of this blinkered approach to reading of a Bible which should in its totality give us such enlightenment on the way God wants us to live our life in the world. In Biblical scholarship, as in most other human endeavours, fashions change. For many years it was fashionable to concentrate on historical traditions in the Old Testament and even in the New, so that other Biblical material escaped attention. One such area of neglect was that kind of reflection on life and its problems that we call Wisdom material, as in books like *Proverbs* and *Job* and parts of the New Testament. The historians in their myopia found this material quaint but irrelevant, though we have since come to see that Jesus is very much a Wisdom figure for his contact with real life. The great contribution that the sapiential, or Wisdom, material in the Bible made was to provide a really universal perspective, including all of creation and not simply one people's historical recollections about themselves. Solomon, the paradigmatic wise man, spoke, like Jesus after him, 'of beasts, and of birds, and of reptiles, and of fish' (*1 Kings* 4.33). The sages, Wisdom composers, saw that all of life falls under the guiding hand of Providence (they pointedly refrained from speaking of the God of Abraham, Isaac and Jacob), who is interested in all peoples and all things.

The healthiness of the sages' universal, this-worldly perspective, as of Jesus', has much to say of our life in a good if imperfect world; Law and Prophets can take us only so far and often fail to reach us where we live. Yet our guides in reading and listening to what should be a revealing Word in the Scriptures often fail to mediate this to us. They could also help us by bringing into focus not only the whole Bible but also something of the other accounts of people's experience of God that do not fall within the covers of our Bible: who is bold enough to say that God has spoken only to Jews and Christians? Not I.

My life in the cosmos

We do not have all the answers to life's questions, to the mystery that is life. Even if we take stock of the sages' and psalmists' meditations on all creation, we are still left to ponder what they could not have known — the immensity of the cosmos that surrounds us in our solar system within but one (albeit mighty) galaxy in hundreds of thousands of such mighty stellar seas. The very thought of it —

9

and we don't often call it to mind — both highlights our relative insignificance as a race on this tiny planet and yet lends each of us great dignity as the object of personal care of the provident Creator. We know now, as the sages did not, that this universe has existed for thousands of millions of years and is midway through its life, that human life in our country stretches back to those Aboriginal inhabitants who have left us relics on the banks of the Nepean River, long before the birth of Jesus and before the European civilisation and Christian religion that ventured to set their mark here a mere two centuries ago. The Columbus quincentenary has led others to similar reflection. It makes you think, doesn't it: what is my life all about in such a vast context? What mark can I leave? What difference will my life make when the universe is cooling right down in another ten thousand million years?

What I can do, of course, is to lead my life on this good earth with as much awareness of that vast historical and cosmic context of my daily minutiae as I can salvage from a busy yet humdrum existence. Can I recognise its significance and insignificance together? Can I discern again something of that underlying pattern to which Jesus directed us and which science now documents? Am I content with the mundane realities of a this-worldly existence of which Solomon and Jesus both spoke, or do I hanker after some release into other-worldly concerns, a flight from the world and painful, incarnational ways to God so as to arrive at a New Age (and ancient Gnosticism) where astrology replaces the down-to-earth acceptance of our limitations? Caring for our human needs and also for our planet while at the same time keeping a sense of our spiritual destiny requires no mean sense of balance; St Augustine might have done us a further service in writing a companion volume to *The City of God*, attentive though he was to that equally elliptical verse from *Hebrews*, 'We have not here a lasting city but must seek one that is to come' (13.14). What chance do we mere mortals have to live life aright in this city, the City of Man, which sages and psalmists and *Genesis* composers assure us is good, ay, very good, for all its imperfections, which we should be working to repair.

The mystery of Christ

Is it all a mystery, then, life in this postmodern age? Well, yes and no. There are plenty of problems and unanswered questions — about religion and religions, Church and the churches, history and its meaning, the Bible and its message, the universe and its origins and future, spirit and matter, City of God and City of Man, and my personal significance in it all. And there is a shortage of informed guides, if no shortage of gurus, to pick out the underlying pattern for us.

But there is a pattern, an underlying design, the 'plan' that Potok's character hungered for to give sense to devastation. We know this intuitively, Jesus told his disciples and others to look for it, and faith provides us with it. Paradoxically, the pattern behind the confusion is a mystery, the mystery of Christ. This book will proceed to unravel the paradox, to outline the mystery which is Christ and the way it gathers up all our questions and offers a solution to our problems.

'The mystery of Christ' is a term which comes to us from the Pauline letters in the New Testament with some indebtedness to earlier Jewish (Aramaic) usage. It occurs more than a dozen times in the letters as a way of speaking of that pattern, design, plan (Paul uses also 'will', 'purpose', 'wisdom' as other synonyms) which helps him understand what was for him in his Jewishness the supreme paradox, a divine choice reaching also to the Gentiles, the basis of his ministry in his new community.

> Surely you have already heard of the commission of God's grace that was given me for you, and how the mystery was made known to me by revelation, as I wrote above in a few words, a reading of which will enable you to perceive my understanding of the mystery of Christ. In former generations this mystery was not made known to humankind, as it has now been revealed to his holy apostles and prophets by the Spirit: that is, the Gentiles have become fellow heirs, members of the same body, and sharers in the promise in Christ Jesus through the gospel (*Eph* 3.2–6).

This extraordinary plan, 'mystery', Paul can never quite digest, meditate on it though he does so frequently. It is a plan in operation 'before the foundation of the world', reaching its climax in the Paschal Mystery (that same usage again, not Paul's but of the Church in our day) of the death and resurrection of Jesus (or Christ Jesus), and continuing on to the eschaton. Paul concentrates on the mystery affecting Church membership, but sees as well the whole universe and all of history coming within its compass, and my place and yours in it, too.

The mystery of Christ, God's design for all he created, includes all those aspects of the postmodern age, or any age, that give rise to questions in us, and provides the basis for response. We shall have

11

to take them one by one and consider each within the mystery. This is an exercise in Christology, in relating all things to Christ as mystery, including the person of Jesus; we saw Paul doing it briefly above, speaking of how it was through Jesus and his Gospel that the converts became fellow heirs and sharers in a plan that had long been the object of promise but not recognised in its entirety.

Questions about Jesus

That relationship of Jesus to the mystery of Christ, to God's whole design, has not always been clear. There are, of course, in our age billions of believers who do not share the views of Christians on this. Who was Jesus? Who is Jesus? Paul does not speak of Jesus as a mystery, because he reserves the word for that divine plan and purpose, but Jesus was literally a stumbling block for him and has been for many people, even within the Christian community.

To prevent this happening to us we have to keep asking, what does the community's tradition say of Jesus? How have his first followers transmitted their experience of him to us? Only in that way — aligning our experience of Jesus with the foundational community's experience — will our faith reflect the community's faith. Paul himself did that after his personal experience on the way to Damascus; extraordinarily personal and authentic though that experience was, he still felt the need to spend time with Peter getting details of Jesus the community possessed that filled out his private revelation.[9]

So for authentic faith in Jesus we turn to the community's tradition of its experience of God's action in Jesus; sound theology does the same. The community offers us this service in various forms: in its scriptures (themselves depending on word of mouth); in its liturgy, or worship, including music and the arts; in its teaching, or doctrine, or dogma (magisterium); in its preaching, or homiletics; in its catechesis; in the lived experience of the community; and in other forms — all are ways of 'passing on what is of first importance' about Jesus, as Paul said of this process to the Corinthians (1 Cor 15.3).

All of this evidence of community tradition about Jesus we can bring together and study to form our own picture. But there is more to Jesus than material for study; like Paul we all have our own experience of him from other sources, such as prayer and meditation and other forms of religious experience, and from others' accounts of their experience of him akin to biblical accounts, helping us determine, Who is Jesus for me? To ensure our faith is the faith of the community we have already, by reference to tradition, determined who is Jesus for them/us. A book like Jaroslav Pelikan's *Jesus through the Centuries. His Place in the History of Culture*[10] provides us with a series of images found appropriate and authentic at different periods for different people, as does John O'Grady's *Models of Jesus*[11]. Here we find Jesus as The Rabbi, as The Light of the Gentiles, The King of Kings, The Son of Man, The Bridegroom of the Soul, The Liberator, The Human Face of God etc. To these Anton Wessels adds the perceptions of Jesus by Moslems and Jews and images of Jesus from non-European cultures: Victor, Chief, Ancestor, Healer (from African cultures, for example).[12] These images and models may help us to understand Jesus and relate to him, as they have helped others.

Jesus in history

Pelikan's survey at least demonstrates that people have seen Jesus differently at different points in history. How does the postmodern age see him, how do we see him? Much contemporary theology, in keeping with the egalitarian tenor of the age, sees him as a liberator, enunciating a policy at the beginning of his ministry in *Luke* 4 that sits well with those of his followers endeavouring to lead others from oppression. Films like *The Mission* highlight this dimension while also allowing that others of his followers recognise another role in him. He has also been seen as a superstar in our time, though at least Mark's Gospel in his time endeavoured to dispel that impression.

Everybody (who knows of him) would concede that the person and teaching of Jesus represent a significant moment in human history. His followers see his coming as the focal point of that history, though we admit that most of the human race does not see things that way; for them history is not 'Before Christ' and 'Anno Domini': 'Before the Common Era' (BCE) and 'Common Era' (CE) is about as far as they are prepared to go. It is helpful to recognise that alternative vision, particularly for us Australians, who prize the fact that the Aboriginal people were in residence here well before Jesus came among us, not to mention the thousands of millions of years of the world's existence. Can we situate Jesus meaningfully within that vast extent of cosmic and human history? Then think also of the billions of people who have followed Jesus into this world and have passed out again without knowledge of him, and of those yet

13

to do so: what does this say of Jesus, his meaning, his mission?

Does the Bible help us much here? How does it see Jesus' significance? We Christians have a Bible that is divided into two: part before Jesus' coming, part after, suggesting again that notion of the Incarnation as the focal point of human history. Living at the close of the second millennium AD we see a certain symmetry in a biblical pattern that began with the patriarchs at the opening of the second millennium BC. Does the symmetry look a little tattered if we refer to that larger context we mentioned before, of a universe beginning billions of years ago and of human beings (not coming within our narrow biblical perspective) living in our land all those thousands of years ago, and of the thousands of years and billions of people lying ahead of our time (in God's providence)? Can we concede that the Bible, with its particular theological perspectives (for they are multiple), has bracketed out so much of human and world history? Perhaps the biblical picture is a distractor if we allow ourselves to be contained within its timeline and dimensions, theologically instructive though they may be. At any rate, to assess Jesus' full significance we may need at times to lift him out of the biblical context, or at least attend to those voices that try to set the wider context, like Paul's; the evangelists are too busy with the small picture to do that.

What, in fact, has been the impact of Jesus on world history and the peoples of the world since the beginning? Pelikan's list of images of Jesus includes The Turning Point of History, The Prince of Peace, The Liberator, The Man Who Belongs to the World. With a growing two-thirds of the world's population even today practically unaware of him, let alone following his person and teaching, perhaps these are partial interpretations. History, they say, is written by the victors, and those civilisations that owe allegiance to Jesus doubtless represent him differently from others: do we know those others' interpretations of him and his impact on their world? Who is Jesus to a Hindu, or a Moslem, or a Buddhist?

Jesus in the Church

It is no surprise that Jesus is not recognised universally for his significance; his followers themselves have interpreted him and his teaching differently and have gone their separate ways — in faith, theology and religion. Instead of seeing one Church encompassing all his followers, the world is presented with a number of churches claiming to represent Jesus and doing so differently, while invoking one form of original tradition or another, and perhaps excluding others of his followers from membership or at least intercommunion. It is enough to raise the question as to whether the founder of all the churches is the same person, and whether he could inspire all the diverse theologies and practices. Can the one Church accommodate all these churches and theologies? Is this the Church outside of which there is no salvation? Or only one of these? How identify it? If all profess faith in Jesus, is it the same faith?

All the followers of Jesus are united in believing one thing: he it is who has brought them salvation. To the question 'Are you saved?' each can answer in the affirmative, whether the participle be aorist, perfect, or present. Each of the churches is built on that truth and operates to mediate that salvation in Jesus. As we have seen, from the time of Cyprian there has been no such unanimity about the salvation of others. The Christian Scriptures themselves are ambiguous: it is the will of the omnipotent God that everyone is saved (1 Tm 2.4), and yet Jesus himself is heard saying, 'The gate is wide and the road is easy that leads to destruction, and there are many who take it' (Mt 7.13).

Those others do not see themselves as dependent on Jesus for salvation of one kind or another; they have developed their own ways to it. His followers, on the other hand, seem not to recognise the validity of those ways, and have from the beginning mounted great missionary efforts to bring the peculiarly Jesuan kind of salvation to Jews and 'pagans'. The egalitarian spirit of the postmodern age discourages them to some extent, as well as a wider appreciation of the riches of other religions. The question resurfaces: how vital is Jesus for religions who owe him no special allegiance? Judaism and Islam recognise his existence, but in no way see him as their saviour. Is there a way to God besides Jesus? Is there a plan, a mystery, capable of bringing salvation to all those Aboriginal people living in the Southern Land of the Holy Spirit long before the birth and death of Jesus? Should we be directing our energies to bringing Jesus to those billions of people following other ancient ways to God, or instead help them and ourselves to discern the wider plan, the mystery of Christ, operating in their lives and cultures as well? Should our accent fall on Christianity in this way rather than on Jesuanity? Or are we thus capitulating before the impossibility of the numbers, in a losing battle, admitting that the world can never be made Jesuan, only Christian (in the way some of the early Fathers, confronting a pagan world, saw the task)?

The choice, an agonising one for pastors feeling responsible for everyone, is open to theological clarification, as it was for the Fathers; we shall attempt to achieve it in the course of this book. In the meantime, we are encouraged to take the 'soft option' (which, however, means adopting the more comprehensive perspective) by Jesus himself, who we recall rarely mentioned the word 'Church', did not set conditions for membership, or insist on baptism or contribution to Peter's Pence. What he did insist on, over and over and over again, was God's value system, his way of running the world, his *basileia* ('kingdom' not so helpful a translation, generally); where he saw it he commended it, where it was lacking he said so, tried to implement it and died in the process. Is there a way of bringing Jesus' teaching, God's plan or mystery for all things and peoples, and Church of salvation together so as to accommodate all within our 'Christian' perspective?

Jesus and the cosmos

You see, it is not easy to relate Jesus to those 'all things': what is the significance of Jesus for our solar system and galaxy and all those other galaxies that have been in existence for millions of years and may be for as long again? In our ecologically sensitive age, does Jesus in the Gospels have anything to say about the ecosystem and conservation, about rainforests and the whales? Not much; he is too busy teaching us about our salvation. After all, he earned his name on that score: the angel told Joseph, 'Call him Jesus (Greek form of Yeshua=Yawheh saves), for he shall save *his people* from their sins' (*Mt* 1.21) — nothing about the environment.

At least Jesus is in touch with the material world and happy with it. A greater than Solomon, he teaches of birds and foxes, fig trees and lilies of the field, good wine and bad fruit — a real Wisdom figure. In Jesus, spirit and matter are not at war; he does not struggle to slough off his humanity as though a burden or, as in the gnostic *Hymn of the Pearl*, a soiled garment. But does that mean we can see him as the highpoint of the evolution of the cosmos? Has the world got better since his time? Are there signs that this is the messianic age, the end of the ages? In what way is the whole world redeemed in Jesus? How do we relate Jesus, our companion on planet Earth, to our whole galaxy and other galaxies? Did he live and die just for us, or for any living beings on other planets?

Jesus for me

Amid all this speculation, my primary task is to develop a relationship with Jesus myself. What does Jesus mean to me, a follower of his, a Jesuan in the way others do not wish to be? Is he friend, or lord, saviour, or refuge, model, teacher, spouse, challenge, foe, or critic — or none of the above because unknown, irrelevant, unnecessary? Am I so out of touch with 'Jesuan' tradition — in the Scriptures, in liturgical celebration, in the lived experience of the Jesuan community — and so out of touch with him in my self-centred daily life that Jesus doesn't really mean anything to me? Or, as many of his followers are able, can I say, 'I have met the Lord Jesus. He is my personal saviour'?

About seven years ago, when I moved into a new home and had to get someone in to repair my heater, Bob came and began to do the job. We chatted, and his first question was not 'May I have a cup of tea' or 'What are you going to pay me?' but 'What's the Catholic position on personal salvation?' Bob was a charismatic, on good terms with the Lord Jesus. His question, a perfectly natural one for him if not what you expect from your Aussie tradesman, had me on the defensive, strangely, as I tried to explain that it was not the kind of question Catholics normally ask, that salvation for Catholics was generally thought of as a package deal, that it came along with a series of duties and obligations and rituals, and was not considered separately. I'm sure I disappointed Bob, who expected something in terms of meeting the Lord Jesus; but he still invited me to the local charismatic group meetings. He certainly set me thinking as to why a personal relationship with Jesus was something I was not accustomed to think or speak about, at least not in those terms. Should it have been? Can I say I have met the Lord Jesus? Does my markedly ritualistic Catholic style of worship give me the opportunity to formalise and verbalise my faith in Jesus, or is it all too mechanical? Is Catholic life just too much a matter of habit? When do we get the chance to express our faith in Jesus?

Why, at our interchurch meetings, do I envy my Protestant friends their ability to pray aloud and invoke the name of Jesus? As far as I remember my upbringing clearly, we did not use the name of Jesus much in home and school; reverence for 'the Holy Name' was stressed to the extent that Jesus was rarely mentioned, being replaced by 'Christ' or 'Our Lord', and when used at all it had to be accompanied with a bow of the head, so better avoided. The result was that 'Jesus' had a Protestant ring about it for me, perhaps ac-

17

centuated by the fact that the Scriptures (which meant the Gospels almost solely in my youth) employ it frequently, and that proved it was Protestant! Another consequence of this usage, for me and I think many Catholics, has been to employ Christ and Jesus interchangeably as though identical in import, unlike Matthew's angel.

Jesus and the mystery of Christ

Paul, too, as we have seen, saw a highly significant distinction between the person of Jesus and the mystery of Christ, even if 'Paul' is not to be applied univocally to all the Pauline letters (as we appreciate in dealing with ancient, and some modern, literature) and if the apostle is not consistent in his usage of Jesus, Christ, Christ Jesus. The distinction enables him to deal with the whole divine plan operating 'from before the foundation of the world' and situate within that design the coming and especially the Paschal Mystery of Jesus (whom other New Testament writings will call Son of the Most High, the Christ, Word, Son of the living God, Lord) — and place all else within that design, too.

In other words, for Paul it *is* all a mystery, the mystery of Christ, 'a plan for the fulness of time, to gather up all things in him, things in heaven and things on earth' (*Eph* 1.10). There is no doubt of the totality, utter comprehensiveness of that plan; Asher Lev's wife Devorah might well have taken *Ephesians* into that sealed apartment with her and read it every day for her sanity and comfort — as we might if ever we have a (forced) time of retreat. No single thing falls outside that design; every item is gathered up — even Jesus himself. The author of the letter (whether Paul himself or a disciple) does not use words idly; the neuter 'things' is used and repeated deliberately, if only to offset the human bias of Matthew's angel. Even more significant is that verb which the NRSV renders 'gather up'. In Greek it is a compound of the word for 'head', and means literally 'to head up', originally of a builder who caps off an archway with the final stabilising stone, the keystone (what a wonderful figure for Jesus, capping off the beautiful divine design so long in the making), and then figuratively of an orator or barrister summing up an argument. The meaning is that within the mystery of Christ every single thing, person, event in history and the cosmos come together, make sense, are united, gathered up, capped off, summed up.

It is a wonderful concept, which we shall shortly examine for its roots and significance; Paul did not stumble on it all by himself. It

18

enables him to come to grips with all those questions which confront us. From time to time thinkers, scientists, theologians, struggling to do justice to the whole of reality, come up with a notion that breaks through previous limitations and more adequately explains what our senses and experience tell us. Copernicus and Newton, for instance, each crossed a frontier (not without resistance from contemporaries) and enabled us to make more sense of the forces of the universe. Paul of Tarsus, 'advanced in Judaism beyond many among my people' (*Gal* 1.14) and yet called to mission among all other peoples, hoping as well that the creation itself would be freed from its bondage to decay (*Rom* 8.21), also crossed a barrier to achieve insight into the whole divine design, the mystery of Christ.

For one thing, he was thus able to understand Jesus better, locating him within a context already well conned to some extent from Jewish upbringing; Luke represents him doing just this for fellow Jews in the synagogue in Pisidian Antioch (*Acts* 13), whereas for members of the Areopagus in Athens the mystery of Christ is presented differently (*Acts* 17) before, in both cases, the resurrection of Jesus is introduced. For one audience the biblical dimension of the mystery of Christ is appreciable; for the other this would make little sense and so a more cosmic setting is outlined by reference not to the God of Abraham but 'the God who made the world and everything in it.'

This task is ours, too: to relate Jesus to the mystery of Christ, as the title of this book suggests. It has been the task of his followers ever since Jesus' coming, from Paul, a Jew among Gentiles, from the early Fathers, endeavouring to interpret the divine design to Jews and pagans unaccepting of the teaching of Jesus to his own yet amenable to the bigger picture in which they themselves figured, to medieval theologians indebted to philosophers coming to God from different directions, up to pastors and teachers and believers in this postmodern age wrestling with its problems. Does the solution to all these problems lie directly in Jesus of Nazareth, or for some of them do we have to fall back on that bigger picture, the whole mystery of Christ?

Can we hope to bring all people to recognise God's action in Jesus and become his followers, or is our task rather to assist them to see God's plan gathering up all things in heaven and on earth in the mystery of Christ? Will the disillusioned and disheartened members of God's various chosen peoples, in the wake of modern and postmodern cataclysms, fall at the feet of Jesus, or rather thrill to read again the pattern of a life-giving plan in their own histories? The splitting of the atom, a man on the moon, the conquest of space: of significance for Jesus, or only within the mystery of Christ? Can we expect the whole of human and cosmic history to make sense merely in terms of the mystery of Christ, or does the person and work of Jesus bear on it all directly and give it a pattern? Are the scriptures of Jesus and his forebears alone revealing of that pattern, or may we turn to all the writings that describe peoples' experience of God? Does the Church in which salvation is found include only the followers of Jesus, or has God in his ages-long economy offered life and love to all? Can my daughter or my son who has abandoned that Jesuan community and its ways of grace expect to find a way home along paths not known to me?

Yes, it's all a mystery — thank God.

Points for discussion

1. Are there times when you fail to make sense of life in the postmodern age? Which features of today's world most tax your ability to find a meaningful synthesis?

2. Politicians have spoken of a New World Order in the wake of the collapse of Communism. Do you recognise it in operation? Does it square with the requirements of our tradition?

3. The third millennium of the Christian era approaches, and yet the world remains largely unresponsive to Jesus. Is there an explanation for this? Should the situation be different?

4. Devorah in Chaim Potok's novel looked in vain for 'a plan' to decipher life's injustices. Should she have been able to find one — in her own tradition, or in yours?

Further reading

C. Birch, *On Purpose*, Sydney: University of NSW Press, 1990.

D. Bonhoeffer, *Letters and Papers from Prison*, Eng. trans., London: Fontana, 1953.

P. Davies, *The Mind of God. The Scientific Basis for a Rational World*, New York: Simon and Schuster, 1992.

H. Küng, *Global Responsibility. In Search of a New World Ethic* (1990), Eng. trans., New York: Crossroad, 1991.

J. Pelikan, *Jesus Through the Centuries. His Place in the History of Culture*, New York: Harper and Row, 1987.

Notes

1. So Arnold Toynbee. Cf Hans Küng, *Global Responsibility. In Search of a New World Ethic* (1990), Eng. trans., New York: Crossroad, 1991, p. 140.

   Templeton Prize winner Charles Birch, under the influence of David Griffin, defines the postmodern worldview: 'As contrasted with the modern worldview which is sustained more by habit than conviction and which has promoted ecological despoliation, militarism, antifeminism and disciplinary fragmentation, the postmodern worldview is postmechanistic and ecological in its view of nature, postreductionist in its view of science, postanthropocentric in its view of ethics and economics, postdiscipline in its relation to knowledge and postpatriarchal and postsexist in relation to society' (*On Purpose*, Sydney: NSW Uni. Press, 1990, p. xvi).

2. A phrase of mathematician Stephen Hawking (concluding his *A Brief History of Time*) taken as the title for his 1992 book, subtitled *The Scientific Basis for a Rational World*, by mathematical physicist Paul Davies (New York: Simon and Schuster). Davies concludes: 'Through my scientific work I have come to believe more and more strongly that the physical universe is put together with an ingenuity so astonishing that I cannot accept it merely as a brute fact. There must, it seems to me, be a deeper level of explanation. Whether one wishes to call that deeper level "God" is a matter of taste and definition' (16). Davies himself does not 'subscribe to a conventional religion.'

3. Such are the findings of archeologists based on the discovery of Aboriginal artefacts dated between 40,000 and 47,000 years old on the basis of radiocarbon and therminoluminescence tests (Gerald C. Nanson, Robert W. Young, Eugene D. Stockton, 'Chronology and palaeoenvironment of the Cranebrook Terrace (near Sydney) containing artefacts more than 40,000 years old,' *Archeology in Oceania*, 22 [1987] pp. 72–78).

4. D. Bonhoeffer, *Letters and Papers from Prison*, Eng. trans., London: Fontana, 1953, p. 108.

5. *Redemptoris Missio*, Rome: Vatican, 1990, #40.

6. *The Future of Man*, Eng. trans., London: Collins, 1964, p. 147.

7. *The Gift of Asher Lev*, New York: Fawcett Crest, 1991, p. 149.

8. For development of this point, its implications and ways to solution, see my *Breaking the Bread of the Word. Principles of Teaching Scripture*, Rome: Pontifical Biblical Institute Press, 1991.

9. *Galatians* 1.18, and particularly the verb 'historein', should be read in that sense (cf J. A. Fitzmyer, *To Advance the Gospel*, New York: Crossroad, 1981, p. 179).

10. New York: Harper and Row, 1987.

11. New York: Image Books, 1982.

12. *Images of Jesus. How Jesus is Perceived and Portrayed in Non-European Cultures* (1986), Eng. trans., London: SCM, 1990.

2

The mystery of Christ

The mystery of Christ is the object of Paul's constant meditation; he speaks thus of God's plan for all things. With support from earlier tradition, he uses the term to denote various dimensions of the divine design, including the salvation of peoples and the destiny of the universe. Within this big picture occurs the life and particularly the Paschal Mystery of Jesus. While the Fathers and the Vatican II Council appreciate Paul's usage and vision, not all magisterial and theological statement recognises the fullness of perspective of the mystery of Christ.

To discern the outlines of the divine design that is the mystery of Christ, to recognise the finger of God tracing it in our lives and in all of history, we need his inspiration. The Church prays for this on the first Sunday of Lent: 'Through our Lenten observance, Lord, deepen our understanding of the mystery of Christ, and make it a reality in our lives.' It was by such inspiration that Paul came to his understanding of the mystery, which we associate particularly with his writings. Pope John Paul II, taking a lead from that seminal statement *The Renewal of the Education of Faith*,[1] acknowledges the apostle in his own exhortation on that subject:

> The primary and essential object of catechesis is, to use an expression dear to Saint Paul and also to contemporary theology, 'the mystery of Christ'. Catechizing is in a way to lead a person to study this Mystery in all its dimensions: 'To make all people see what is the plan of the mystery ... comprehend with all the saints what is the breadth and length and height and depth ... know the love of Christ which surpasses knowledge ... (and be filled) with all the fulness of God' (*Eph* 3.9,18–19).[2]

You could be pardoned for failing to detect the Pauline and indeed scriptural character of this notion in some theological writing, despite the Pope's acknowledgement. Karl Rahner, in commenting on a draft of a Vatican II text which became #16 of *Optatam Totius*, the decree on the formation of priests, recognised the foundational role of the mystery of Christ in underpinning 'the basic and central discipline of theological formation', as the Council document recommended. If this is accepted, he says,

> then the *mysterium Christi* is seen automatically as the mystery opera-
> tive in the priestly ministry, without this aspect simply degenerating
> into a small, individual dogmatic or edifying point which would really
> have little to do with an *introductio generalis* to the whole of theology.
> The transcendental reflection on the conditions of the possibility of
> faith — which must always also reflect on the ultimate reason for this
> faith, viz. God's self-communication in grace understood as a per-
> manent existential dimension — shows immediately and in an original
> manner that the *mysterium Christi* suffuses and finalises the whole his-
> tory of mankind, so that this supernatural transcendentality appears
> ever more clearly in history until it finds its highest and unsurpassable
> manifestation in Christ.[3]

Some reference to Paul's thinking here, in the manner of the Pope, one feels, would have better reflected the Council's concern expressed a few lines earlier in that document that theology had lost its soul, the study of the Scriptures, and might have better expli-cated the sense of that mystery.

Paul's understanding of the mystery

So it is to Paul we should turn for an understanding of the mystery of Christ, besides praying with the Church about it. In the letters the singular *mysterion* occurs about a dozen times in the sense of the mystery of Christ, or of God's plan, depending on variant manuscript readings; in three other places this sense is slightly nuanced. In the plural the meaning is quite different, and not relevant here. We should look at those dozen occurrences in both proto-Pauline letters (those more directly associated with his literary activity, in scholarly estimation) and deutero-Pauline.[4]

Rom 11.25   I want you to understand this mysterion: a hardening has come upon part of Israel, until the full number of the Gen-tiles has come in.

Rom 16.25   According to the revelation of the mysterion that was kept secret for long ages but is now disclosed, and through the prophetic writings is made known to all the Gentiles, according to the command of the eternal God, to bring about the obedience of faith.

1 Cor 2.1   I did not come proclaiming the mysterion/martyrion of God in lofty words or sophia.

1 Cor 2.7   We speak God's sophia in mysterion, the hidden sophia which God decreed before the ages for our doxa [a more literal translation of the Greek than the NRSV].

Eph 1.8ff   With all sophia and insight he has made known to us the mysterion of his will, according to his good pleasure that he set forth in Christ, as an oikonomia for the fulness of time, to gather up all things in him.

Eph 3.3ff   the mysterion was made known to me ... enable you to perceive my understanding of the mysterion of Christ. In former generations this mysterion was not made known to humankind ... ; to make everyone see what is the oikonomia of the mysterion hidden for ages in God who created all things; so that through the church the sophia of God in its rich variety might now be made known.

Eph 6.19   that a message may be given to me to make known with boldness the mysterion of the gospel.

Col 1.25ff   God's oikonomia that was given to me for you, to make the word of God fully known, the mysterion that has been hidden throughout the ages and generations but has now been revealed to his saints. To them God chose to make known how great among the Gentiles are the riches of the doxa of this mysterion, which is Christ in you, the hope of doxa.

Col 2.2f   the knowledge of the mysterion of God/Christ,[5] in whom/which are hidden all the treasures of sophia and knowledge.

Col 4.3f   God will open to us a door for the word, that we may declare the mysterion of Christ, for which I am in prison, so that I may reveal it clearly, as I should.

1 Tm 3.9   they must hold fast to the mysterion of the faith with a clear conscience.

1 Tm 3.16   The mysterion of our religion is great: He was revealed in the flesh, vindicated in spirit, seen by angels ...

What Paul understands by the mystery of Christ emerges pretty clearly from these many passages from different points in his ministry and from different parts of the spectrum of authorship we class as Pauline; attention to the context of each fills it out even further. A pattern of divine action, discernible only obscurely in the past, has now been made clear to the apostle, who must preach and help to implement it, especially as regards Jesus' role and the place of the Gentiles within the plan, for whom it is good news. The fact of its erstwhile obscurity and the need for revelation is an integral but not predominant note of *mysterion* in these passages, enabling Paul to contrast two dispensations; regrettably, as we shall see, some readers have allowed that note to monopolise their thinking, so that (even in otherwise good translations, for instance) a version as 'secret' was offered, quite corrupting the sense Paul is conveying.

Besides *mysterion*, other key terms recur in the above passages: *oikonomia* (a term which will become basic to patristic thinking on the Incarnation and is important for Orthodox theology today) as the plan in operation;[6] *sophia*, wisdom, which we shall see denoting a particularly comprehensive version of God's dealings with all of his creation; *doxa*, glory, a share in the divine nature to which the mystery introduces us — the last two terms of such significance to Paul's readers familiar with the Jewish Scriptures (in the Greek translation made in late Old Testament times).

Paul employs *mysterion* in three other places referring not to the whole divine design but an aspect of it. At *1 Cor* 15.51 it is the resurrection that is in focus: 'Listen, I will tell you a mystery! We will not all die, but we will all be changed.' At *Eph* 5.32 use of the term makes possible, cryptically, the most beautiful theology of marriage in all the New Testament, where one relationship reflects another and in fact the whole divine plan: 'This a great mystery, and I am applying it to Christ and the Church.' The obverse of that plan is spoken of at *2 Thes* 2.7, everything intended by the Father frustrated by sin: 'The mystery of lawlessness is already at work.' In these more limited applications (as well as in three 'Pauline' occurrences in the book of *Revelation*: 1.20; 10.7; 17.5), too, the basic sense of the term appears that emerges in its fullness when Paul speaks of the mystery of Christ.

Nowhere else in the New Testament does 'mystery' occur — with one most intriguing exception: it is evidently a term to be avoided, and reasons suggest themselves, which we must look at carefully. That exception is in Jesus' mouth at *Mark* 4.11, which the other evangelists hasten to adjust. It is a highly significant occurrence, serving to bridge Paul's earlier usage and Jesus' own talk of his mission. We shall have to examine it closely, thankful that it survived the distaste for it shown by Matthew and Luke, for it provides us with a valuable scriptural datum for relating Jesus to the mystery of Christ.

Origins and associations

One could hazard a guess as to why we are having to rely on Paul and give credit to him for this theological concept of the mystery of Christ, which magisterium and theologians are at one in highlighting as the fundament and matrix for adequate theological formation and education in the faith. Usually only in the Reformed tradition does Paul outrank the evangelists. Our educated guess would be that in choosing, for whatever reason, a word with a tainted religious history, Paul was departing from accustomed usage. Association with pagan mystery religions and cults, notorious for excess and depravity in the ancient world, was something Christian literature and ritual would want to eschew; and the educated rabbi of Tarsus should have known that.

In fact, our guess would be wide of the mark. Paul was faithful to sound religious tradition in using 'mystery' — in the singular — for this sense of God's plan, will, purpose (the plural, we noted, is a different matter). The background to the word has been investigated thoroughly in the last fifty years since the work of K. Prümm. More recently Raymond E. Brown,[7] Gunther Bornkamm[8] and Chrys Caragounis[9] have demonstrated the roots of the Pauline 'mystery' in apocalyptic and sapiential literature in the Old Testament, intertestamental literature and the writings found at Qumran on the Dead Sea. We look, for instance, at *Daniel*, that late apocalyptic book which in the Christian Bible stands at the head of The Twelve, the minor prophets, but in the Hebrew Bible is more properly placed among The Writings. Chapter 2 tells of Nebuchadnezzar's dream (the author harking back all those centuries for his apocalyptic message), which Daniel has both to divine and to interpret at the risk of his life.

> Daniel told (his companions) to seek mercy from the God of heaven concerning this mystery, so that Daniel and his companions with the rest of the wise men of Babylon might not perish. Then the mystery was revealed to Daniel in a vision of the night (2.18–19).

Revelation through dreams is a normal component of Wisdom and apocalyptic; we recall the Joseph of both testaments. God allows Daniel to come to a knowledge of the dream and interpet it in terms of the four ages of world history under the figure of a mighty statue made of four metals. The Aramaic word for this mystery (this section of *Daniel* being now extant in Aramaic — a strange feature of the book) is *raza*, derived from Persian; in the Greek translation of the Old Testament (current at the time of Jesus and Paul when the original languages were not well known) it becomes *mysterion*. Interpretation of world history in this way Daniel attributes to God, and the king is greatly astonished, even if the message is hardly comforting.

> 'But as for me, this mystery has not been revealed to me because of any wisdom that I have more than any other living being, but in order that the interpretation may be known to the king' (2.30).

A similar usage can be found frequently in the hymns of the Dead Sea community, perhaps contemporary with *Daniel* in the second century before the time of Jesus:

> In the mystery of Thy wisdom
>   Thou hast opened knowledge to me,
> and in Thy mercies
>   [Thou hast unlocked for me] the fountain of Thy might.[10]

In the light of this more ancient religious literature of Israel, commentators summarise the usage of *mysterion* Paul (and his disciples) was tapping into. Caragounis says that the notion in *Daniel* 'is God's purpose, it is eschatological, it has cosmic dimensions, and it is a unified plan' [11] — and we can see how precisely that is what Paul had in mind from his post-Damascus perspective, and how that serves him eminently as a context in which to situate and evaluate Jesus. Bornkamm, who like us can see the connection in Pauline passages like the above between mystery and wisdom (we noted, and will further examine, Paul using them synonymously), paraphrases *mysterion* as 'the mysterious wisdom of God' which, he says, is

(a) prepared before the world was (*1 Cor 2.7*),

(b) concealed from the aeons (*1 Cor 2.8; Eph 3.9; Col 1.26; Rom 16.25*, a later doxology),

(c) hidden in God, the Creator of all things (*Eph 3.9*).
     The mysterion of the will of God (*Eph 1.9*) is brought by God himself to execution (*oikonomia, Eph 3.9*) and manifestation. As the divine *mysterion* is fulfilled in Christ, the creation and consummation, the beginning and the end of the world are comprised in Him and taken out of the sphere of their own control and apprehension. The times come to their end in the revelation of the divine mystery (*Eph 1.10*).[12]

THE MYSTERY OF CHRIST

Our 'educated guess' was wrong, then, that Paul in employing 'mystery' was, alone among the New Testament writers, straying into the language of pagan religion and bringing with it associations of those abhorrent cults. Quite the contrary: he was aligning himself with a solid biblical and extra-biblical (but still religious) tradition that provided him with a superb matrix for theologising about all the Christian data and all of creation, a *Weltanschaung* that would be required for bringing together Israel's experience of God and the Jesus event as well as sapiential and apocalyptic notions of the cosmos. Pope and theologian concur with his judgment of the adequacy of his matrix for theological formation and education in faith. As we shall see from looking at Gospel usage, not all sacred authors were prepared to run the risk of listeners/readers responding to less savoury connotations of 'mystery', but in that choice they lost more than they gained. Writers in the following few centuries, we are assured, did not respect their sensitivity. '*Mysterion* is regularly used in the singular without any connotation of cult, and designates God's counsel to save the world, at first hidden and inscrutable, then revealed and realized in Christ ... Nor do we uncover any presentation of the Christian message which would have parallels in the mystery cults.'[13]

We shall look more fully in Chapter 4 at patristic usage on the mystery of Christ. Let us simply take a trustworthy synopsis of that period from its classic commentator, the late Henri De Lubac: 'If one can say that [in the Fathers' view] everything, in the biblical history, is brought about "in mystery", it is that it is brought about in a unique mystery, "in the mystery of Christ".'[14] De Lubac documents this summary of patristic attitudes with reference to Origen's commentary on the prayer of Jesus in *Matthew* 24.20 that flight from the final cataclysm would not be on the sabbath, where Origen explains the real meaning of sabbath rest, quoting Lamech's reason in *Genesis* 5.29 for naming his son Noah (thought by the popular etymology of the time to mean 'relief') and commenting: 'Lamech gave this name to his son Noah in the mystery of Christ.'[15]

A multifaceted mystery

So, on all the evidence, particularly from Paul himself as the originator of the term, as well as from its religious background, from his commentators and from other usage in the early Church, we can grasp something of what *the mystery of Christ* denotes: 'a vast sacred reality, an immense design, in the mind of God "from before the foundation of the world", reaching its focal point at "the end of the ages" in (the Paschal Mystery of) Jesus, for the benefit of all people and the cosmos, something we could only know through revelation.'

Paul himself does not treat equally of all these notes to the concept in the letters. He is primarily a missioner, not a theologian at his desk, and certain missionary concerns dominate the letters composed on the run and sent to particular communities to meet certain situations. Hence it is the ecclesial dimension of the mystery that is mostly on his mind, that aspect of the plan which involves its human beneficiaries (in this he does resemble Matthew's angel), and particularly the relative claim on membership in the community of salvation ('Christian' community in the wide sense) of Jews and other people. Failure to recognise this preoccupation of his (reaching its highpoint in *Romans* 9–11) vitiated Reformation debate on justification; for Paul a 'pangs of conscience' approach, the question of *my* place as a sinner in the scheme of salvation, arises only within that larger context, as Protestant scholars like A. Schweitzer, W. D. Davies, C. K. Barrett, K. Stendahl and E. P. Sanders have come to see. Related to this concern about the respective value of two dispensations are his teachings on true knowledge (especially in *Colossians*) as opposed to something gnostic, and on true wisdom (in *1 Corinthians* and elsewhere) in place of that embodied in the Mosaic Law or in pagan sophistry.

This communal, ecclesial, missionary dimension of the mystery of Christ, however, is but one of its many dimensions, as Paul acknowledges — hence its value as a matrix for thinking and theologising (theology in the sense of 'faith seeking understanding'). The letters are explicit about this. In that classic essay on the mystery in *Ephesians* the dawning awareness of the multifaceted design is beautifully expressed.

> Although I am the very least of all the saints, this grace was given to me to bring to the Gentiles the news of the boundless riches of Christ, and to make everyone see what is the plan of the mystery hidden for ages in God who created all things; so that through the church *the wisdom of God in its rich variety* might now be made known to the rulers and authorities in the heavenly places. This was in accordance with the eternal purpose that he has carried out in Christ Jesus our Lord (3.8–11).

We have touched on some of the synonyms for mystery that occur in the letters: plan, purpose, will, and (as here) wisdom. The significance of wisdom as a synonym will not fully emerge until we look at the whole biblical picture in the next chapter, and particularly the contribution of Wisdom material from both testaments (not to mention extrabiblical material of the period). The phrase I have emphasised above from the NRSV appeared in this fine translation's predecessor in an insipid version, 'the manifold wisdom of God'; the Jerusalem Bible did better with 'comprehensive', and William Barclay got right to the essence in saying 'the many-coloured wisdom of God'.[16] The word at issue in the Greek has an interesting history. It has to do with colour and texture. We recall the coat Jacob made for Joseph that caused all the trouble; it was special in this way (though the Hebrew is obscure, and is sometimes rendered 'with long sleeves'), and the Greek Bible has *poikilos* to denote this special colour and texture (*Gn* 37.3). Likewise in *Ezekiel* 16 the Lord makes for his beloved, if wanton, daughter Jerusalem a *poikilos* robe. In the New Testament *1 Peter* speaks of the many gifts that come from the variegated, *poikilos*, grace of God (4.10), applying the word figuratively.[17] But in *Ephesians* to denote the mystery of Christ, God's plan, wisdom, even this figure is found inadequate, and so a neologism is coined, *polypoikilos*, *multi*coloured, *many*faceted, of *many* dimensions; the NRSV's 'in its rich variety' renders the Greek perfectly.

The implication, of course, is that the biblical mould has been broken, that what once seemed (to Paul and his Jewish associates) a monochrome design encompassing one chosen people only is now recognised as technicolour, of a rich variety, embracing all (also chosen) peoples (and material creation as well). That news would be as acceptable to some as the original coat was to Jacob's other sons — but unfolding plans are like that: obscure realisation can be more comfortable. The mystery of Christ has in fact many dimensions beyond this *community* dimension: a *biblical* dimension, which we shall shortly explore, which itself recounts (partially) an *historical* dimension; a *cosmic* dimension in the sense of including 'all things, things in heaven and things on earth'; a *personal* dimension in allowing and challenging me to look for my place and role in the mystery of Christ. We might also speak of a *theological* dimension if we consider the attempts (such as that we are making here, and as have believers and thinkers and theologians from the time of the primitive community) to come to grips with the implications of the mystery of Christ and particularly to relate Jesus of Nazareth to it, as Paul had to do. And there could be other dimensions to the mystery, for it is truly *polypoikilos*.

The big picture

When Paul speaks of the mystery of Christ in this way, he is plainly studying a wider canvas than simply the life of Jesus, even if for him as a believer the pattern reaches a high point or focal point (or whatever is the appropriate geometrical expression) in the death and resurrection of Jesus (*1 Cor* 15.1–5), and if the benefits that God wishes us (and the universe) to receive from his plan come to us 'through his blood' (*Eph* 1.7). But we were chosen 'in Christ' before the foundation of the world (*Eph* 1.4), before the ages (*1 Cor* 2.7). We might say that the (total) mystery of Christ encompasses more than the (individual) mystery of the Incarnation. The dimensions of this plan — cosmic, historical, ecclesial — betray Paul's indebtedness to the apocalyptic and sapiential material which provided him with the term 'mystery'. They also lay out for Paul and us the 'big picture' in which the Jesus event occurs and may be evaluated against the backdrop of eternal purpose, human and cosmic history. The evangelists — in a conscious reaction of concern, some would say[18] — later reduce the dimensions in a relatively microscopic study of Jesus' person, life and teaching in a smaller picture which has the effect of shrinking (even perhaps losing from sight) the wider context.

This matter of *perspective* is an important one for us in our study of Jesus and the mystery of Christ, and we shall return to it particularly in Chapter 4 when focusing more closely on the person of Jesus; our title and Introduction highlight the need to recognise the difference in perspectives. The bigger picture that Paul draws in the mystery of Christ has attracted those from earliest times concerned to find a place for all people (and things) within a divine plan of salvation. Paul had an obvious missionary reason for preferring it. The Fathers, particularly those confronting a pagan world and not simply sorting out doctrinal differences among the followers of Jesus, opted for the wider screen; we shall look at these early apologists and catechists later, mentioning here only Theophilus of Antioch in the second century, who in his three books to the pagan Autolycus[19] developed what might be called a Christology without Jesus, as did other apologists of his time.

In our day missionaries and students of world religions have found help in a similar approach, trying to find a meaning in the bigger Pauline picture that the smaller 'Jesuan' picture provided by the Gospels does not allow them. One thinks of Raimundo Panik-kar, priest, scientist, son of Christian mother and Hindu father, endeavouring within an Asian culture to reconcile religious traditions, and concluding that 'Christ the Saviour is ... not to be restricted to the merely historical figure of Jesus of Nazareth ... Hence, for Christianity, Christ is already there in Hinduism in so far as Hinduism is a true religion; Christ is already at work in any Hindu prayer as far as it is really prayer; Christ is behind any form of worship, in as much as it is adoration made to God.'[20] All of these thinkers deserve our closer attention if we wish to investigate that vital relationship.

Church as mystery

It was the ecclesial dimension of the mystery, we have seen, that was of special interest to Paul in his missionary role. The mystery of Christ furnished him with a catholic understanding of Church, arising in a particular way from Old Testament Wisdom, that could include all peoples and reach back to the beginnings of humanity and forward to the time when the full number of the Gentiles would come in and all Israel, too, could be saved (*Rom* 11.25–26) — a mystery in any sense of the word. Not all in the primitive community shared this catholic vision; *Galatians* and *Acts* show Paul struggling to make inroads into an attitude that took up where Jesus' saying (now found in *Mt* 10.5–6) left off, a community of salvation confined to the lost sheep of the house of Israel. Eventually Paul's vision of the mystery, which took ecclesiological expression in another terminology which he also cannot take complete credit for, the body of Christ,[21] was grudgingly accepted, and the outreach to the Gentiles began.

Even by the time of the Pastoral letters, of course, institutionalisation of Church is quite evident, as was to be expected. It developed throughout history as the community spread, until we reach its definition in the post-Reformation Catholic community in Bellarmine, an ecclesiology that Dulles tells us remained official policy for close on four hundred years and in which the Pauline sense of mystery is scarcely visible:

> The one and true Church is the community of men brought together by the profession of the same Christian faith and conjoined in the communion of the same sacraments, under the government of the legitimate pastors and especially the one vicar of Christ on earth, the Roman pontiff.[22]

I have written elsewhere[23] of the recovery in our time of the Pauline theology of Church as mystery, thanks to the revival of biblical and patristic studies, evidenced so conspicuously in the work of those great traditionalists (tradition in the sense we outlined above on p. v) Henri De Lubac and Yves Congar, whose initially unpopular pioneering work on Church eventually influenced the bishops at Vatican II. The climax of this change in attitude was the teaching of the Council's foundational document on Church, *Lumen Gentium*, which gives pride of place not to institutional characteristics but to 'The mystery of the Church'. That opening chapter begins by referring to Christ and spelling out the biblical and historical dimensions of the mystery as the story of the origins of the Church and relating it also to the creation of the world and the benefits intended for human recipients, pre-eminently the gift of divine life. The documentation here is predictably Pauline and patristic.

Though this notion of Church as mystery was not fully understood owing to lack of appreciation of Paul (Avery Dulles[24] and Pope Paul VI in his *Ecclesiam Suam*[25] might serve as examples of overemphasis on the secret character of the mystery — a common misreading, as we shall shortly see), the magisterium has generally continued to follow the lead of *Lumen Gentium*. Twenty years after the close of Vatican II a Synod of Bishops in 1985 examined the intervening period and repeated the Council's presentation of Church as mystery, with particular insistence from German curial bishops, whose motives and understanding of mystery make one wonder if they were respecting Paul's intentions. Cardinal Mayer, prefect of Roman bodies to do with sacraments and liturgy, told the Synod that 'the Church, as the Council emphasised, can be understood in her specific form only in relation to the mystery of Christ,' [26] and went on to call for renewed recognition of 'the value of reverence, of the sacred and of silence' — that popular misconception of mystery. Cardinal Ratzinger lamented the amount of attention since the Council to structural matters: 'The Church has been reduced to its institutional aspect. It is essential, therefore, to put forward the Church as *mysterium*, transcending itself towards Christ.' [27]

So when the Synod gave its Message to the People of God, its endorsement of Church as mystery was slanted in the direction of interiority, spirituality — which is not what Paul had in mind altogether:

We are aware that the Church cannot renew herself unless this spiritual note of mystery is more deeply rooted in the hearts of Christians. This note has as its first characteristic element the universal call to holiness which is addressed to all the faithful as well as to those who, according to their state in life, follow the evangelical counsels. The innermost reality of the Church must be understood in this way if we are to avoid false sociological or political interpretations of the nature of the Church.[28]

Following the 1987 Synod on the laity, however, Pope John Paul II wrote to the Church in *Christifideles Laici* in terms that showed a more adequate appreciation of Paul's theology of Church as well as picking up the 1985 Synod's contribution, Church as communion:

> The reality of the Church as communion is, then, the integrating aspect, indeed the central content of the 'mystery', or rather, the divine plan for the salvation of humanity (19).

The Pope thus brings together two scriptural notions of Church, *mysterion* and *koinonia*, that have received attention in contemporary ecclesiology, the latter thanks particularly to the statements by the Anglican–Roman Catholic International Commission (ARCIC I and II).[29] As the Pope suggests, they allow Church to be seen as a mystery or plan for life (with which Paul — and John — would agree), the beneficiaries being all 'humanity'.

The world in the mystery

But though that represents a great advance in understanding Church, in seeing somehow all humanity coming within the compass of Church, it still leaves the world out in the cold. Not, of course, if by 'world' we understand human beings, which is one way of taking it, found also in the New Testament (for *kosmos*), where we are sometimes warned against 'the world' in the sense of the evil people in it. Television viewers of the Seoul Olympics may have noticed, as I did, a large white billboard displayed trackside day after day by someone who had gone to the trouble of purchasing an expensive ticket just for the sake of holding up at a spot known to be within camera-range a sign which read simply and boldly: 'JOHN 3.16'. Bible lovers or those around the world with an inquisitive bent would have found that that verse reads, 'God so loved the world that he gave his only Son, so that everyone who believes in him may not perish but may have eternal life.' That apostle of the Word had thus seized on a summary of the Johannine and indeed evangelical message, and no doubt succeeded in awakening others to it who could crack the code; he was at work again at the 1990 World Cup in Rome, presumably satisfied to be out of pocket if only a few viewers got the message of God's love for humankind.

At other places in the Scriptures the world includes all the rest of creation, and, as we have seen, Matthew's angel and many other figures are not concerned with it — just with humanity. It is all a matter of perspective, we agreed; no one is condemning the world in the sense of God's creation — just not seeing it as a high priority when it comes to the plan of salvation. Paul again, though as a missioner also concerned about priorities, could see that the mystery of Christ 'gathers up' all things, and that these things have a fulfilment awaiting them, too, connected somehow with ours (*Rom* 8.19–23). His use of wisdom as a synonym for mystery also connotes that cosmic, material, this-worldly dimension to the plan.[30]

It is, of course, important for us dwellers in this world that the divine plan for life does take this world seriously. Otherwise, we should join gnostics and New Agers in looking out into space and seeking guidance from astrology and 'the elemental spirits of the universe' — tendencies not unknown to the intellectual world of the early Church. We cannot afford any such dualism that wars against incarnation. The Christian East has always looked seriously and optimistically at the world in its theology, perhaps unlike Augustinian emphasis on the City of God (and sin). Clement of Alexandria says, 'Just as the will of God is an act and is called the world, so also his intention is the salvation of people and is called the Church.'[31] We could perhaps quarrel with Clement's distinction between Church and world but not with his vision of both within the divine plan, which fascinates Eastern theologians still today:

> The relationship of the world to its absolute Creator and Sustainer defines and augments its character as a mystery. In its existence the power of its Creator and Sustainer is manifested even though, on the one hand, he transcends it. The mystery of the world and the mystery of humanity are seen as an active presence of the absolutely Transcendent in their existence. But the world's own relationship with the Transcendent is itself a mystery ... This bond between the world and its creator is 'participation' according to St Athanasius of Alexandria ... God brought the created world into being as a form of existence (other

than his own) only in order to permit it to be filled with his perfections.[32]

Vatican II did Western Christians a service by writing an affirmative Constitution on the Church in the Modern World entitled encouragingly *Gaudium et Spes* (Joy and Hope) that reflects the vision
and optimism stemming from (Jewish Wisdom and) Paul and the
Eastern Fathers and more recent theologians. We need reminding
that the world, too, falls within the divine plan, the mystery of
Christ. Jesus, as a Wisdom figure, we noted, was very happy to be
with us in this real world, and rooted his teaching in the day-to-day
realities of this created world — *kosmos* in that sense. Just how Jesus
and the material universe come together in a meaningful synthesis
within the mystery of Christ we need to examine in detail in Chapter 6. New Agers and a wave of millenarianism that is likely to
wash over us in the last years of this century[33] will tend to call in
question such a synthesis.

The mystery about mystery

One obstacle to a proper understanding of the mystery of Christ,
which we have noticed already in connection with theologising
about Church, is that for most people the term 'mystery' means
what it meant to Agatha Christie — a puzzle, a secret, something
beyond understanding — except that Agatha usually got to the bottom of her puzzles and solved her riddles. So we saw popes and
theologians presenting the Church as something beyond our understanding (no doubt true), and wanted us to interpret the Church as
mystery in that sense — which, with Paul's guidance, we agreed did
not do justice to the extensive religious background of the term, even
if we could also see where the less adequate notion might come from.

Unfortunately, much theological literature (extending even to
magisterial statement) is bedevilled by this inadequate understanding of Paul's term — a misunderstanding that has no proper
excuse now that work has been done to provide the necessary
clarification. My wife frequently shows exasperation with
preachers who discharge themselves of the responsibility of breaking the bread of the Word fruitfully to us by throwing up their
hands and exclaiming piously of the topic for discussion, 'O, it's a
mystery,' and bailing out at that point — whereas a little solid
study (perhaps by reference to the many good commentaries available) would enable the sacred reality ('mystery' in that sense) to be-

come amenable to clear presentation and explanation and the community thus duly nourished. Paul certainly believed we could, with help from on high, gain a real understanding of the mystery of Christ, and the Incarnation suggests we take practical steps to gain that understanding.

The Fathers of Vatican II, at least in places, got it right, thanks to some good preparatory work. So the Church appears in *Lumen Gentium* right from the outset as mystery — not as puzzle but as great divine design arising in God's eternal decision and finally gathering in all good people from Abel to the last of the elect (in Gregory's and Augustine's words) — exactly the way Paul would have spoken of Church had he been there. The Council Fathers, we noted, were thus reflecting the good ground work of soundly traditional theologians like De Lubac, who with their thorough knowledge of biblical and patristic tradition could write so adequately (and feelingly) of Church:

> The mystery of the Church is all mystery in little; it is our own mystery par excellence. It lays hold on the whole of us and surrounds us; for it is in his Church that God looks upon us and loves us, in her that he desires us and we encounter him, and in her that we cleave to him and are made blessed.[34]

In other places the Council employs the more limited (but still accurate) sense of mystery as one aspect of the whole pattern, especially of the life of Jesus, as it does in the Constitution on the Liturgy when it tells us that 'within the cycle of a year, the Church unfolds the whole mystery of Christ [=Jesus], not only from his Incarnation and birth until his ascension' (#102). The sense here has been current in English at least from the time we began speaking of the mysteries of the Rosary, or of Mystery Plays in early English drama — nothing secret or puzzling being intended, just (part of) the divine plan of salvation, revealed to us though it had to be.

Since composers of magisterial statements are not always of the calibre of Paul or De Lubac, we were not surprised (though disappointed) to find the 1985 Synod bishops, for their own passing concerns, moving back in the direction of Agatha Christie by seeing the mystery of the Church denoting particularly 'the universal call to holiness'. They could have claimed the support of scholars who should know better, like an eminent commentator on *Ephesians*, Markus Barth, who recognises the letter's drift but suddenly distorts the sense of *mysterion* in the text: 'It is impossible to demonstrate that at any place in the NT it signifies an insoluble puzzle or incomprehensible — and yet believed — mystery, though the English translation "mystery" may suggest this meaning. To avoid confusion with such a puzzle the term "secret" has been chosen in our translation.' [35] Why capitulate before ignorance and opt for error, and not rather endeavour to educate the reading public to the true sense of mystery?

This is not to move in the direction of rationalism and ignore the transcendent in our theologising; it is just to heed Lonergan's reminder that 'mystery is not be confused with problem' [36] and that 'transcendence can be over-emphasized.' [37] We heed John Shea's statement that 'we are inescapably related to Mystery, ... this transcendent yet permeating reality,' while also following him in distinguishing mystery from both mysticism and rationalism.[38] We accept the apophatic tradition in theology that proceeds by negatives rather than positives, and are aware that St Thomas begins his *Summa* with an admission, confirmed in Fourth Lateran and First Vatican Councils, that we can more readily say what God is *not* than what he is.[39] We are aware of the nice differences between theologians of the eminence of Lonergan and Karl Rahner about the proper object of theology.[40] There is, however, no dispute about the process of theology, definitively stated by Anselm in his *Proslogion* in the eleventh century after study of Augustine's similar conclusion in the 5th, 'faith seeking understanding'. For our present discussion the implication is that recourse to the available fruits of theological study on 'mystery' is *de rigueur* for us all, and to treat the term as synonymous with the unknowable, a secret, a problem, a puzzle is no longer respectable for scholars, though frequent refuge is taken in this direction.

The result of such lazy refuge-taking has been that we get a lot of loose talk in theology about 'the mysteries of religion' where the intention is to suggest realities that are utterly incomprehensible and thus not worth the effort to study and plumb — like that manual that has been influential in the formation of the ministers of the Word of the type criticised above who give up too readily on the plea of 'mystery', namely, Matthias Scheeben's *The Mysteries of Christianity*. A further irony is that Scheeben proceeds to quote, in support, Paul and even Jesus at that critical occurrence at *Mark* 4.11, who in fact confute him:

> Christianity entered the world as a religion replete with mysteries. It was proclaimed as the mystery of Christ (*Rom* 16.25–27; *Col* 1.25–27), as

the 'mystery of the kingdom of God' (*Mk* 4.11; *Lk* 8.10). Its ideas and doctrines were unknown, unprecedented; and they were to remain inscrutable and unfathomable.[41]

This is just outdated scholarship, and leads to the kind of pious agnosticism that leaves the faithful in the dark needlessly.

Fortunately, other writers have troubled themselves to tap into the fruits of scholarship, or like G. K. Chesterton have simply been more perceptive about English usage. In *The Innocence of Father Brown* Chesterton has his priestly detective make one of his characteristic distinctions: 'The modern mind always mixes up two different ideas: mystery in the sense of what is marvellous, and mystery in the sense of what is complicated.' [42] To arrive at this insight Father Brown did not have the opportunity to become aware of his namesake's later research into the Pauline mystery, which may have helped more recent writers like Andrew Greeley, who distinguishes thus: 'By "mystery" I do not mean something that is hard to cope with because it is obscure and baffling; I mean something that is hard to cope with because it is so bright and dazzling' [43] — which reminds one of Chesterton's further remark, 'startling but simple'. Gabriel Moran comes even closer to an adequate appreciation of mystery in Paul's sense:

> Nothing should be more evident (though we constantly tend to obscure it) than the fact that the word 'mystery' as it pertains to revelation does not signify unintelligibility and lack of meaning for the Christian life. On the contrary, the word 'mystery' as it is used here has exactly the opposite meaning, that is, it signifies a superluminous intelligibility, an inexhaustible depth of meaning.[44]

Those phrases he parallels with others from F. X. Durrwell in his book *In the Redeeming Christ*: 'Anyone we cannot love remains a mystery to us, a house closed and impenetrable. Christ is a mystery too, but rather for the infinity of his openness, his unlimited comprehensibility.' It is not clear whether Moran and Durrwell in speaking of Christ have, like Paul, a more comprehensive reality in mind than the person of Jesus, and this reservation could be applied also to John F. O'Grady in his *Models of Jesus*. O'Grady clarifies well and in similar terms the sense of mystery:

> If at the outset of this work I choose to speak of mystery, then, it is because I am aware that any theologian faces inexhaustible intelligibility as he or she tries to encounter in a personal way the meaning of Jesus the Christ.[45]

Glenn F. Chesnut in a book with similar scope, *Images of Christ. An Introduction to Christology*, also feels the need to set an adequate definition of mystery, without quite managing to throw off the incubus of the old distortion:

> It is a great Mystery of which we speak, in fact the greatest of all. By this is meant Mystery in the proper sense — not dishonesty, or special pleading, or obscurantism. Mystery is what invariably, ultimately appears when one is resolutely logical, scientifically honest, and courageous enough to pursue truth to the end. Practising scientists know what this means, particularly in the fields of chemistry, astronomy, and the strange, disorienting world of modern physics. On the other side of our theories lies at all times a reality which our schematizations and models do not fully comprehend.[46]

All of these thinkers resist the temptation to accept an inadequate inherited notion of mystery in their theologising about a vast reality that has been revealed to us, particularly those who speak of superluminous intelligibility, inexhaustible depth of meaning, unlimited comprehensibility, inexhaustible intelligibility. As Paul realised, the fact that the whole divine design requires a revelation from above to discern does not make it obscure: we are recipients of an enlightenment in the Jesus event that it would be a mockery of Providence to dismiss and revert to the obscurity of former 'ages and generations'. We do enjoy an insight, like Paul and thanks to him, into the mystery of Christ, and we can deepen our understanding of its inexhaustible/unlimited/superluminous/infinite depths and riches if we are prepared to work at it and not take refuge in pious humbug or lazy scholarship. We saw John Paul II recommending catechists to lead people to study this mystery in all its dimensions (*Catechesi Tradendae* 5); agnosticism is not the appropriate response. Let us heed this direction, and direct our study now to one such dimension of this multifaceted, *polypoikilos* mystery in preparation for proceeding with our Christology.

Points for discussion

1. Paul's Damascus experience and missioning to other races helped him discern a pattern in divine workings not previously clear. Can you point to such an illuminating experience in your life to the same effect? Is there need of some such vision?

2.   Are there occasions in life when we need to have recourse to a bigger picture, a wider perspective than our normal workaday situation? Should we be grateful for the diversity of perspective offered by our tradition? Think of Church life, worldly involvement, family troubles, personal achievement.

3.   Do you feel our community has benefited from the tendency of preachers and teachers to declare the truths of faith to be 'mysteries'? In what sense do they normally use the word? How far is their usage legitimate?

4.   Pope John Paul II nominates the mystery of Christ as 'the primary and essential object of catechesis'. In your experience, does education in faith enjoy such an illuminating and enriching synthesis?

Further reading

G. Bornkamm, *mysterion* in G. Kittel (ed.), *Theological Dictionary of the New Testament* IV (1952), Eng. trans., Grand Rapids, Eerdmans, 1967.

J. Hamilton, 'The Church and the language of mystery. The first four centuries,' *Ephemerides Theologicae Louvanienses* 53 (1977 No.4), pp. 479–94.

C. Hill, 'The mystery of Christ: clue to Paul's thinking on wisdom,' *The Heythrop Journal* 25 (1984), pp. 475–83.

John Paul II, *Christifideles Laici*, Sydney: St Paul Publications, 1989.

The Renewal of the Education of Faith, Sydney: Dwyer, 1970.

Notes

1.   Australian edition, Sydney: Dwyer, 1972, #102: 'The mystery of Christ, which is what catechesis is all about, ...' Cf ##69, 73, 80, 96, ...

2.   *Catechesi Tradendae* #5.

3.   'The intellectual formation of future priests,' *Theological Investigations* 6, London: DLT, 1974, pp. 132–33. Likewise, in the article on 'mystery' in his *Encyclopedia of Theology. A Concise Sacramentum Mundi* (1975), Eng. trans., London: Burns and Oates, 1975, pp. 1000–1004, Rahner does not acknowledge Paul's sense, but dwells on 'mysteries' and God's incomprehensibility as the one mystery underlying them.

4. A similar examination has been conducted in my articles 'The mystery of Christ: clue to Paul's thinking on wisdom,' *The Heythrop Journal* 25 (1984) pp. 475–83; 'Synoptic *basileia* and Pauline *mysterion*,' *Estudios Biblicos* 45 (1987) pp. 309–24.

5. The manuscripts offer a wide range of variant readings here, without much difference in meaning.

6. Cf Claude Tresmontant, *Saint Paul and the Mystery of Christ*, Eng. trans., London: Longmans, Green & Co, 1957, p. 47: 'To express the 'plan' of God's work, its effective means and their carrying out, Paul uses the word *oikonomia*.'

7. *The Semitic Background of the Term 'Mystery' in the New Testament*, Philadelphia: Fortress, 1968.

8. *mysterion* in G. Kittel (ed.), *Theological Dictionary of the New Testament* IV, 1952, Eng. trans., Grand Rapids: Eerdmans, 1967.

9. *The Ephesian Mysterion* (Coniectanea Biblica, NT series 8), Lund: Gleerup, 1977.

10. G. Vermes, *The Dead Sea Scrolls in English*, 3rd edn, Sheffield: JSOT, 1987, p. 198.

11. *The Ephesian Mysterion*, p. 134.

12. *mysterion, Theological Dictionary of the New Testament* IV, p. 820.

13. J. D. B. Hamilton,'The Church and the language of mystery. The first four centuries,' *Ephemerides Theologicae Louvanienses* 53 (1977 No.4) p. 482. The plural is common in this period for pagan religious rites.

14. *Exégèse Médiévale. Les Quatre Sens de L'Ecriture* II, Paris: Aubier, 1964, p. 81.

15. *Comm. on Mt* 45, in E. Klostermann (ed.), *Origenes Matthäuserklärung* II, Berlin: Akademie-Verlag, 1976, p. 91.

16. *The New Testament. A New Translation* (1968), London: Fontana, 1976, p. 407.

17. Cf William Barclay, *New Testament Words*, London: SCM, 1964, *poikilos*, pp. 235–37.

18. Cf E. Käsemann, *New Testament Questions of Today*, Eng. trans, London: SCM, 1969, p. 63: 'The reversion to the form of the Gospel narrative, to the story of the Palestinian preacher, to the "once upon a time" as against the "once-for-all", to a historicizing presentation within the framework of the kerygma and, last but not least, to Jesus as he wandered through Palestine; all this occurred as a reaction — theologically relevant and therefore initiated and maintained by the Church — directed towards restoring the autonomy of the Christ, of the Spirit and of faith itself.'

19. R. M. Grant (ed.), *Theophilus of Antioch, Ad Autolycum*, Oxford: Clarendon, 1970. Among Christologists Wolfhart Pannenberg is most attentive to the perspective of the Fathers.

20. *Salvation in Christ* (privately published, 1972, p. 62; quoted by P. Knitter, *No Other Name?*, London: SCM, 1985, p. 155); *The Unknown Christ of Hinduism*, 1st edition, London: DLT, 1964, p. 17 (cf rev.edn, 1981, p. 49).

21. Cf Käsemann, *op.cit.*, 128: 'The theme — which may well go back behind Paul — of the Church as the body of Christ is a precise expression of a relevant theology for the very reason that it emphasizes better than any other conception of the Church the world-wide nature of a Christianity which is breaking through to the Gentile mission and the universality of the redemptive happening which this break-through indicates.'

22. Quoted by A. Dulles, *Models of the Church*, Garden City: Doubleday, 1974, p. 14. Cf E. Schillebeeckx, *Church, The Human Story of God* (1989), Eng. trans., New York: Crossroad, 1990, p. 198.

23. 'The Church as mystery,' *Compass Theology Review* 23 (1989 No.1) pp. 37–44; *Mystery of Life. A Theology of Church*, Melbourne: Collins Dove, 1990.

24. 'The term mystery ... implies that the Church is not fully intelligible to the finite mind of man' (*Models of the Church*, 15).

25. 'That doctrine concerns the origins of the Church, its own nature, its own mission, its own ultimate destiny, a doctrine never sufficiently investigated and understood, inasmuch as it contains the "publication of a mystery, kept hidden from the beginning of time" ' (English Catholic Truth Society edition, 1964, #9).

26. Quoted in *The (Sydney) Catholic Weekly*, December 11, 1985, p. 7.

27. *L'Osservatore Romano*, November 26, 1985.

28. *Message*, II. This is the kind of refuge criticised by Steven T. Katz in his article, 'The language and logic of "mystery" in christology,' in *Christ, Faith and History*, ed. S. W. Sykes and J. P. Clayton, Cambridge: CUP, 1978, p. 248: 'The tremendous price paid for the escape into mystery is not generally appreciated by those who seek to utilize this theological gambit.' Katz himself shows no awareness of the Pauline sense of mystery.

29. Cf *The Final Report*, London: CTS/SPCK, 1982; *Church as Communion*, 1991.

30. Cf R. C. Hill, 'The perspective of Wisdom,' *Scripture Bulletin* 21 (1991 No.2) pp. 16–20.

31. *Paedagogus* I, p. 6 (*Patrologia Graeca* pp. 8, 281).

32. Dumitru Staniloae, 'The mystery of the Church,' in G. Limouris (ed.), *Church, Kingdom, World. The Church as Mystery and Prophetic Sign* (WCC Faith and Order Papers No.130), Geneva: World Council of Churches, 1986, pp. 51–52.

33. One notes already among booksellers' 'New Titles' Sir George Trevelyan's *A Vision of the Aquarian Age*, Peter Spinks's *A Christian in the New Age*, George Maloney's *Mysticism and the New Age*, Charles Cummings's *Eco-Spirituality*, and *Nostradamus. The End of the Millennium. Prophecies: 1992–2001* by V. J. Hewitt and P. Lorie.

34. *The Splendour of the Church*, 2nd edn, Eng. trans., Glen Rock: Paulist, 1963, p. 28.

35. *Ephesians 1–3* (Anchor Bible 34), Garden City: Doubleday, 1974, p. 124.

36. Bernard Lonergan, *Method in Theology*, 2nd edn, London: DLT, 1973, p. 345.

37. *Ibid.*, p. 110.

38. *Stories of God*, Chicago: The Thomas More Press, 1978, pp. 13–17.

39. *Summa Theologiae* Ia, q. 3.

40. Cf K. Rahner, 'Reflections on methodology in theology,' *Theological Investigations* 11, London: DLT, 1974, p. 84; A. J. Kelly, 'Is Lonergan's *Method* adequate to Christian Mystery?' *Thomist* 39 (1975) pp. 437–70; J. Thornhill, 'Is religion the enemy of faith?' *Theological Studies* 45 (1984) pp. 254–74.

41. London-St Louis: Herder, 1946, p. 2.

42. Harmondsworth: Penguin, 1950, p. 145.

43. *The Great Mysteries: An Essential Catechism*, New York: Seabury, 1976, pp. xvi–xvii. Such a title prepares us for a disappointment in Greeley's understanding of mystery when he proceeds: 'The Greek word from which "symbol" and "mystery" come can also be translated as "secret". St Paul is frequently translated as speaking of the great 'secret' hidden from the ages and revealed in the Lord Jesus' (*loc.cit.*) — which suggests Greeley has looked at neither Father Brown.

44. *Theology of Revelation*, New York: Herder and Herder, 1966, p. 133.

45. Garden City: Image Books, 1982, p. 22.

46. Minneapolis: Seabury, 1984, p. xiii.

3

Biblical dimension of the mystery

The scriptural tradition of our community traces the story of God's word and action, particularly in Jesus; other communities, orally or in writing, record their own experiences of God. Old and New Testaments try to get behind the facts to the truth — a theological exercise because done in faith. The fact that all peoples are not represented suggests we may not have the *whole* truth, the mystery of Christ in its fullness. We are at least offered in our Scriptures a double perspective, one focusing on Jesus, the other taking a wider Christological view to include the welfare not only of people but of all things.

Human communities generally develop their own tradition, a body of lore accumulated through experience that is transmitted to later generations. Depending on the technology available, this tradition can take the form of a permanent record, such as writing, though the effect of writing on oral tradition can be more influential than merely recording and fixation,[1] and some communities have evidenced reluctance to allow record and translation of their lore. Over time, major religious communities have developed a written, scriptural, biblical form of tradition of their experience of God, sometimes parallel to other forms of transmitting this story, such as ritual and familial tradition. It is an unfortunate development if this fixed written record comes to be seen as something separate from the overall traditional process. As Orthodox theologian John Meyendorff says, 'Scripture, while complete in itself, presupposes Tradition, not as an addition, but as a milieu in which it becomes understandable and meaningful ... There cannot be, therefore, any question about "two sources" of Revelation.'[2]

Religions of the book

So we have scriptures and bibles and sacred books in various religious communities — Hindu, Jewish, Christian, Islamic. In this sense we speak of religions of the book, communities that have in some literary way registered their experience of God's dealing with them. Paul, who knew well his original community's sacred writings and contributed to an incipient literature of his new community, also insisted on the valid experiences of God even by other peoples resisting divine truth.

> For what can be known about God is plain to them, because God has shown it to them. Ever since the creation of the world his eternal power and divine nature, invisible though they are, have been understood and seen through the things he has made. So they are without excuse; for though they knew God, they did not honour him as God or give thanks to him, but they became futile in their thinking and their senseless minds were darkened (*Rom* 1.19–21).

It suits Paul's theme in this letter on God's grace to highlight peoples' desperate need of it; in doing so he presupposes their experience of him well before the revelations to Jewish and Christian communities — in fact from the creation of the world, a timeline appropriate to the whole mystery of Christ.

The fact of the wide diversity in the written traditions of these communities' experience of the one God reflects not only cultural and historical differences but also marked differences in perspective. You would expect such different expression in literatures composed *by* individual communities *for* these communities: they reflect the viewpoint of the particular communities. Commentators assure us, for instance, that the picture given above by Paul of the pagans' failure to acknowledge and reverence God is an echo of current Jewish thinking,[3] just as he will proceed in the letter to deliver a Christian reflection on Jewish infidelity. The English proverb, 'history is written by the victors', suggests that bias can affect all writing, especially that of embattled groups. No Catholic teaching on biblical inspiration requires that it eliminate all human characteristics — strengths and weaknesses — of biblical composers. We accept the Bible as the truth, nothing but the truth — but the *whole* truth? That's a different question. Even the notion of biblical truth we Catholics have had to qualify: 'that truth which God wanted committed to the sacred writings for the sake of our salvation.'[4] And what that *truth* is does not always easily emerge from a particular text; it certainly does not in many cases square with the *facts*.

Our understanding of Incarnation, that pre-eminent exemplar of divine revelation which underlies the great patristic commentaries on Scripture in the Christian community, obliges us to reject any idea of scriptural revelation coming in a wrapped package unrelated to the human situation of the composers, including bias and ignorance. We need some understanding of truth that allows for discrepancy with fact; as Australian biographer Alan Marshall says, 'I try to get beyond the facts to the truth,' as does any good writer: we have all witnessed the marshalling of facts to obscure truth, especially by politicians. We also need to recognise that the *whole* truth may lie elsewhere, beyond a particular writer's or community's perspectives; we are not surprised to find in the Jewish scriptures little sympathetic attention to other peoples' experience of God, the view that 'chosen' applies to them alone — something grist to Paul's mill in *Romans* chapter 1 but not in chapters 9–11. If we want to find the religious literature of ancient Egyptian, Canaanite, Phoenician, Mesopotamian peoples, we do not turn to the Hebrew Bible for it, though we would find there many negative comments about those peoples.

Finding the big picture

Each religious community, then, that has left a written account of God's dealings with them writes from its own perspective and for the benefit of its own members. That parochial viewpoint does not disappear from Jewish and Christian scriptures even when the Catholic community holds for the inspiration of all the composers concerned in them (without saying anything of other communities' composers). Even Jesus, we have seen, had to point out to Jewish readers of their (inspired) scriptures that the small picture represented there needed a wider hermeneutical reference to be valid — the big picture of the mystery of Christ. 'The Jews' in *John* 5 (a technical term in that Gospel for those who failed to respond) and the two disciples on the way to Emmaus in *Luke* 24 certainly pondered the Jewish scriptures, but failed to see there the bigger picture in which full significance lies. I suggest the risen Lord (speaking in both evangelical loci) is calling both groups, and us, to find in those writings not simply his person (by some sort of fragmentary typology) but the meaningful pattern which is the whole mystery of Christ — as Paul after Damascus was able to recognise it and so write to the Romans with a perspective that begins 'from the creation of the world' or even before it.[5]

Collated in the Christian Bible are the literatures of two religious communities, commonly known (for lack of more satisfactory terminology)[6] as Old Testament and New Testament.[7] Like other extant religious literatures, they serve to document the story of these communities' experience of God's dealing with them. The latter is composed in the knowledge and light of the former (by the Jew Paul, for instance), but both are generally ignorant and unconcerned about other communities (Paul an exception to an extent, Matthew's angel not). The perspective of each, and in particular the earlier, predictably, is limited; the small picture only is in focus, except where a theologian like Paul stands back and surveys the whole scene, and we have seen evangelists reacting to correct that tendency. In other words, we cannot expect all the composers from these particular communities to adopt a universal viewpoint; biblical revelation and biblical inspiration are faithful to the economy of incarnation and do not require miraculous expansion of vision on the part of individual composers. Not all have a Damascus experience.

And yet there are some few who do, who can stand back and glimpse the big picture. And there are many who pause to reflect in the pages of both testaments, who struggle to see the truth beyond the facts and perhaps even slant or select the facts to bring out the truth. Jesus, we saw, wanted his listeners to find this truth. What we ourselves need to do is to attempt that hermeneutical exercise, to survey the whole of the Christian Scriptures, Jewish included, depending on those reflective composers and particularly the rare visionaries like Paul to see a pattern emerging from all the Scriptures, a pattern that he calls the mystery of Christ. It is only a beginning, taking two communities' reflections; under guidance it should be possible to go on to other peoples' records and engage in a similar Christological exercise there.

Christ in the Old Testament

So let us begin that task by looking at Old Testament material to find Christ there. This is to trace the biblical dimension of the mystery. We must not be selective, but need to take a comprehensive view, considering all types of composition — torah, history, prophecy, psalmody, apocalyptic and sapiential material — whether in prose or verse, pre-exilic and post-exilic, Palestinian or diaspora in provenance. But we should concentrate on those passages where the composer, in his own mouth or through a mouthpiece[8], pauses to reflect on the pattern, the significance (as we are now) — truth, in other words, as distinct from facts.

50

Some further initial considerations. Apropos of canon, we can attend either to the significance of layers of composition in the case of reworked material, or regard the text as the final religious product of a community irrespective of its history[9] — though the latter attitude seems to forfeit valuable and relevant theological information from a range of contributors, and also seems to beg the question as to which community is responsible — perhaps several, as in the case of the Torah. Secondly, the understanding of the formation of the Christian canon of the Old Testament has undergone development in recent years at the hands of Protestant scholars Albert Sundberg, James A. Sanders and others;[10] with them we are not content with the limits placed by Pharisaic Judaism in the post-70 period on material available to Jesus fifty years before, and therefore opt for that wider body of material inaccurately called the Alexandrian canon and accepted generally throughout Christendom before Luther's rejection of it for polemical reasons in 1519.

In looking for a pattern in these Scriptures, for a mystery, a story, we are not adopting a basically historical approach such as has come under attack from those dissatisfied with *Heilsgeschichte* as an adequate hermeneutic.[11] Ours is a theological, indeed Christological, study, and we are looking for the evidence of theologians speaking in or contributing to the text. The question of the adequacy of a salvation history approach to the Christian Scriptures need not be argued here. We are concentrating on the mystery of Christ, which is a Pauline theological construct, and are interested to see if the Old Testament can be interpreted in those terms as Paul believed.[12]

Let the text speak

Taking account of these considerations, let us read (or, better, listen to) the text of the Old Testament and let it speak for itself of its central message. We shall begin with something ancient and basic: the cultic credos found in the Torah and Former Prophets. It was the great German literary critic Gerhard Von Rad who drew attention to these compositions now embedded in the text — a text which because of modern technology all looks so uniform, an impression that masks the complex literary history of our pages and conceals the innumerable contributors to a tradition that was at first oral and only at a later stage fixed in written form (and even then subject to revision). A glance at our timeline (see appendix II) may help us understand this lengthy process, particularly true of the composition of the Torah (or Pentateuch, in the Christian Bible). In fact, in reading all this biblical material we need to recognise the differences between ancient authorship, when technology was so much more limited, and modern composition. The question, 'Who wrote the Torah?', cannot be answered so simply as a question about the author of *The Name of the Rose* or even *The Merchant of Venice* — unless we are prepared to settle for an uncritical, fundamentalist reply ignoring all the evidence.

Scholars like Von Rad,[13] then, suggest that a passage like *Deuteronomy* 26.5–9 represents a recital of a creed in ancient times in a paraliturgical situation like the presentation of harvest first fruits to the priest (and now inserted into our composite text). A catechesis occurs in the paraliturgy, allowing the individual to recite belief in some way like our credal recitation, stating who is the people's God and what is the relationship between them — a belief basic to any religion:

> A wandering Aramean was my father [i.e., the patriarch Jacob];
> > he went down into Egypt and lived there as an alien, few in number,
> > and there he became a great nation, mighty and populous.
> When the Egyptians treated us harshly and afflicted us, by imposing hard
> > labour on us, we cried to the Lord, the God of our ancestors;
> The Lord brought us out of Egypt with a mighty hand and an
> > outstretched arm, with a terrifying display of power,
> > and with signs and wonders;
> and he brought us into this place and gave us this land,
> > a land flowing with milk and honey.[14]

The creed contains three main items:

- God's *choice, election, promise* to the people (in the patriarchs);
- God's *deliverance* of them from slavery: the *Exodus*; and
- their *entry into the Land*.

We find the same basic elements in other such creeds (which we should read to validate the point, but space does not allow in this book): *Dt* 6.20–23 (where the situation is even more catechetical) and *Joshua* 24 (where a ceremony of covenant rededication seems to be enacted). They will recur over and over again throughout the Old Testament, even as other items enter the pattern in the course of time; if we are looking for pattern — and we are — one is emerging. What is also interesting and relevant is the absence of some items from the pattern we might have thought likewise basic:

– some mention of creation of the world instead of immediate
   concentration on the (single) people; and
– (Sinai) covenant, which looms large in the OT as a whole (but
   which belongs to a different tradition from the Exodus
   tradition represented here).

Having looked at some basic parts of Torah and, with *Joshua*,
Former Prophets (Historical Books, in the Christian Bible) in prose,
let us turn our attention to some verse pieces of the OT — often
older for that fact. Also from the Torah, in *Exodus* 15, we have a
song of Moses recounting, with poetic elaboration, the marvels of
the Exodus that also fascinated the Deuteronomic author. We
should read it all, at least down to these verses where the theological message is formulated:

> Who is like you, O Lord, among the gods?
> Who is like you, majestic in holiness, awesome in splendour, doing
>   wonders?
> You stretched out your right hand, the earth swallowed them.
> In your steadfast love you led the people whom you redeemed; you
>   guided them by your strength to your holy abode (11–13).

It is, in fact, theology we are reading, not simply expressions of
faith. The people over time have had the opportunity to mull over
the events of the Exodus, probably to elaborate them as good tales
told over time tend to get embroidered, and to bring out their significance — a theological exercise, as resulted also in those cultic
credos (as our Christian creeds are the result of much 'heavy'
theologising, less accessible than their biblical counterparts). The
theological judgment in both cases is identical: God has chosen and
cared for a people, and the principal index of this is the Exodus.
This theology emerges also from another verse passage, one of
several salvation history psalms in our Psalter (others include *Pss*
78, 104, 135, which also could be read, glancing at our timeline for
the information that the psalms come from a lengthy period of
Israel's history). *Psalm* 136 is a litany of praise/thanksgiving, an-
tiphonal in form; its interest for our theme is that while thanking
God for favours we have seen as traditional, especially the marvels
of the Exodus, the litany begins with material creation as grounds
for praise:

> O give thanks to the Lord of lords, ... ;
> who alone does great wonders, ... ;

> who by understanding made the heavens, ... ;
> who spread out the earth on the waters, ... ;
> who made the great lights, ... ;
> the sun to rule over the day, ... ;
> the moon and stars to rule over the night, ... ;
> who struck Egypt through their firstborn, ... (3–10, antiphon omitted).

That interest in the cosmos as integral to the divine plan, which occurs elsewhere as a theme in the *Psalms*, will disappear as we return to historical material; for those composers it is secondary in importance to the fortunes of the people.

A developing pattern

The theological pattern of the cultic credos had in time to accommodate further developments in Israel's history if these were to be seen as part of God's providence in their regard. The monarchy was one such. At first, through the eyes of a composer (perhaps from the north, and thus) unsympathetic to a (Jerusalem) king, the new institution is seen as religiously decadent and pragmatically regrettable. The Lord consoles Samuel, 'They have not rejected you, but they have rejected me from being king over them' (*1 Sm* 8.7). And Samuel proceeds to lecture the people on 'the ways of the king who will reign over you', a very unflattering portrait indeed — but insufficient to dissuade the people from their demands (8.10–22). Further on in the Former Prophets, however, at *2 Sm* 7, where the composer (probably from the south) is sympathetic, not only is monarchy now permissible but it has become so much a part of the divine design for Israel as to be an eternal dynasty. The Lord through Nathan assures David:

> I will raise up your offspring after you, who shall come forth from your body, and I will establish his kingdom. He shall build a house for my name, and I will establish the throne of his kingdom forever (7.12–13).

Later developments, like exile and return from exile, also had to be incorporated in the pattern. The Chronicler,[15] in a remarkable survey of Israel's history in the book of *Nehemiah*, develops a theological pattern with which Paul would resonate, with a point–counterpoint sequence of fidelity–infidelity: the Lord's continuing fidelity to his promises, the people's equally consistent infidelity. The survey, rehearsing the traditional items from the viewpoint of the restored community, is noteworthy also for substantial inclusion of the Sinai covenant:

... You came down also upon Mount Sinai, and spoke with them from heaven, and gave them right ordinances and true laws, good statutes and commandments, and you made known your holy sabbath to them and gave them commandments and statutes and a law through your servant Moses. For their hunger you gave them bread from heaven, and for their thirst you brought water for them out of the rock, and you told them to go in to possess the land that you swore to give them.
BUT they and our ancestors acted presumptuously and stiffened their necks and did not obey your commandments; they refused to obey, and were not mindful of the wonders that you performed among them ...
Here we are, slaves to this day — slaves in the land that you gave to our ancestors to enjoy its fruit and its good gifts ... [16]

For a prose survey of Israel's history that is similar in its theology while representing a quite different category of 'historical' composition we could look at the deuterocanonical book of *Judith*, a late piece of religious literature unashamedly mixing up facts of history to bring out its pious message. The author tests our credulity, while highlighting a theology that does cohere with the rest of the Old Testament, by putting into the mouth of the Ammonite general Achior a typical survey of Israel's salvation history in the manner of *Joshua* 24, concluding with the grave advice to the invader (later beheaded by the pious Judith, paragon of Jewish fidelity) that only infidelity will betray the people (ch. 5).

The message of the prophets

From a selection of reflective material from Torah and Former Prophets, prose and verse, pre-exilic and post-exilic, representing northern and southern sympathies, we can discern a pattern on the part of theologians pondering God's dealings with the people (and, in a minor key, with the whole universe). The pattern is strong on truth, theological significance, less so on fact; *Judith* is the classic example of this, but to an extent all the composers have filtered the data to bring out the message. From Paul's vantage point it is (a version of) the mystery of Christ that is being sketched, but 'in former generations this mystery was not made known to humankind' (*Eph* 3.5), at least in those terms. It is also a partial version, looking at one people's story — naturally.

The pattern is known also to the Latter, or Writing, Prophets of the Hebrew Bible; in fact, it is basic to their message. To underpin their call to fidelity, which is their staple teaching, the prophets refer their listeners to that tissue of divine favours that served The Chronicler so powerfully to document his thesis of fidelity–infidelity. Eighth-century Hosea (see timeline), using marital imagery which the story of his own unhappy marriage in ch. 1 reinforces, refers to wilderness and covenant themes in ch. 2 to call the northern people back to observance before it is too late. His version of the Lord's lament over an unresponsive northern kingdom is full of pathos as it is of references to favours of the past:

> When Israel was a child, I loved him,
>   and out of Egypt I called my son.
> The more I called them,
>   the more they went from me;
> they kept sacrificing to the Baals,
>   and offering incense to idols.
> Yet it was I who taught Ephraim to walk,
>   I took them up in my arms;
>   but they did not know that I healed them.
> I led them with cords of human kindness,
>   with bands of love.
> I was to them like those
>   who lift infants to their cheeks,
>   I bent down to them and fed them (11.1–4).

With the north fallen through unrepentant infidelity (in the theological judgment of the biblical authors), prophets in Judah who sensed a like fate for that kingdom also had recourse to the familiar pattern to urge repentance and fidelity. Jeremiah under King Jehoiakim preached a religion of the heart mindful of God's favours since the Exile:

> For in the day I brought your ancestors out of the land of Egypt, I did not speak to them or command them concerning burnt offerings and sacrifices. But this command I gave them, 'Obey my voice, and I will be your God, and you shall be my people.' ... From the day that your ancestors came out of the land of Egypt until this day, I have persistently sent all my servants the prophets to them, day after day; yet they did not listen to me, or pay attention, but they stiffened their necks. They did worse than their ancestors did (7.22–23,25–26).

The Chronicler, we saw, would later concur in this analysis, as would Paul. Jeremiah has finally to admit that the original covenant on Mt Sinai, the original attempt at relationship, has failed on the people's part, has been externalised instead of reaching the heart. The pattern of divine action — the mystery — has proved ineffectual: nothing more damning and hopeless could be said. So a new covenant, a new attempt at relationship that will be interior, of the heart, will be necessary — something the New Testament will see fulfilled in Jesus. It is a unique admission in the Hebrew Bible:

> The days are surely coming, says the Lord, when I will make a new covenant with the house of Israel and the house of Judah. It will not be like the covenant that I made with their ancestors when I took them by the hand to bring them out of the land of Egypt — a covenant that they broke, though I was their husband, says the Lord. But this is the covenant that I will make with the house of Israel after those days, says the Lord: I will put my law within them, and I will write it on their hearts; and I will be their God, and they shall be my people (31.31–33).

Even after the fall of Judah, prophets continued to remind the people in exile of the pattern of divine favours that followed from their original choice, Ezekiel and Second Isaiah among them; in that pattern, and particularly in covenant relationship, lay hope. The mystical Ezekiel, obsessed with the holiness of God, who would vindicate his name, confirmed Jeremiah's promise of a new, interior relationship:

> I will take you from the nations (says the Lord), and gather you from all the countries, and bring you into your own land. I will sprinkle clean water upon you, and you shall be clean from all your uncleannesses, and from all your idols I will cleanse you. A new heart I will give you, and a new spirit I will put within you; and I will remove from your body the heart of stone and give you a heart of flesh. I will put my spirit within you, and make you follow my statutes and be careful to observe my ordinances. Then you shall live in the land that I gave to your ancestors; and you shall be my people, and I will be your God (36.24–28).

Occupation of the land, a theme recurring in all recitals of sacred history, is particularly central to the Priestly material in the Hebrew Bible, with which Ezekiel has an affinity. Hope in this credal article was kept alive among the exiled community by reminders also from the Isaian prophet we call Second Isaiah after his eighth-century namesake. The good news about return from exile preached by 'this impressive evangelist'[17] was couched in terms of the original exodus, itself such a cornerstone of Israel's belief: the pattern, the mystery, could not fail to inspire.

> Thus says the Lord,
>   who makes a way in the sea,
>   a path in the mighty waters,
> who brings out chariot and horse,
>   army and warrior;
> they lie down, they cannot rise,
>   they are extinguished, quenched like a wick:
> Do not remember the former things,
>   or consider the things of old.
> I am about to do a new thing;
>   now it springs forth, do you not perceive it?
> I will make a way in the wilderness
>   and rivers in the desert (43.16–19).

Deutero-Isaiah, repeating a theme that surfaces elsewhere before him in these scriptures only in his namesake, warns the people that the salvation now being brought to them is being offered also to the *goyim*, those other nations so often spurned. This universal offer is to be mediated through a mysterious figure (also so significant for the New Testament) of a Suffering Servant, who becomes light to the nations, the *lumen gentium* that Vatican II would take as its clarion call. (The prophetical book *Jonah* will, of course, develop this theme in a major key much later.)

> Here is my servant, whom I uphold,
>   my chosen, in whom my soul delights.
> I have put my spirit upon him;
>   he will bring forth justice to the nations ...
> I have given you as a covenant to the people,
>   a light to the nations,
>   to open the eyes that are blind,
> to bring out the prisoners from the dungeon,
>   from the prison those who sit in darkness (42.1,6–7).

The perspective of Wisdom

As we have read those major divisions of the scriptures of the Jewish people, Torah and Prophets and some of the Writings, a theologised pattern emerged of the major concerns of the community. It was a limited perspective on God's dealings with them

and their world: they were at centre stage, other peoples rarely seen
in a good light as objects of the divine favour demonstrated so
markedly in their own story, while the universe as a whole was
generally out of focus. Perhaps it is a perspective typical of any
people reflecting on history; the whole story, the whole truth, 'was
not made known to humankind,' as Paul says of the mystery of
Christ. It is the overall perspective, the pattern we are looking for as
the biblical dimension of the mystery of Christ; we are not interested in any typological procedure that in a very partial way looks
for figures and events that might be thought to point ahead to the
person of Jesus.

We are especially thankful, therefore, as Paul was, for the expansion of this introspective biblical viewpoint achieved by the Wisdom composers of the Old Testament (and here we take particular
advantage of the fresh appreciation of its canon encouraging us to
include *Sirach, Wisdom of Solomon* and *Baruch* along with *Job,
Proverbs* and *Ecclesiastes*, not to mention sapiential material in other
books). These composers, who before the Exile and particularly in
the wake of it drew on traditions from human experience generally,
even from outside Israel, gave such a new dimension to community
thinking as to earn the displeasure of biblical theologians committed to a narrow historical tradition.[18] Von Rad and his many disciples could even claim that 'its theological base and interest were
too narrowly fixed,' [19] and Walter Zimmerli remark that 'Wisdom
has no relation to the history between God and Israel.' [20] Quite the
contrary is true: the anthropological, cosmic, epistemological,
moral, religious, theological, traditional, thematic and social viewpoints of Wisdom have the effect of achieving for Israel a universal
perspective[21] that, while certainly different from the introspection
of Torah and Prophets, lends to the pattern a comprehensiveness
that wins Paul's approval to the extent of becoming synonymous
with God's will, purpose, plan, mystery in the letters. Yet even
today, though there has been quite a reversal of appreciation of this
material, commentators on Wisdom can be satisfied to point to
literary forms as its distinctive characteristic, neglecting its remarkable theology.

It is the sages' theological perspective we are interested in. Von
Rad is right in observing that the God of these books is not the God
of the patriarchs; instead, it is a Providential Lord of history and the
cosmos, who governs all peoples and all things. Not that the sages
are unaware of Israel's history: *Sirach* devotes chapters 44–50 and

Wisdom of Solomon the final ten of its 19 chapters to a survey of that history — but not on the model of patriarchal and deuteronomistic history. These sapiential surveys reach beyond Abraham, father of Israel, back to the primeval history, to Enoch (*Sir* 44.15) and 'the first-formed father of the world' (*Wis* 10.1 in a litany of figures of wisdom left deliberately anonymous so as to be universal); it is all humankind that is of interest, not simply one people. One can understand how this perspective (plus the Greek language of *Wisdom* and their late composition) would encourage the rabbis late in the first century AD to relegate these books from their canon.

For example, look at the reworking (midrash) of the *Genesis* creation stories in *Sirach* 16.26–17.17. The author follows the regular movement of the Priestly version from creation of the universe, its stocking with living things, and then the appearance of human beings. But in this sage's version it is to all of these human beings — not just one chosen people — that he grants his various gifts, including (God forbid!) the Sinai covenant, reported in the language of *Exodus*:

> He bestowed knowledge upon them
>   and allotted to them the law of life.
> He established with them an eternal covenant,
>   and revealed to them his decrees.
> Their eyes saw his glorious majesty,
>   and their ears heard the glory of his voice.
> He said to them, 'Beware of all evil.'
>   And he gave comandment to each of them concerning the neighbour.

Only after this universal picture of God's intentions for his creation does Sirach revert to type (in fact, he is a very devout, if generally catholic, Israelite) and agree that Israel enjoys special attention:

> He appointed a ruler for every nation,
>   but Israel is the Lord's own portion (17.11–14,17).

So the theological anthropology of Wisdom (with a capital W: it is interested in more than wisdom) regards people not as Jew and Gentile but in the most universal categories, good and evil. Yet Wisdom has a cosmic, this-worldly dimension to its thinking, too, that distinguishes it from the rest of the Old Testament and gives scandal to those commentators spoken of above. Not only does its epistemology and morality depend on experience in the real world as distinct from Sinai epiphanies and other such revelation, but it takes this world seriously: Solomon, the paradigm of wisdom, speaks (as Jesus will later) 'of trees, ... of animals, and birds, and reptiles, and fish' (*1 Kgs* 4.33). Further, in a Pauline perspective 'from before the foundation of the world', it sees wisdom hypostatised (no simple personification here) being active in creation:

> The Lord created me at the beginning of his work,
>   the first of his acts of long ago.
> Ages ago I was set up,
>   at the first, before the beginning of the earth.
> When there were no depths I was brought forth ...
> when he marked out the foundations of the earth,
>   then I was beside him, like a master worker
> (*Prv* 8.23–24,29–30; cf *Sir* 24.1–12).

Wisdom can speak at length and with obvious affinity and pathos of natural marvels and beauties in a way thought irrelevant by most of the Old Testament from its narrower perspective: read the Lord's lectures to Job on his transcendence (e.g., chs. 38–39) or that beautifully pathetic picture of declining energies in old age painted by quaintly dyspeptic Qoheleth (*Eccl* 12.1–7), not to mention the psalms we adverted to and others like *Ps* 8.

When we add to this the further extension of the 'traditional' pattern achieved by the insight into immortality for the just in *Wisdom of Solomon*, it is not surprising that Paul can see in wisdom a synonym for his theological matrix and say, 'We speak God's wisdom in mystery' (*1 Cor* 2.7). The debate in that letter to the Corinthians is about true wisdom, which Paul sees not encapsulated in mere pagan sophistry or in the rabbinic view (represented in pious *Sirach* and *Baruch*) that 'she is the book of the commandments of God' (*Bar* 4.1), the Mosaic Law, but in God's whole design, the mystery of Christ, and particularly its focal point, the Paschal Mystery of Jesus, 'a stumbling block to Jews and foolishness to Gentiles, but to those who are called, both Jews and Greeks, Christ the power of God and the wisdom of God' (1.23–24). Yes, true wisdom is in mystery, in the mystery of Christ. For Paul, wisdom denotes an interpretation of God's designs that sees all people within them, not just one people chosen, and that includes as well the whole universe — something the Old Testament otherwise ignores and gnostic creation myths (such as *The Apocryphon of John*)[22] and some intertestamental literature (such as Ethiopian *Enoch*)[23] reject.

Not surprisingly, commentators have found in the creation

stories of *Genesis* the hand of the sages, even if the stories in-
dividually have been attributed to Priestly and Yahwistic com-
pilers/editors. The repeated emphasis on the goodness of created
realities in the former, which we saw Sirach found grist to his mill,
is thoroughly sapiential. It helps to fill out the theology of the
Hebrew scriptures, as an element missing from those cultic credos,
which like all creeds come to be normative, as we found.

Christ in the New Testament

We noted earlier that, of the scriptures composed by Jews and
Christians, the latter had the former at hand in the work of composition. Moreover, most of the contributors to the New Testament
came from Judaism, and were aware of those normative creeds. It is
therefore not surprising if, as well as presenting the life and person
of Jesus, they reflect on and indeed duplicate the well-rehearsed
pattern found in the Old. They are naturally concerned to suggest
that whatever was said of the people of one dispensation could be
said in a major key of the people of the new relationship. We have
seen the Jew Paul doing just that, stating that the pattern which
emerged in Old Testament history and literature without the actors
and reporters fully grasping its significance was now, in the light of
the Paschal Mystery, clear as to its intended scope and true
beneficiaries. Not that all New Testament contributors, without a
Damascus experience, themselves see the pattern that Paul sees, the
mystery of Christ; we noted Matthew's angel, for instance, being as
myopic as the Deuteronomist about the beneficiaries of God's
favours. Those we shall focus on are theologians who step aside
from the action to reflect on significance, truth, pattern, mystery;
evangelists, by nature of their (reactionary) concentration on Jesus,
do not often number among these, theologians though they be.

The result is that we find ourselves referring largely to epistolary
literature, more reflective than kerygmatic, for documenting the
biblical dimension of the mystery of Christ in the case of the New
Testament — Peter and particularly Paul. Paul it is, for instance,
who is adamant that the pattern should be less obscure with the
coming of Jesus: the veil over the face of Moses (2 *Cor* 3.13) — or
over the minds of the Jewish people (3.15) — has been removed for
those who turn to the Lord. So the *Acts* represents him (and
Stephen at 7.2–53) doing just what Nehemiah and so many others
in the Old Testament did, rehearsing the familiar pattern from the
patriarchs onwards, before crossing to Jesus, particularly his death

and resurrection (cf *Acts* 13.17–33), and claiming the pattern has reached fulfilment.

The ancient creeds began with election of a people (creation, we saw, being of secondary importance), and New Testament authors are thus anxious to see a new choice, a new election and promise to a new people of God. For Peter the key scriptural references to this (*Exodus* 19, *Isaiah* 42, *Hosea* 1) can be applied to converts to the new community:

> But you are a chosen race, a royal priesthood, a holy nation, God's own people, in order that you may proclaim the mighty acts of him who called you out of darkness into his marvellous light.
> Once you were not a people,
>   but now you are God's people;
> once you had not received mercy,
>   but now you have received mercy (*1 Pt* 2.9–10).

Paul the Jew, beginning that essay in *Romans* which is the kernel of his message, agonises over this same fact — that to the Gentiles goes the election to a destiny that his people of birth enjoyed in wondrous fashion. True pathos is here in this acceptance of the mystery of Christ:

> I am speaking the truth in Christ — I am not lying; my conscience confirms it by the Holy Spirit — I have great sorrow and unceasing anguish in my heart. For I could wish that I myself were accursed and cut off from Christ for the sake of my own people, my kindred according to the flesh. They are Israelites, and to them belong *the adoption*, the glory, the covenants, the giving of the law, the worship, and *the promises*; to them belong the patriarchs, and from them, according to the flesh, comes the Messiah [*Christos*], who is over all, God blessed forever. Amen (9.1–5).

The wrenching pathos for Paul, of course, is that in the mystery of Christ he, while so conscious of the prerogatives of his own people (at least as instilled into him by his biblical upbringing), has the mission of administering a plan, an *oikonomia* that acknowledges the partiality of that biblical view and admits a much wider range of beneficiaries.[24] It is only Jesus, however, who can speak for the God of the glory and the covenants, and announce the criteria on which that more comprehensive election (determined 'from before the foundation of the world') is made. These criteria constitute his fundamental message: God's *basileia*, value system, will, kingly rule (less happily 'kingdom'). Of all his teaching, these criteria, these values are expressed in the Gospels most formally (as kernel of all parables and miracles) at the opening of the great sermons:

> Blessed are the poor in spirit, for theirs is the *basileia* of heaven.
> Blessed are those who mourn, for they will be comforted.
> Blessed are the meek, for they will inherit the earth.
> Blessed are those who hunger and thirst for righteousness, for they will be filled.
> Blessed are the merciful, for they will receive mercy.
> Blessed are the pure of heart, for they will see God.
> Blessed are the peacemakers, for they will be called children of God.
> Blessed are those who are persecuted for righteousness' sake, for theirs is the *basileia* of heaven.
> Blessed are you when people revile you and persecute you and utter all kinds of evil against you falsely on my account. Rejoice and be glad, for your reward is great in heaven.[25]

Completely in the tradition of biblical Wisdom, Jesus steps away from any notion of racial exclusiveness and challenges all people to gain membership in God's people. The evangelical *basileia* is a divine policy statement, a manifesto, that we shall see all the great major religions of the world endeavouring, unconscious of its Jesuan expression, to replicate; its implementation, however, will naturally prove as difficult for them as it has for the followers of Jesus. As a theological matrix related to Paul's notion of the mystery of Christ, it supplies the moral basis on which people can be confident of finding a place within the divine plan for all. For us in our study of the biblical dimension of the mystery, we see it supplanting the inadequate criteria for inheritance of God's blessings enunciated in earlier credos.

A new relationship

The central message of the Old Testament, we saw, was that God so cared for the people of his choice as to (deliver and) relate himself to them; even sages like Ben Sira and Baruch felt constrained to admit this special relationship. So the New Testament theologians are concerned to show that Jesus' principal task and achievement is to forge a new relationship, a new covenant, as Jeremiah and Ezekiel had foretold. For Paul, with his sights on Judaism and his continuing problems from Judaizers in the community, the deliverance, the new Exodus Jesus achieves (referred to also by Peter above) is from (sin, ignorance and) the burden of the Mosaic Law. At one time for that people the Law[26] served the negatively protective role of a gaoler, he tells the Galatians (3.23–24); with the coming of Jesus and the achievement of true freedom it is only an incubus to be removed along with subjection to any other false influence or discrimination, racial or sexual:

> When the fulness of time had come, God sent his Son, born of a woman, born under the Law, in order to redeem those who were under the Law, so that we might receive adoption as children. And because you are children, God has sent the Spirit of his Son into our hearts, crying, 'Abba! Father!' So you are no longer a slave but a child, and if a child then also an heir, through God (*Gal* 4.4–7).

What relationship could be closer than children to father? A new covenant indeed, as intimate and permanent, as proof against externalising as Jeremiah and Ezekiel could want.

John the evangelist, quite capable of interposing in his own narrative to comment on significance, also highlights Jesus' achievement in terms of exodus and covenant. When he reports Caiaphas' comment on the appropriateness of one man dying for the people, John interrupts to endorse the accuracy of this remark: it is exactly what is happening in terms of the old pattern, but with the reshaped dimensions of the new covenant:

> He did not say this on his own, but being high priest that year he prophesied that Jesus was about to die for the nation, and not for the nation only, but to gather into one the dispersed children of God (11.51–52).

So when the Gospels (and Paul) reach the climax of the Paschal Mystery, they report Jesus deliberately evoking echoes of *Exodus* and *Jeremiah* on covenant. That is what he is doing in that mystery:

> And he did the same with the cup after supper, saying, 'This cup that is poured out for you is the new covenant in my blood' (*Lk* 22.20; cf *1 Cor* 11.25).

A new people

Jesus would achieve that intimate relationship for the people — but it would be a new people, differently composed, of 'all the scattered children of God'. The old model has gone, the Light of the nations has come. Paul, missioner to the nations, can never forget this, the remarkable fact that, in the mystery of Christ, despite all the insistence of his upbringing, these nations gain entrance to the plan — and he is charged to ensure it! We continue to detect in him, despite his acceptance of the newly constituted single people of God, an 'us and them' mentality, deepening the pathos. He continues to speak of 'my own people' even while addressing pagan converts:[27] it appeared in the beginning of the essay in *Romans* above as it does at the close in ch. 11, when he highlights instead the gain of the Gentiles at the expense (and possible emulation) of the Jewish people:

> Now I am speaking to you Gentiles. Inasmuch then as I am an apostle to the Gentiles, I glorify my ministry in order to make my own people jealous, and thus save some of them. For if their rejection is the reconciliation of the world, what will their acceptance be but life from the dead! ... Brothers and sisters, I want you to understand this mystery.[28]

The letters to the converts from paganism in the communities at Ephesus[29] and Colossae also stress the remarkably new dimensions of (Paul's understanding of) the mystery, the pattern:

> I became the servant [of the Church] according to God's commission that was given to me for you, to make the word of God fully known, the mystery that has been hidden throughout the ages and generations but has now been revealed to his saints. To them God chose to make known how great among the Gentiles are the riches of the glory of this mystery, which is Christ in you, the hope of glory (*Col* 1.25–27; cf *Eph* 3.1–12).

The mystery and the cosmos

Remarkable though this redimensioning of the old pattern is, to include the nations within the bounds of God's people, yet the New Testament picture is more striking still. Paul spoke to the Romans above (11.15) of the mystery as we now know it involving 'the reconciliation of the world', the *kosmos*, as though reconciling the other nations to God has somehow led to the complete reconciliation of the whole universe to him. This is to follow Israel's sages down an avenue they opened up with their wider perspective. Paul's thinking on the mystery of Christ, we observed, owes much to this Wisdom theology; he insists that the mystery 'gathers up all things, things in heaven and things on earth' (*Eph* 1.10). So the notion of reconciliation extending to the whole of creation is found elsewhere in his thinking:

So if anyone is in Christ, there is a new creation: everything old has passed away; see, everything has become new! All this is from God, who reconciled us to himself through Christ, and has given us the ministry of reconcilation; that is, in Christ God was reconciling the world to himself.[30]

The New Testament generally does not follow Paul down that sapiential avenue; Matthew's angel and Paul's fellow contributors are not of that mind, even though Jesus himself we have seen to be completely in the tradition of Solomon in his attitude to the real world. The evangelists, however, do not present him speaking on cosmic redemption but rather on the human beneficiaries. Paul it is who principally gives us evidence of an expansion of the biblical dimension of the mystery of Christ in the New Testament, thanks to Wisdom. There is that hymn about Christ in *Colossians* 1.15–20, clearly a composition anterior to the letter, that speaks in Wisdom terms of God reconciling all things to himself (v. 20) and presents a figure, who is 'before all things' and reminiscent of hypostatised wisdom's role in creation in *Proverbs* 8 and *Sirach* 24:

He is the image of the invisible God,
   the firstborn of all creation;
for in him all things in heaven and on earth were created,
   things visible and invisible, …
   all things have been created through him and for him.
He himself is before all things,
   and in him all things hold together.
He is the head of the body, the church;
   he is the beginning, the firstborn from the dead,
   so that he might come to have first place in everything.
For in him all the fullness of God was pleased to dwell,
   and through him God was pleased to reconcile to himself all things,
   whether on earth or in heaven,
   by making peace through the blood of his cross.[31]

The hymn, of disputed origin, clearly owes much to Wisdom, and has been adapted; some inconsistencies are evident, moving from the place of the cosmos in the mystery of Christ to the work of Jesus for the Church. Despite that, the dimensions of the divine plan, reaching its focal point in Jesus (a typically Pauline emphasis), reach out beyond its human beneficiaries.

Paul, himself very much in the business of bringing those human beneficiaries to reach salvation, nevertheless explores in one rarefied vision the relation between their destiny and that of all created things. It is a remarkable insight, if in keeping with his understanding of the mystery of Christ elsewhere. His remarks in ch. 8 of *Romans* on a Christian life lived in the Spirit and destined for glory despite present suffering lead him to associate that destiny with the end awaiting the rest of creation. In his excitement he mingles two figures to convey this apocalyptic vision of the world's future: *deliverance* from bondage and *delivery* of a child struggling to be born.

> I consider that the sufferings of this present time are not worth comparing with the glory about to be revealed to us. For the creation waits with eager longing for the revealing of the children of God; for the creation was subjected to futility, not of its own will but by the will of the one who subjected it, in hope that the creation itself will be set free from its bondage to decay and will obtain the freedom of the glory of the children of God. We know that the whole creation has been groaning in labour pains until now; and not only the creation, but we ourselves, who have the first fruits of the Spirit, groan inwardly while we wait for adoption, the redemption of our bodies (8.18–23).

As apocalyptic usually does, Paul glances both back to the (biblical account of) beginnings and forward to the eschaton, neither of which is clear and precise, nor is his meaning when he talks of the primordial subjection of creation. But we get his general drift: creation, now in a condition of frustration,[32] as we are, will be delivered from it and attain a glorious destiny akin to ours. The mystery of liberation/redemption/reconciliation extends to the universe as a whole.

The breadth of the vision of God's plan for all his creation is breathtaking; animate and inanimate beings are gathered up into it. Like all such visions it is as short on detail as it is novel in its outline. The linear dimension of the pattern as Paul sees it is equally extensive, reaching forward to the eschaton, and equally sketchy. Like the people of God in the Old Testament, who struggled on from one unfulfilling realisation of the 'promised land' to another, our pilgrimage in salvation history still stretches ahead, in Paul's view. We are now, with the coming of Jesus the Christ, in the messianic age, 'the end of the ages'; there is an urgency about this present age,[33] the values are so much more clarified than in pre-Jesuan ages, response called for more urgently. So what is the recipe for life in the world with the end in sight? Detachment, says

Paul; in a series of hyperbolic paradoxes he recommends (not withdrawal — no ghetto mentality for him — but) a life that restores the intended relationship of human beings to the material world in *Genesis* that was distorted by Adam's choosing to invert the Priestly pyramid:

> I mean, brothers and sisters, the appointed time has grown short: from now on, let even those who have wives be as though they had none,
>> and those who mourn as though they were not mourning,
>> and those who buy as though they had no possessions,
>> and those who deal with the world as though they had no dealings with it.
>
> For the present form of this world is passing away (*1 Cor* 7.29–31).

The 'ministry of reconciliation' given to us in respect of the world should not be undermined by our absorption in the material realities we are necessarily involved with in this life. Like Wisdom, Paul sees the great danger in excessive preoccupation with things, good in themselves, whose transformation depends on our distancing ourselves somewhat from them. It is another brief, if pregnant, insight, rounding off the biblical picture of the mystery of Christ.

Pattern or person?

The New Testament thus reshapes or at least reinterprets the pattern of God's action in favour a people recognised and recorded in the Jewish scriptures. Just as the later body of tradition found the earlier blinkered, myopic, so other religious communities would record their own experience of God differently. Even Christians have continued to represent their experience since the close of the New Testament canon; *Part III. The Christian Testament since the Bible*[34] is one such attempt to suggest that revelation and story have not ceased in the Christian community. Likewise, many other religions have a body of lore that invites our study to discern the pattern of God's action among them: Moslems, Hindus, Buddhists, Sikhs, Zoroastrians, Taoists, Confucians,[35] even if for some eastern communities it is an 'oral scripture'[36] that is preserved. It would be relevant, though outside the scope of this essay, to read or listen to all this lore from the viewpoint of the mystery of Christ — to submit it, that is, to a Christological scrutiny.[37]

One feature of those other scriptures would be the place of Jesus: in most he would not appear, or would be relegated to a less prominent position; the human history they recount does not adhere to a BC ... AD polarity. Jesus is clearly the distinguishing figure of the Christian scriptures and Christian movement. These could more accurately be described as Jesuan when one considers that within the overall pattern — the mystery of Christ, in Paul's phrase — described similarly in Old and New Testaments, Jesus comes and acts. It is the significance of Jesus within that pattern to which all the second testament authors address themselves, some (like the evangelists, unlike Paul) even losing sight of the context, the big picture, to study the focal protagonist of the smaller picture. Even for Paul, however, right from *1 Thessalonians* it is 'our Lord Jesus Christ' whose grace he wishes his listeners (5.28), as right from Luke's angel it is 'the Christ, the Lord' (2.11) who is coming in the birth of Jesus; both authors are equally Jesuological if not equally Christological. It is faith in Jesus that leads them to compose and that they have in mind to nourish in their believing communities. These scriptures are generated by and for the body of Jesus' followers.

In our Christology, then, we need to keep in focus all of this scriptural reflection on God's creation and providence: an emerging pattern in Deuteronomist, Prophets, psalmists and sages, a climax to the pattern in chroniclers of Jesus' coming and going, a different pattern in the scriptures of other religious communities appreciative of divine action but not equally appreciative of the Jesus event. Which leads us to look more closely at the place of Jesus in the mystery of Christ, the nub of our Christology.

Points for discussion

1.   'I try to get beyond the facts to the truth,' says biographer Alan Marshall. Is there some correlation between this attempt and Paul's presentation of biblical history as the mystery of Christ?

2.   Are there any grounds in reading the Bible for concurring with the view, 'history is written by the victors'? To what extent does the *whole* truth about God's designs for all people and things appear?

3.   The evangelists stress Jesus' inauguration of God's value system, *basileia*. Can you see a connection between this emphasis and the Pauline presentation of the mystery of Christ?

4.   How well do you know the sacred writings of other religions? Why would this be advisable if you are to grasp the full pic-

ture of the mystery of Christ? Does the division of history into BC–AD make sense in the fuller picture?

Further reading

J. Barr, 'Biblical theology,' *Interpreter's Dictionary of the Bible, Supplement.*

W. Graham, 'Scripture' in M. Eliade, *The Encyclopedia of Religion* 13, New York: Macmillan, 1987, pp. 133–45.

B. Griffiths, *A New Vision of Reality. Western Science, Eastern Mysticism and Christian Faith* (1990), London: Fount, 1992.

C. Hill, *Breaking the Bread of the Word. Principles of Teaching Scripture*, Rome: Pontifical Biblical Institute, 1991.

D. Knight and G. Tucker, *The Hebrew Bible and its Modern Interpreters*, Chico CA: Scholars Press, 1985.

K. Rahner, 'Towards a fundamental theological interpretation of Vatican II,' *Theological Studies* 40 (1979) pp. 716–27.

Notes

1. Cf my *Breaking the Bread of the Word. Principles of Teaching Scripture*, Rome: Pontifical Biblical Institute Press, 1991, pp. 11–12; 'From Good News to Holy Writ. The share of the text in the saving purpose of the Word,' *Estudios Biblicos* 51 (1993).

2. *Living Tradition. Orthodox Witness in the Contemporary World*, Crestwood NY: St Vladimir's Seminary Press, 1978, p. 16.
   In the Catholic community, under the pressure of Counter-Reformation reaction to the Protestant stand on 'scriptura sola', the separation Meyendorff regrets became apparent. Though during the Second Vatican Council a Two-Source approach to the document on Revelation was formally rejected, the later text and continuing theological (and magisterial) statement still contain relics of that thinking, indicative of and contributory to a widespread misunderstanding of tradition in the community. 'Tradition' (with a capital) is thus often equated with doctrinal tradition, seen as separate from (and even opposed to) scriptural tradition, whereas both are forms of the community's transmissional process.

3. Cf J. A. Fitzmyer, 'Romans,' *New Jerome Biblical Commentary*, Englewood Cliffs: Prentice Hall, 1990, p. 835.

4. Vatican II Constitution on Divine Revelation *Dei Verbum* (1965), #11.

5. Cf Pierre Grelot, *La Bible Parole de Dieu*, Paris: Desclée, 1965, p. 253: 'All the history which precedes Christ, all that takes its course in constituting sacred history, thus gains its meaning by reference to Christ

... In saying *by reference to Christ,* one does not understand only Christ as Head considered from the point of view of his individual life, which occurs in the time from his Incarnation up to his cross and reaches its consummation beyond the time of his entry into glory. One envisages the mystery of Christ in all its extent, including the historical development which occurs here below in the Church and is consummated on the last day in the glory of the resurrection. Such is the *Reality* to which is related all history previous to the first coming of Christ.'

Grelot, while appreciating the difference in biblical perspectives, could elaborate it more clearly by distinguishing Jesus from Christ, one feels. He would also need to realise that the mystery, the reality, is not only linear but has a dimension of breadth as well; it is not only Jews and Christians who have their place in 'sacred history' (to say nothing of inanimate creation) — as later chapters will investigate.

6. There is a call today on the part of some groups sensitive to Jewish attitudes (generally in the US) to replace these terms. The alternatives proposed seem at least as unsatisfactory: 'Jewish and Christian Scriptures' obscures the fact that from the beginning the Christians spoke of Jewish writings, and not simply the NT, as their own; 'First and Second Testaments' seems equally discriminatory if discrimination is the problem. The Vatican's 1985 Notes on *Nostra Aetate,* Vatican II's Decree on Non-Christian Religions, addressed the issue, concluding that the current terminology is traditional and does not subscribe to displacement theology, treating the Old Testament as dépassé. Certainly there is no major unease with the traditional terminology: in 1990, for instance, two important biblical publications appeared that did not consider the issue worth even a mention: the *New Jerome Biblical Commentary* and the *New Revised Standard Version* of the Bible containing a preface by Bruce Metzger listing issues of concern to the revision committee. Our library shelves are full of journals and OT and NT Introductions that refer in their titles to these testaments, hardly a one that is entitled Hebrew Scriptures, Christian Scriptures. It would therefore be misleading to students, for instance, to encourage in them a usage not current, especially if current usage is not generally thought objectionable.

7. One real drawback of current usage is that 'testament' is a very ecclesiastical term that does not speak to the normal person unaware of its biblical background in *berith* (Heb.) and *diatheke* (Grk) and of the political figure employed there for a personal relationship. It would not be feasible to try to switch terminology to Old Relationship and New Relationship, nor appropriate if one considers that that term itself has become undervalued in today's sexually liberal times.

8. In the absence of evidence that in the biblical cultures women did take a literary role.

9. Cf Brevard Childs, *Introduction to the Old Testament as Scripture*, London: SCM, 1979: 'The history of the canonical process does not seem to be an avenue through which one can greatly illuminate the present canonical text (67) ... Although I do not deny that such a historical enterprise is legitimate and at times illuminating, it is my contention that the study of the history of Hebrew literature in the context of the ancient Near East is a different enterprise from studying the form and function of the Pentateuch in the shape accorded it by the community of faith as its canonical scriptures' (128).

10. See A. C. Sundberg, *The Old Testament of the Early Church*, Cambridge MA: Harvard Uni. Press, 1964; 'Reexamining the formation of the Old Testament canon,' *Interpretation* 42 (1988) pp. 78–82; J. A. Sanders, *Canon and Community. A Guide to Canonical Criticism*, Philadelphia: Fortress, 1984.

11. Cf Mary C. Boys, *Biblical Interpretation in Religious Education. A Study of the Kerygmatic Era*, Birmingham AL: Religious Education Press, 1980. Suggesting that the issue is susceptible of review, Boys concludes: 'During the early stage of my research and writing, I was acutely conscious of the theological and educational limitations of salvation history. Now, some three years later, I am no less aware of these problems, but I am also much more appreciative of its significance ... We can, nevertheless, discover that the concerns lying at the heart of *Heilsgeschichte* are timeless' (339).

12. There has been a considerable debate about the usefulness of biblical theology, including its accent on *Heilsgeschichte*, arising partly out of canonical criticism of the kind elaborated by Brevard Childs (note 8 above) and itself found wanting; see Childs' *Biblical Theology in Crisis*, Philadelphia: Westminster, 1970, and a helpful corrective to this reaction in James Barr's article, 'Biblical theology,' esp. ##13,14, in *Interpreter's Dictionary of the Bible, Supplement* (1970).

    For our purposes it is important to note that our accent lies on the theological attitude of the composers of the text, not on those of biblical commentators. It is vital to 'let the text speak' for itself.

13. Positions reached by the great pentateuchal scholars of a half century ago, like Von Rad and Martin Noth, have naturally undergone revision in the meantime. For a review of such recent scholarly work on the various divisions of the OT, see a work like D. A. Knight and G. A. Tucker (ed.), *The Hebrew Bible and Its Modern Interpreters*, Chico CA: Scholars Press, 1985 (pp. 268–72 for more recent pentateuchal positions).

14. It is important that we have a sound, preferably fairly literal translation, like the NRSV or NJB, so as to bring out not just the sense but the basic rhythms of the text (e.g., the Deuteronomic repetitiveness), which we may then recognise in other material calling upon the same source.

15. The unity of composition of the four books, *Chronicles 1 & 2, Ezra* and *Nehemiah*, is also a matter on which modern scholars have a range of positions; cf Knight and Tucker, *op.cit.*, pp. 305–308.

16. *Neh* 9.13–17,36. The composer's point–counterpoint procedure makes effective use of adversative adverbs, which in recitation (it is a homily that is being delivered at this point) deserve emphasis.

17. Cf W. Zimmerli, *The Law and the Prophets*, Eng. trans., Oxford: Blackwell, 1965, p. 87.

18. See my 'The dimensions of salvation history in the Wisdom books,' *Scripture* 19 (1967) pp. 97–106.

19. G. Ernest Wright, *God Who Acts: Biblical Theology as Recital*, London: SCM, 1952, p. 104. Cf G. Von Rad, *Old Testament Theology* I (2nd edn, 1957), Eng. trans., Edinburgh: Oliver and Boyd, 1962, pp. 445–46.

20. 'The place and limit of Wisdom in the framework of Old Testament theology,' *Scottish Journal of Theology* 17 (1964) p. 147.

21. See my 'The perspective of Wisdom,' *Scripture Bulletin* 21 (1991 No.2) pp. 16–20.

22. See B. Layton (ed.), *The Gnostic Scriptures*, London: SCM, 1987, pp. 23–51.

23. See H. F. D. Sparks (ed.), *The Apocryphal Old Testament*, Oxford: Clarendon, 1984, pp. 169–322. In *1 Enoch* 42 wisdom declines to take up a dwelling on earth, as she agreed willingly to do in *Sirach* and elsewhere in biblical Wisdom: 'Wisdom found no place where she could dwell, and her dwelling was in heaven. Wisdom went out in order to dwell among the sons of men, but did not find a dwelling; wisdom returned to her place and took her seat in the midst of the angels' (Sparks, p. 225). The world is unworthy, spoiled — a dualistic attitude found widely in contemporary thinking.
  For a modern Asian version of this story, rid of its dualism, Korean theologian Chung Hyun-Kyung spoke to the Seventh Assembly of the World Council of Churches in Canberra in 1991 in these terms: 'For me the image of the Holy Spirit comes from the image of *Kwan In*. She is venerated as Goddess of compassion and wisdom by East Asian women's popular religiosity. She is *bodhisattva*, enlightened being. She can go into Nirvana any time she wants to, but refuses to go into Nirvana by herself. Her compassion for all suffering living beings makes her stay in this world enabling other living beings to

achieve enlightenment … Perhaps this might also be a feminine image of the Christ who is the first born among us, one who goes before and brings others with her?' ('Come Holy Spirit, Renew the whole creation,' Assembly document no. PL 3.3, p. 7).

24. Karl Rahner, in estimating the key significance of Vatican II to be the transformation of a European Church into a world Church, parallels it with only one other such transformation, 'the transition from Jewish to Gentile Christianity', which he credits Paul with achieving — 'the transition from the Christianity of the Jewish Jesus to the Christianity of Paul' ('Towards a fundamental theological interpretation of Vatican II,' *Theological Studies* 40 [1979] p. 723).

25. *Mt* 5.3-11; cf *Lk* 6.20-23 for a less aetherealised version of the conditions of election — and a series of corresponding Woes. (Luke speaks of the *basileia* being God's; Matthew with his Jewish sensitivities avoids easy reference to the divine name and substitutes 'heaven'.)

26. Paul is not opposed to all law. In *Galatians*, while upholding freedom from the Mosaic Law, he can see no problem in imposing the Law of Christ (6.2) in its place.

27. Cf J. A. Fitzmyer, 'The Letter to the Romans,' *New Jerome Biblical Commentary*, p. 860: 'Though a Christian, Paul still looks on himself as a member of the race of the Jews. He calls them literally "my flesh", and thereby gives vivid expression of his solidarity with them.'

28. *Rom* 11.13–15,25. Brendan Byrne, *Reckoning with Romans* (Good News Studies 18), Wilmington: Glazier, 1986, p. 203, remarks of this reversal of fortunes: 'This view precisely reverses the standard Jewish apocalyptic expectation where the Gentiles stream to an already glorified Sion.'

29. Not all manuscripts of this letter mention the traditional destination; perhaps it was a circular letter rather than one meant for just one community.

30. *2 Cor* 5.17–19. Fitzmyer remarks of this passage: 'Reconciliation has not only an anthropological dimension, but a cosmic dimension too' ('Pauline theology,' *NJBC* p. 1399) — though one has to allow the possibility of an anthropological reference in *kosmos* here as we noted in the Johannine writings (cf p. 36).

31. *NRSV* translation, with a suggested verse form.

32. Cf B. Byrne, *Inheriting the Earth. The Pauline Basis of a Spirituality for Our Time*, Sydney: St Paul Publications, 1990, p. 88: 'By "futility" is meant frustration of its true purpose … Landscapes devastated by war, fertile areas reduced to desert by over-grazing, cities rendered uninhabitable by atmospheric pollution, irreplaceable forests cut

down: all these modern symptoms of human misuse of creation would precisely correspond to "futility" in Paul's understanding.'

33. It seems preferable to see this sense, rather than a merely temporal one, in Paul's statements about the endtime.

34. Introduced by Mark Booth, Harmondsworth: Penguin, 1986.

35. Cf William A. Graham, 'Scripture,' in M. Eliade, *The Encyclopedia of Religion* 13, New York: Macmillan, 1987, pp. 133–45.

36. Walter Ong regrets that such terms have been made necessary by our failure to develop concepts to deal with oral art forms, especially in other than Western cultures (*Orality and Literacy. The Technologizing of the Word*, London-New York: Methuen, 1982, p. 10). See my 'From Good News to Holy Writ'.

37. In this postmodern age we find extraordinarily arrogant the attitude of Jean Daniélou towards these religious traditions: 'There is in history a furrow made by God. This is the great proof of Catholicism, and is one of the most astonishing facts to come out of any objective study of the world. God intervenes in history to accomplish a certain plan ... The essential difference between Catholicism and all other religions is that others start with man ... But in Catholicism there is a contrary movement, the descent of God towards the world, in order to communicate His life to it. The answer to the aspirations of the entire universe lies in the Judaeo–Christian religion' (*The Salvation of the Nations* [1948], Eng. trans., Notre Dame: UND, 1962, pp. 7–8).

For an entirely more holistic approach to other (particularly eastern) religions and especially their scriptures, see Dom Bede Griffiths, *A New Vision of Reality. Western Science, Eastern Mysticism and Christian Faith* (1989), London: Fount, 1992. A further merit of this book is that it does in fact endeavour to submit these other scriptures to Christological analysis.

4

Jesus and Christology

Definitions of Jesus in our tradition, scriptural and dogmatic, have not always achieved a satisfying adequacy. The New Testament offers a range of portraits of Jesus; the Gospels and Paul present a double perspective of person and mystery. The early Apologists capitalised on the wider perspective to present Christianity in their pluralist world; pastors and Councils later concentrated on the person of Jesus, generally neglecting the more comprehensive mystery of Christ on which mission to Church and world depends.

The cover story of the August 15 1988 issue of *Time* magazine was devoted to the question, 'Who was Jesus?' The editors were impressed by the number of letters they received on the story, the largest since they had startled the world by naming Ayatollah Khomeini their Man of the Year in 1980. Beyond the degree of interest in the topic, they were also impressed by the number of readers suggesting a rephrasing: 'For the "well over a billion souls" who worship Jesus as God, the question is "Who *is* Jesus?", not "Who *was* Jesus?",' wrote a reader from Florida.

Members of other faiths have also raised this question over the ages, and in some cases their sacred literatures address it.[1] The question is not settled for Christians, either, at least in its extended form, 'Who is Jesus for me?' An undergraduate student of mine, a country lad perhaps being exposed to some Christological considerations for the first time as a young adult, left me with this unsophisticated admission of enquiry and uncertainty:

> The day had dawned, but
> still he did not come
> from behind the tree.
> My eyes are wide; I see —
> but nothing can be seen.

A touch, a handshake,
that's all I ask.
I go to Mass
and stare at statues
and read his book —
but my faith is still lingering.
O Jesus, open my eyes
and let me see you.
I turn over and touch the switch:
there is dark.
There is always darkness.
I wish there wasn't.

A.D.

Limits of a definition

The light had not yet dawned fully for Anthony, as it perhaps has not for any of us, despite all our reading of the Jesuan scriptures and the definitions of Church councils. Have our biblical and dogmatic traditions served us well in this regard? We note that our most recent Church council, Vatican II, did not aspire to improve upon earlier conciliar definitions of Jesus but instead settled for longer, more discursive descriptions of him.[2] Was that because the formula of Chalcedon in 451[3] could not be improved upon, or because the 'simplicity and clarity' that have been claimed for that very carefully worked formula[4] would still be beyond the modern readers of a pastoral document? Jesus, we recall from the New Testament, was not for pinning everything on terms or definitions, perhaps aware that formulas can be quoted by adversaries in quite opposite senses, as the history of heresy and dogma well illustrates. Anthony was right to admit to some agnosticism.

There is one place in our Gospels, however, an intriguing exception to their avoidance of the term 'mystery' that we left out of our earlier survey of the term with a view to close study here, where Jesus attempts self-definition in formula style. It, too, has the effect of such formulas, deluding or at least dismaying even other evangelists. It occurs in ch. 4 of *Mark*, and is situated at present (though probably originally from another part of Jesus' ministry) in the Galilean ministry, following immediately on the parable of the Sower. *Mk* 4.10ff reads as follows, translated literally:

(10) When he was alone, those around him with the Twelve asked him about the parables. (11) He said to them, 'To you the *mysterion* of God's

basileia has been given, whereas to those others outside everything is in parables, (12) so that

"Looking they may look and not see,
  and hearing they may hear and not understand,
 lest they be converted and forgiven" [*Is* 6.9–10].
(13) He said to them, 'Don't you understand this parable? How will you grasp all the parables? (14) The Sower sows the word … '

Commentators[5] have observed that there are some strange features of the passage as it now stands — vocabulary, phrasing, the 'intolerable' interpretation of the purpose of parables, the lack of correspondence between question and answer — so that there is likelihood that the self-definition of Jesus in 4.11a came originally from another part of the ministry, and was mistakenly brought into service here on the question of the meaning of parables in general.

What Jesus is asserting in this dominical saying preserved in *Mark* (and we note that his classic commentator Vincent Taylor sees Pauline influences on this evangelist), taking into account an adequate understanding of the two Greek terms, is this: *we/the disciples have been given a share in the wonderful reality that is Jesus himself as inaugurating God's reign and value system, and we are invited to accept the gift.* That is the marvellous statement about Jesus' role that is obscured by its placement in its present context. It is further obscured by translations such as 'secret', as we have seen before. Commentators more discerning grasp Mark's true intention: 'Mark indeed pre-supposes an age-long purpose of God, which he traces back to the beginning of creation (10.6; 13.19), a phrase which — not incidentally — Mark shares with *Dn* 12.1.' '*Mysterion* … is wholly appropriate to the context of *Mk* 4.11–12, which reflects on the disclosure of God's purposes.' Unlike these commentators, the other synoptic evangelists, who reproduce the pericope of Mark, hasten to alter Jesus' self-definition as though something shocking — for reasons we can understand, having seen something of other associations of 'mystery'. In both *Matthew* (13.11) and *Luke* (8.10) it appears in this denatured version: to you it has been given to know the mysteries of the *basileia*. They thus turn the gift of Jesus to us/the disciples into a merely 'cognitive experience' (as Fitzmyer says) by using mystery in the plural, by inserting the verb 'to know', and using the verb 'to give' in the sense of permit (uniquely) — losing the beautiful role definition of Jesus. So much for the fate of definitions.

New Testament perspectives

The overall message of the New Testament, as distinct from such isolated self-definitions, is that Jesus comes principally to announce and inaugurate God's *basileia*, his reign, will, value system; the Paschal Mystery, 'of first importance' to Paul (*1 Cor* 15.3), is subsumed in this mission.[6] This intention emerges in the structure of all Gospels as it does in the 'mini-Gospels' and briefer New Testament statements of Jesus' role such as *1 Cor* 2.1–2, *Phil* 2.5–11, *Rom* 5.6–11, *1 Pt* 1.18–21; 3.18–22. The mini-Gospels, those less casual attempts to encapsulate Jesus' life and work, replicate the concentration in these one-liners on the Paschal Mystery, but begin like the Gospels with ministry and preparation for ministry; Peter's sermons in *Acts* exemplify the kerygmatic form.

> You that are Israelites, listen to what I have to say:
> Jesus of Nazareth, a man attested to you by God with deeds of power, wonders and signs that God did through him among you, as you yourselves know —
> this man, handed over to you according to the definite plan and foreknowledge of God, you crucified and killed by the hands of those outside the law.
> But God raised him up (2.22–24; cf 1.21–22; 10.36–41).

The same kerygma underlying our Gospels results in an identical structure in all four:

— *preparation for ministry* (including Baptism and Temptations);
— *ministry in Galilee* (and movement to Jerusalem); and
— *THE PASCHAL MYSTERY.*

Within this preset pattern, which does not include birth stories as an integral element, individual evangelists feel free to adapt, especially John, whose Jesus, the Way, must appear more frequently in the centre of worship. But the stress still falls on function, soteriology.

Where Paul does differ from these Gospels is in setting a context, the mystery of Christ, 'the age-long purpose of God' (to quote the above Marcan commentator), within which the individual contribution of Jesus, the mystery of Jesus,[7] occurs; the Gospels, we saw, by way of reaction to the bigger picture, reduced the focus, though Mark in that verse 4.11a allows some suggestion of it to be retained — much to the alarm of the later evangelists. There is no contradiction between Paul and evangelists, merely a question of focus, perspective. Paul, with his broad focus and his indebtedness to

other scriptures, particularly Wisdom, can admit that the whole pattern, the mystery of Christ, is more comprehensive than the life and
work of Jesus (though to him as a follower this is of utmost importance). In his terms, that mystery is *polypoikilos*, multifaceted, 'of a
rich variety', with many dimensions — historical, ecclesial, cosmic;
these he explores to some extent, even if (as in the case of cosmic
reconciliation) cryptically, whereas he tells us nothing of the ministry of Jesus — not a single parable or miracle — before the Supper.
'The Jesus of history is apparently dismissed' by Paul, says
Günther Bornkamm with pardonable exaggeration.[8]

For some theologians the wider scope is acknowledged in the
phrase 'Christ-event', perhaps as open to misunderstanding as the
more biblical 'mystery of Christ'. Rudolf Bultmann, John Knox and
John Macquarrie find it helpful, even if not using it univocally.
They admit what we have found in Paul to be biblical, historical
and ecclesial dimensions of the mystery of Christ 'in seeing the
Christ-event as something larger than the career of Jesus of
Nazareth. In that larger reality there were joined inseparably the
career of Jesus and its impact on the believing community, the history of Israel and the history of the church, the tradition of the past
and the experience of the participants in the event. They are inseparably joined because each lends meaning to the other. This is in
no sense to downgrade Jesus Christ.'[9] Macquarrie is right: it is
simply a difference of perspective, of focus, which in theological
discussion it is helpful to preserve for the purpose of precision. To
achieve similar breadth of perspective, Indian theologian Raimundo Panikkar has adopted the term 'Christophany' to avoid the
limitations of a 'tribal Christology' failing to recognise that 'Christ
infinitely surpasses Jesus, the gate for christians to the christian
mystery.'[10]

We are grateful both for wider scope and for narrower focus; the
distinct contributions supply us with a key to an adequate Christology. We may not pick and choose like shoppers in a supermarket;
each scriptural theology fills in part of the picture, as Moltmann
reminds us.[11] Had we only the Jesuology of the Synoptics (John, we
shall see, does not respect the distinction), we should not have been
able to contextualise Jesus and appreciate his significance in at least
two communities' experience of God. Were the community of
Jesus' followers deprived of his 'vital statistics' in the Gospels,
there would be little basis for contact with the person in whom is
divine grace and truth and who for us is righteousness and

sanctification and redemption; nor without the Gospels would we come to see the central importance of the divine value system in all (valid) religious communities.

We can also appreciate how religious communities not sharing our faith in Jesus would yet find meaningful a Christology (doubtless in different terminology) that encompasses their story and experience of God as well as others', and includes also the story and welfare of the universe, while promoting as well the values of the Beatitudes. Pope John Paul II recently met in audience for the first time in 30 years the bishops of Burma (now officially Myanmar), and acknowledged their presence within a people largely following the form of Buddhism known as Theravada; he reminded the bishops that this religion makes people sensitive to values found in Jesus' life and teaching, 'a spiritual attitude which emphasises renunciation, self-giving and peaceful relations with all.' [12] We recall the efforts of the early apologists who constructed Christologies without mentioning the name of Jesus[13] yet upholding those values.

Jesus in Jesuan scriptures

It is thus important to acknowledge that our scriptural tradition about Jesus, whether the narrower Jesuology of the (Synoptic) Gospels or the more comprehensive Christology of commentators like Paul, is framed by one community for that community.[14] This is so even if, as in the case of Paul, there is consideration of the situation of (some) other peoples: the message is still directed to followers of Jesus. Faith in Jesus and acceptance of him as saviour is at least implicit. Until recently we have tended to read our scriptures as universal statements composed without reference to particular recipients, as though the Deuteronomist's message of fidelity and retribution did not have in focus a community on the brink of punishment in exile, or the Johannine accent on love and unity was not directed to a divided community in the province of Asia.[15] Our Bibles today are on sale at the corner store anywhere; in antiquity the text was intended for recital within one particular group.[16]

Magisterial statements like the Pontifical Biblical Commission's Instruction on the Historical Truth of the Gospels, *Sancta Mater Ecclesia*, in 1964,[17] endorsed at Vatican II, have helped alter our fundamentalist mindset on this matter; and of course it is a right hermeneutical attitude we should bring to all traditional statements of the community, such as doctrinal and dogmatic definitions. Faith does not remove the responsibility to be discriminating, critical (in the etymological sense) about purpose and occasion in the use of language.

Correlatively, we need to recognise the diversity of theologies about Jesus (the 'cloud of witnesses' of which Frances Young speaks)[18] in the various strands of our scriptural tradition. Not all composers, we have noted, see him identically in the same breadth of context, for example, while all yet being believers. Hence, in his *Christological Catechism* Fitzmyer responds with some warmth to the question, 'Are there different interpretations of Jesus as the Christ (or different Christologies) in the New Testament?' 'There are, indeed, and the sooner that readers of the New Testament learn to respect them, the better their comprehension of the New Testament will become. The tendency in the past to harmonise the data has been the cause of much misunderstanding about Jesus and his status as the God-man.'[19] We have done anything but harmonise the data above, being at pains to remark on the deliberate (even reactionary) change of focus of the evangelists in the wake of Paul's broad canvas.

Even amongst the Gospels there is diversity in depicting Jesus, for the good reason of the different composers and their different viewpoints dictated by their recipients' different situations and needs, as was emphasised by the 1964 Instruction and the Commission's later *Scripture and Christology*.[20] We have noted the Synoptics' accent on Jesus' role of announcing and implementing (not his own, but) God's kingly rule, *basileia*, on which John is silent, preferring to concentrate on the *basileus*, the king himself.[21] That notable departure suggests a wider theological difference: whereas the 'Synoptic' evangelists earn their name for the similar viewpoint they reveal in focusing on the doings of the Jesus of Nazareth (whom they in fact believe to be the Messiah), John's Jesus is introduced, acts and speaks as the King in person, the divine Logos, the Word (made flesh). Mark, for instance, is much concerned to dispel in his community any notions of Jesus as superstar, wonderworker; so he sandwiches the extraordinary event of the Transfiguration in ch. 9 between dire predictions of passion and death for the Son of Man (8.31; 9.31; 10.33), and secrecy about Jesus' messianic status is constantly enjoined. No such secrecy about status for John's Jesus: he comes as a pre-existent divine figure, he speaks in a series of divine 'I am' affirmations, he goes to death debating kingship with his judge without mention of suffering or crucifixion, only coronation, exaltation.[22]

That tone of divinity is so typically Johannine and so conspicuously missing in the Synoptics that when at one place in *Matthew* and *Luke* (in discourse material not available to Mark) Jesus for once speaks like Wisdom incarnate — a posture exemplified a score of times in *John*[23] — commentators remark on its oddity and term it 'a bolt from the Johannine firmament':

> I thank you, Father, Lord of heaven and earth, because you have hidden these things from the wise and the intelligent and have revealed them to infants; yes, Father, for such was your gracious will. All things have been handed over to me by my Father; and no one knows the Son except the Father, and no one knows the Father except the Son and anyone to whom the Son chooses to reveal him.
>
> Come to me, all you that are weary and are carrying heavy burdens, and I will give you rest. Take my yoke upon you, and learn from me; for I am gentle and humble in heart, and you will find rest for your souls. For my yoke is easy, and my burden is light.[24]

Likewise we note the difference in perspective between Jesus' commissioning of the Twelve to work only among the lost sheep of the house of Israel (*Mt* 10.5ff), a predictable Matthean perspective, and the Great Missionary Commission to all nations by the Danielic Son of Man now standing as the close of Matthew's Gospel.[25]

Jesus and Christ

Are we, when noting the different perspective and theological accent of John's Logos, the Light of the World, when compared with the Synoptic Jesus who — generally — works among Israel's needy and lost sheep, justified in speaking of a more Christological as distinct from Jesuological perspective? Is John, like Paul in places, adopting a wider viewpoint, conscious of the bigger picture, while still keeping the central figure in focus? This is not to question the faith in Jesus of the other evangelists and their audiences, but rather to admit the relative limitation of their viewpoint in concentrating on that Jesus whose task was principally to do with kingly rule among a new people of the divine King. How other people — all people, past and future — and the whole cosmos might respond to him was not their immediate concern, whereas it is integral to Paul's conception of the mystery of Christ.

Distinguishing these perspectives is likewise not simply a process of noting in New Testament accounts of Jesus pre-Easter and post-Easter viewpoints, as commentators usually do. Sean

Freyne says of a 1985 Christology by Juan Luis Segundo, *The Histori-cal Jesus of the Synoptics*: 'His own perspective is to look for signs of post-[P]aschal eschatological and ecclesiological concerns retrojected back on to the accounts of Jesus' career, and to separate the one from the other.' [26] This process is valuable in alerting us, for example, to the differences in Synoptic and Johannine portraits of Jesus. But the Pauline mystery of Christ is still more comprehen-sive; not simply pre-Easter and post-Easter, it is as well pre-Jesus and post-Jesus and side by side as well. A linear dimension is not sufficient for its theological compass — *polypoikilos*, the *Ephesians* calls it.

In suggesting that the focus in some New Testament authors is more on Jesus (a personal name) than on Christ (connoting the whole divine design, mystery, in which the Incarnation occurs) on ac-count of their purpose at the time, we are not following an adoptionist line suggested by John Hick and others impatient of an 'incarnational' Christology, who want us to see myth replacing reality:

> The need arises from growing knowledge of Christian origins, and in-volves a recognition that Jesus was (as he is presented in *Acts* 2.21) 'a man approved by God' for a special role within the divine purpose, and that the later conception of him as God incarnate, the Second Per-son of the Holy Trinity living a human life, is a mythological or poetic way of expressing his significance for us.[27]

Though there is value in the biblical notion of myth as a figurative overlay applied to a person or event to highlight its inner sig-nificance (such as referring to a person as a New Moses — as Jesus is presented by Matthew, but as also are other, especially political, figures by other writers in other ages) — any suggestion that the difference between human and divine in Jesus is only poetic is not true of the New Testament. John shares the same faith as the Synop-tics and Paul, whatever differences of theology emerge for the needs of the time. Those differences are associated with differences in perspective, and to this extent we are encouraged to speak of a Jesuology in one author and a more comprehensive Christology in another (in places: Paul can alter focus as suits).[28] That is also true of writers, theologians, artists, believers in other ages; the mystery, after all, is multifaceted.

Jesus and Christ in the Fathers

The Fathers, especially apologists and theologians but not so much pastors concerned about popular misunderstanding, found the distinction helpful. We shall see Justin, Clement of Alexandria and Tertullian employing it when considering the salvation of non-Christians. Origen applies it more generally, on biblical evidence:

> The Gospels know that the one who in Jesus says, 'I am the Way, the Truth and the Life' has not been circumscribed so as to occur nowhere outside the body and soul of Jesus — a fact that is clear from many instances, a few of which we cite here.[29]

And in support of this distinction he quotes places in the New Testament where Jesus speaks with Johannine authority, such as that Great Missionary Commissioning we remarked on in *Matthew* and also *Mt* 18.20 ('For where two or three are gathered in my name, I am there among them'), as well as John the Baptist's words about Jesus at *Jn* 1.26. For Origen it was from the Incarnation (*oikonomia* in patristic terminology) that the soul and body of Jesus formed one being with the Logos of God (cf also *Contra Celsum* 4, 5; 5, 12); he speaks interchangeably of Logos and Christ as distinct from Jesus, a usage not original to him but of rich potential for later theologians.

That distinction in usage would have helped Augustine, too (not to mention theologians generally), who saw the real distinction in reference. He was obliged, in the course of his scriptural hermeneusis, to recognise a wider reference[30] in passages of the Bible, including the *Psalms*. Unwilling to see the reference limited to Jesus, he seeks another way to express himself (on *Ps* 3.9):

> This psalm can be taken to refer to the person of Christ another way, namely, that the whole Christ is speaking. I mean by 'whole' with his body, of which he is the head ... In the inspired author, then, at once there speaks the Church and her head, constituted as she is throughout the whole world amidst storms of persecution.[31]

> All those passages (of Scripture) speak of Christ. The head now ascended into heaven along with the body still suffering on earth is the full development of the whole purpose of the authors of Scripture, which is well called Sacred Scripture; we should not believe there is anything narrated in the context of the prophetic books which lacks future reference.[32]

We have mentioned Theophilus, bishop of Antioch in the late second century, whose three books to his pagan friend Autolycus were classed by Eusebius in his survey of Christian (or Jesuan) literature in the *Church History* a century later 'three elementary works' — a verdict his modern editor endorses.[33] Realising he cannot count on faith in Jesus in his friend, Theophilus avoids mention of him, his Incarnation or resurrection; he even derives the word 'Christian', not from Christ, but directly from its root *chriein*, to anoint: 'We are actually called Christians because we are anointed with the oil of God' (I, 12). Instead, he speaks of the provident God and his Logos, by whom all things were made and who is the executor of all the works of God. What is essential to Christianity is faith; Christians distinguish themselves also by truth and right living (what the New Testament would refer to as *basileia*). His more sympathetic modern commentator, J. Bentivegna, refers to Theophilus' work as 'achristological' while wanting to see the work as 'a Christianology', 'a Christianity without Christ'.[34] We would suggest he could be more precise about the distinction he draws regarding the apologist's purpose if he spoke in terms of Jesus and Christ, Jesuology and Christology, Jesuan and Christian, Jesuanity and Christianity; again it is a matter of the focus this early theologian thinks it appropriate to adopt in dialoguing between two communities. Theophilus' recourse to a Logos Christology would be found helpful in continuing this dialogue, though dyed-in-the-wool monotheists like Athanasius would scent the whiff of heresy that way and discourage the distinction.[35] It will be ever thus with concerned pastors.

Blurring a distinction

It is the concerned pastors who were generally responsible for formulations about Jesus (and, less frequently, Christ), even in the patristic period when bishops were theologians and theologians often bishops. We have seen that theological precision depends on perspective, and pastoral concern does not always allow for breadth of perspective, as in the case of Athanasius and another Alexandrian pastor, Cyril. A certain degree of tolerance and freedom is required for theologians to move from one perspective to another without the cry of 'heresy' being raised, a word which originally carries no sense of heterodoxy, just the choice of one position rather than another, but which later with the firming up of positions into (often limited) formulas comes to be a pejorative label.

When one considers the origins and early situation of the followers of Jesus, right from persecution under Nero and unsympathetic co-nationals and the death of Peter and Paul around 67, and as well the religious and philosophical diversity of the Roman world, it is both quite predictable that the fine line of 'orthodoxy' took some long time to be drawn, and also quite regrettable that, like all fine lines, it did not allow for breadth of perspective. In that early period of some centuries, the biblical diversity we have highlighted gave way to, even encouraged, diversity in theologising about the mystery of Christ and the person of Jesus. The value of latitude for theological experimentation is that it allows for development of previous positions, perhaps complementary without being contradictory (such as Pauline and Synoptic), tracing their relationship and also finding the paths not to follow in the case of either. Premature judgment and fixation under the pressure of temporary pastoral concerns can shortcircuit this valuable process.

The Jesuan community in the apostolic and subapostolic periods[36] took advantage of this latitude to exemplify, identify and in some cases reject early attempts to relate Jesus to the mystery of Christ or reconcile both to current cosmologies and religious systems. The New Testament texts already show unease about gnostic and docetic theologising, and early Fathers like Ignatius and Irenaeus tell us more of them. The former tendency, illustrated in *The Gospel According to Thomas* (containing elements deriving from traditions possibly as antique as the canonical Gospels) and the later *Apocryphon of John*,[37] fell short of the biblical accounts of both Jesus (the gnostic Gospel eschews completely the centrepiece of the kerygma, the Paschal Mystery) and the mystery of Christ (the gnostic creation myths caricaturing hypostatised wisdom as the source of a tainted material creation). This dualism regarding creation and the humanity of Jesus in particular as well as the scriptures of both Jewish and Jesuan communities characterised also docetism and then manicheism, not to mention later variants to our own day, which contain this hereditary suspicion of the material, the human. Wholesome Jesuological and Christological perspectives that accommodate things in heaven and things on earth, spirit and matter, life and death, joy and suffering could not accept these systems.

Naturally, for all the Jesuan community, and particularly for its pastors, the threat these aberrant systems posed to an adequate understanding of Jesus was uppermost; the loss of the broader perspective in which Jesus stands was more imperceptible and thought less urgent. The New Testament calls for antidocetic discernment of spirits: 'Every spirit that confesses that Jesus Christ has

come in the flesh is from God,' the Johannine community is reminded
(1 Jn 4.2). Along with this assertion of his humanity is felt the need
to oppose any Jesuologies that undermine divine status; the opening to the *Hebrews* represents the opposition in full flight. It is that
latter reaction that predominates in theological debate (especially
outside of Antioch, more committed to defence of Jesus' humanity)
and Council formulation. It not only succeeds in blurring the biblical distinction in perspective but has been styled by reductionist
theologians as entrenching the incarnational myth. Maurice Wiles
asks, 'Does Christology [meaning Jesuology] rest on a mistake?'

> Traditional [C]hristology rests on a mistake in this sense. It arose be-
> cause it was not unnaturally, yet nonetheless mistakenly, felt that the
> full divine character of redemption in Christ could only be maintained
> if the person and act of the redeemer were understood to be divine in a
> direct and special sense.[38]

Wiles, Hick and others who tend to identify reality with myth
are as little concerned about the loss of a truly biblical and fully
Christological perspective as the early community; the debate is
about Jesus, and Jesus ontologically, not functionally, whereas we
saw the New Testament's overall insistence on what was 'of first
importance', Jesus' Paschal Mystery. Now attention switches to the
conception and birth — from Easter to Christmas, if you like — as
the moment of 'hypostatic union' of human and divine, to use the
language of the philosophy of the day. Nicea and Constantinople
devise one term, *homoousios*, to do justice to Jesus' equality of status
with the Father; the 'astonishing medley of rival meetings' [39] at
Ephesus in 431 that goes down in history as the Third General
Council keeps the focus narrow; Chalcedon opts for the philosophical categories of person and natures to speak of Jesus and settles on
four negative adverbs to head off deviation from the fine line of orthodoxy about the union: 'unconfusedly, unchangeably, undivided-
ly, inseparably'.[40] We have moved from plurality of perspective on
Christ and Jesus to conformity of terminology, philosophy and
theology about the latter. From working within one faith community with little acknowledgement of other communities we have
moved to a specialist nucleus within that one group, articulating its
microscopic perspective in formulas scarcely appreciable by the
simple faithful and intolerant of legitimate alternatives.

We can concede, with Rahner, that such conciliar definitions
achieve 'the possibility of teaching and doctrinal certainty'.[41] But

when one considers, from the viewpoint of an adequate Christology in the Pauline and even evangelical senses, what has been lost of the multifaceted mystery of Christ — the 'Christ-event' — and the simplicity and directness of emphasis in the Jesus-event Gospel accounts of passover and *basileia* in these debates, formulas and creeds, one finds it hard to appreciate the unqualified enthusiasm of a Grillmeier about them:

> We seem to have come a long way from the Bible. Nevertheless, it is remarkable how the content of so decisive a concept as hypostasis is determined precisely by the way it is used in *Heb* 1.3 …
>
> We believe that to a certain extent we have made it clear that the simple, original proclamation of Christ, the revealer and bringer of salvation, the proclamation of Christ the Son of God can be heard in undiminished strength through all the *philosophoumena* of the Fathers.[42]

It is not for any querulous attitude to magisterium or through reductionist tendencies that one finds such partiality badly focused, not through any wish to go along with the sentiment of Mary Magdalen in *Jesus Christ Superstar*, 'he's a man, he's just a man.' It is simply regret that early Councils and this latterday historian have forfeited the enriching perspective of the mystery of Christ, and without feeling a sense of loss have moved from the Jesus of Calvary and the Mount of Beatitudes to the 'ecclesiastical Christ', as Don Cupitt says,[43] which we find reflected also in the remoteness of Byzantine Cristos (like the cover to this book). Creeds and formulas have their role and occasion,[44] but when they have the effect (perhaps by being imperfectly understood — and, *pace* Rahner, they are hardly 'simple and clear') of drastically paring back a comprehensive biblical theology, they have pastoral limitations within the community — hence Vatican II's welcome shift in style and purpose. They also do little to dissipate the darkness that at the opening of this chapter we saw Anthony lamenting.[45] We are thus inclined to find John Macquarrie's evaluation more perceptive, if still shortsighted:

> One has got to ask whether the tendency to concentrate on doctrinal formulas has not diminished the existential and soteriological understanding of faith in Jesus Christ, and indeed whether the whole discussion has not been in danger of slipping into artificial disputation over minutiae and fine distinctions. Alongside the intellectualizing tendency goes another. This is the tendency to assimilate Jesus Christ more and more to the being of God, and to obscure his humanity.[46]

In other words, it was no longer current to speak of Jesus except as Christ, and vice versa — to the detriment of theology through the blurring of a biblical distinction. No patience here, either, with the fine line drawn by a modern theologian from the subcontinent sensitive to interreligious dialogue: 'The reality of Christ cannot be restricted to the historical Jesus.' [47]

Need of a restatement

One thinks of those believers in Jesus, including a large number of intellectual and literary figures in Australia and doubtless other countries,[48] who flatter themselves that, while not responding well to the teaching and practice of established churches, they nonetheless retain a respect for and even observance of the Jesuan manifesto. Tom Collins, in his classic *Such is Life*, was one of these. In his view:

> ecclesiastical Christianity vies with the effete Judaism of olden times as a failure of the first magnitude ... The Church quibbles well, and palters well, and, in her own pusillanimous way, means well, by her silky loyalty to the law and the profits.

> Yet there is nothing Utopian in the charter of that kingdom — in the sunshiny Sermon on the Mount. It is no fanciful conception of an intangible order of things, but a practical, workable code of daily life, adapted to any stage of civilisation, and delivered to men and women who, even according to the showing of hopeless pessimists, or strenuous advocates for Individualistic force and cunning, were in all respects like ourselves — delivered, moreover, by One who knew exactly the potentialities and aspirations of man. And, in the unerring harmony of the Original Idea, the outcome of that inimitable teaching is merely the consummation of prophetic forecast in earlier ages. First, the slenderest crescent, seen by eyes that diligently searched the sky; then, a broader crescent; a hemisphere; at last, a perfect sphere, discovered by the Nazarene Artisan, and by him made plain to all who wish to see. But from the dawn of the ages that orb was there, waiting for recognition, waiting with the awful, tireless, all-conquering patience for which no better name has been found than the Will of God.

> History marks a point of time when first the Humanity of God touched the divine aspiration in man, fulfilling, under the skies of Palestine, the dim, yet infallible instinct of every race from eastern Mongol to western Aztec. 'The Soul, naturally Christian,' responds to this touch, even though blindly and erratically, and so from generation to genera-

tion the multitudes stand waiting to welcome the Gospel of Humanity with palms and hosannas, as of old; while from generation to generation phylactered exclusiveness takes counsel against the revolution which is to make all things new.[49]

One can pardon the acerbity of criticism of institutional religion (perhaps recalling the acrimony and intolerance of conciliar debate) for the awareness in this writer (Collins) not only of the centrality of the *basileia* in Jesus' teaching but also of the context in which it occurs, the Will of God from the dawn of the ages, and of the relevance of both to every race. We resonate as well with Collins' familiarity with Tertullian's *Apology*, which appropriately deals with the natural respect of all people for God as judge, prompting this apologist to exclaim, '*O testimonium animae naturaliter Christianae!*',[50] which the Fathers of the Church translation well turns, 'O testimony of the soul, which is by natural instinct Christian!' For Tertullian, as for Collins, the mystery of Christ, that Will of God operative from the dawn of the ages, before the coming of the Nazarene Artisan, was working, if obscurely, for the benefit of Mongol and Aztec and Aborigine as it is working now for all people, who by natural instinct and divine aspiration can be Christian, even if not Jesuan. The values of the *basileia*, that charter of the kingdom, do not belong exclusively to the followers of the Nazarene.

It is not only litterateurs and the self-justifying lapsed who ask for a more generous statement of Jesus and the whole mystery of Christ, nor are we intent on a lowest-common-multiple approach to dogma to suit the requirements of unschooled youth like Anthony. Yet what Moltmann says of an exclusively biblicist justification of Christological statements is true also of the conciliar approach we have seen: 'It would no longer be able to relate these statements therapeutically to people in the wretchedness of their present situation. The hermeneutics of christology's origins must therefore be complemented by the hermeneutics of its effects.' He believes we can do justice to both precision and relevance by asking, 'Is Jesus really the Christ? Who really is Jesus Christ for us today?'[51]

Our concern here is with the former criterion and former question, though expanding precision to include adequacy, in the belief that relating Jesus to the mystery of Christ will provide a theological matrix for us (as it did for Paul) to speak of Jesuans and other religious communities, Church and salvation (for all), individual welfare and universal destiny. Patristic debate and conciliar definition exemplified precision but not within an adequate context;

perspective was foreshortened, as other theologians (including even Rahner) lament. 'A strange and unconscious line of thought all too often and too easily asserts itself by which Jesus comes simply to be identified with God.' [52] 'The simple equation Jesus=God not only fails to represent what Christian tradition has claimed, but is distinctly odd.' [53] 'The truth of the humanity of Christ got left more and more in the shade in the course of the centuries, and in practice Jesus was seen only as God. So there occurred something like a concealment or a clear Monophysitism in Christian piety.' [54] 'Would it be a delusion to suppose that the abstract formalism of Christology has also contributed to a decrease of interest in a theology of the mysteries of Christ's human life?' [55] Rahner, Young and Ratzinger are not here compromising on faith in Jesus — just appealing, as we are, for retention of a biblical perspective.

Christology and Jesuology

Our concern is to be clear enough in our Christological and Jesuological thinking to enable us to think of and use the terms Jesus and Christ with sufficient discrimination to reflect adequately the reality, the mystery, in each case. Employing them interchangeably does not do that, as we have seen: for one thing, evangelical and Pauline perspectives are merged, blurring a significant distinction. Retaining the distinction is necessary for dealing with the theological realities mentioned above: salvation, religion, Church, world — dimensions of the mystery of Christ, in our terminology. Karl Rahner, for instance, in his comparison of the achievement of Vatican II with other councils', sees it in the recognition that other communities than the Jesuan need to be addressed (he could be clearer if he distinguished, like Tertullian and Origen and Theophilus, between Jesuanity and Christianity):

> None of us can say exactly how, with what conceptuality, under what new aspects the old message of Christianity must in the future be proclaimed in Asia, in Africa, in the regions of Islam, perhaps also in South America, if this message is really to be present everywhere in the world.[56]

The conceptuality that suggests itself for this task is the Pauline one, especially as the challenge is similar; repetition of Nicene, Constantinopolitan or Chalcedonian formulas and their underlying theologies will not suffice because the challenge is different. We respectfully note that in his encyclical on the permanent validity of the Church's missionary mandate *Redemptoris Missio* John Paul II, while allowing that 'it is legitimate and helpful to consider the various aspects of the mystery of Christ,' does not encourage adoption of the distinction of Tertullian, Origen, Theophilus and others in missionary attitudes; where the Fathers saw grounds for distinction, the Pope speaks simply of separation:

> To introduce any sort of separation between the Word and Jesus Christ is contrary to the Christian faith. St John clearly states that the Word, who 'was in the beginning with God', is the very one who 'became flesh' (*Jn* 1.2,14). Jesus is the Incarnate Word — a single and indivisible person. One cannot separate Jesus from the Christ or speak of a 'Jesus of history' who would differ from the 'Christ of faith'. The Church acknowledges and confesses Jesus as 'the Christ, the Son of the living God' (*Mt* 16.16): Christ is none other than Jesus of Nazareth; he is the Word of God made man for the salvation of all (#6).

We have acknowledged that pastors are not always in a position to allow room for theological precision and exploration, especially in an area where lived experience in the field is a necessary stimulus for rethinking. Small wonder if practising missionaries responded to this unnuanced call for old recipes on the basis of an old 'conceptuality' by seeing it as inducing 'schizophrenia',[57] pitting theology against practice.

As we shall see in the next chapter, approach to missionary work within the whole question of salvation obliges one to have as a basis an adequate Christology. Wolfhart Pannenberg points out that Tillich has things in reverse order when he maintains that 'Christology is a function of soteriology.'[58] Paul needed to have a sound Christological basis for his theologising about Jews and Gentiles and his missionary work among some few peoples. Recitation of conciliar formulas or even isolated biblical definitions framed by one faith community for its own members will hardly measure up to the religious diversity of the wider world, as some of the Fathers already admitted. Living and working among different peoples and religions brings this home to one. We have mentioned Raimundo Panikkar, son of Jesuan mother and Hindu father, scientist, theologian. Like other theologians,[59] but with keener existential stimulus from his Indian situation, he resists the identification of Christ with 'Jesus only':

> Even from right within Christian faith, such an identification has never been asserted. What the Christian faith does affirm is that Jesus of

Nazareth has a special and unique relationship with what Paul, following Old Testament usage, calls the Uncreated Wisdom, what John, following Philo, calls the Logos, and Matthew and Luke, following Judaism,
call the Holy Spirit, and what all later tradition has called the Son.[60]

Panikkar sees that proper relations between Jesuans and followers of other religions depend on acknowledging the distinction
between the particular Jesus and the universal Christ.[61] This is not
to abandon the 'steadfastness' in upholding one's own tradition
that Hans Küng sees as a necessary correlative of the capacity for
dialogue with other religions;[62] it is rather, on the basis of biblical
and patristic tradition, to develop an adequate Christology as a
basis for that dialogue (something Küng neglects to do at that
place). Once I have that Christological basis, I can admit the
legitimacy of other religions, admit with Tertullian that all people,
while not followers of Jesus, are by natural instinct Christian,
whereas for me as a Jesuan (in Panikkar's words) 'this Lord whose
Lordship can appear in innumerable forms has taken for me an ultimate form which is indissolubly connected with Jesus of
Nazareth.' [63] For me the whole divine design, the mystery of Christ,
reaches its focal point in Jesus; from his teaching and particularly
his Paschal Mystery salvation and special revelation of God's purposes come to me. This is the faith also of Paul, the evangelists and
all the Jesuan community.

As Paul also understood, an adequate Christology involves as
well appreciation of the ecclesial and cosmic dimensions of the
mystery of Christ. And so we turn in the following chapters to
studying the relationship of Jesus to Church and world in that
divine design. These are questions dear to Orthodox theology. John
Zizioulas, Metropolitan of Pergamon, speaks of our need for adequate understanding of Jesus and Christ in those terms:

> If the Church disappears from his identity, he is no longer Christ, al-
> though he will still be the eternal Son. And yet the 'mystery hidden
> before all ages' in the will of the Father is nothing else but the incor-
> poration of this other element, of us, or the many, into the eternal filial
> relationship between the Father and the Son. This mystery amounts,
> therefore, to nothing but the Church ...
>
> The ecclesiological question receives its fullest treatment if it is placed
> also in the light of the significance of the Church of [sic] the entire
> cosmos.[64]

It is a direction we should now follow.

Points for discussion

1. Where in our tradition about Jesus do you find the most satisfying statement about him? Where the least satisfying? (Consider Scriptures, Fathers, Councils, creeds, liturgy, ...)

2. Church Councils from the beginning have concentrated on clarifying the person and significance of Jesus; some of these efforts appear in our creeds (see others in manuals and Vatican II documents). What precisely is achieved by these definitions?

3. To what extent does the world of the early Fathers correspond to ours in its religious and philosophical diversity? Does their approach to presenting Christianity in their world offer us any model for our stance towards our world?

4. Look again at Tom Collins' words from *Such is Life* (p. 91). How accurately does he grasp the significance of Jesus and the mystery of Christ, do you think?

Further reading

J. Fitzmyer, *A Christological Catechism. New Testament Answers*, New York: Paulist, 1981.

A. Grillmeier, *Christ in Christian Tradition* I, 2nd edn, Eng. trans., London: Mowbray, 1975.

J. Macquarrie, *Jesus Christ in Modern Thought*, London: SCM, 1990.

J. Moltmann, *The Way of Jesus Christ. Christology in Messianic Dimensions* (1989), Eng. trans., London: SCM, 1990.

R. Panikkar, *The Hidden Christ of Hinduism*, revised edn, Maryknoll: Orbis, 1981.

W. Pannenberg, *Jesus God and Man* (1962, revised edn), Eng. trans., London: SCM, 1968.

J. Thornhill, *Making Australia. Exploring our National Conversation*, Sydney: Dwyer, 1992.

Notes

1. Cf Anton Wessels, *Images of Jesus. How Jesus is Perceived and Portrayed in Non-European Cultures.*

2. For example, Constitution on the Church in the Modern World *Gaudium et Spes*, 22,38,45.

3. For the text of the formula, see my *Faith in Search of Understanding. An Introduction to Theology*, Melbourne: Collins Dove, 1989, p. 28.

4. Cf Karl Rahner, 'Chalkedon — Ende oder Anfang?' *Chalkedon* III, 3: 'If the formula is thus an end, the result and victory which bring about simplicity, clarity, the possibility of teaching and doctrinal certainty, then in this victory everything depends on the end also being seen as a beginning.' Cf Rahner's 'Current problems in Christology', *Theological Investigations* 1 (1954), Eng. trans., London: DLT, 1961, p. 149. For a more nuanced appreciation of the achievement of the formula, see John Macquarrie, *Jesus Christ in Modern Thought*, London: SCM, 1990, p. 14.

5. For details of these, see my 'Synoptic *basileia* and Pauline *mysterion*,' *Estudios Biblicos* 45 (1987) pp. 309–24.

6. Paul uses *basileia* differently from the Synoptics: for him it is a future experience, to be inherited or deserved. See 'Synoptic *basileia* and Pauline *mysterion*' for details of usage.

7. Which A. Grillmeier, and so many other theologians who do not read Paul thoroughly, calls the mystery of Christ: 'The church must regard the *mysterium Christi* as a reality which is continually to be thought through afresh,' he says of the Jesuological controversies of the fourth and fifth centuries (*Christ in Christian Tradition* I, 2nd edn, Eng. trans., London: Mowbray, 1975, p. 556). The result is considerable, unnecessary confusion in Christological perspective.

8. *Paul* (1969), Eng. trans., London: Hodder and Stoughton, 1971, p. 110.

9. J. Macquarrie, *op.cit.*, pp. 19–20.

10. 'A Christophany for our times' (Bellarmine Lecture 1991), *Theology Digest* 39 (1992 Spring) p. 11.

11. 'People who restrict the Christian faith to "the historical Jesus" or — more recently — to "Rabbi Jesus", dispensing with the allegedly "high Christology" of Paul, John and the ancient church, do not only lose the Christian faith in the resurrection. At the same time they cast away the faith in God that is specifically Christian' (*The Way of Jesus Christ. Christology in Messianic Dimensions* [1989], Eng. trans., London: SCM, 1990, pp. xvi–xvii).

12. Quoted in *The Tablet*, 7 September 1991. Karl Rahner suggests 'that dogmatic Christology might pay a little attention to the general history of religions … For the first time since the patristic era, this history is becoming a reality for the West again, in the perichoresis of all cultures and historical movements which is in fact taking place today' ('Current problems in Christology,' 189 & n.1).

13. Cf R. M. Grant, *Theophilus of Antioch, Ad Autolycum*, Oxford: Clarendon Press, 1970, p. xvii: 'His (Theophilus') understanding of the work of Jesus Christ can be recovered only from allusions, for like other apologists of his time he never openly speaks of him.' The

remark of another commentator, J. Bentivegna, on the work of
Theophilus as 'a Christianity without Christ' would have been more
accurately and more helpfully phrased 'a Christology without Jesus'
('A Christianity without Christ by Theophilus of Antioch,' *Studia
Patristica* 13 [1971] pp. 107–130). Bentivegna tries again with 'a
Christianology' (130). There is obviously need to provide some
neologisms for a reworked theology in this area, as theologians like
Macquarrie and Panikkar are endeavouring to do.

14. I note that these terms, Jesuology and Christology, which probably
suggest themselves to anyone endeavouring to register the different
(biblical) perspectives, are used somewhat differently by
J. Moltmann, *op.cit.*, 55: 'Anthropological christology is simply Jesuology and nothing else. Jesuology is not the opposite of christology.
The term is used for the modern christology which is also called
"christology from below". The centre of this christology is the human
being Jesus of Nazareth, not the exalted or pre-existent Christ. That
is why we talk about Jesuology.'

15. Cf Raymond E. Brown: 'Without an appreciation that every word in
the Scriptures has been uttered by human beings in fixed circumstances to communicate a message, one may misread them, applying
their words to solve problems to which they do not speak' ('Communicating the divine and human in Scripture,' *Origins* 22 [1992
No.1] 3; an address to the US National Catholic Educational Association, St Louis, April 20, 1992).

16. Which is not to say these particular texts as Word of God do not
have a relevance to us as readers today.

17. For text and commentary see Joseph A. Fitzmyer, *A Christological
Catechism. New Testament Answers*, New York: Paulist, 1981, pp. 95–
140.

18. 'A cloud of witnesses' in J. Hick (ed.), *The Myth of God Incarnate*, London: SCM, 1977, pp. 13–47. (The phrase is borrowed from *Heb* 12.1.)

19. *A Christological Catechism*, 62–63. James Dunn agrees on the need for
a corrective: 'What many Christians both past and present have
regarded as orthodox christology may be regarded (not altogether
unfairly) as a curious amalgam of different elements taken from different parts of first-century Christianity — personal pre-existence
from John, virgin birth from Matthew, the miracle worker from the
so-called 'divine man' christology prevalent among some Hellenistic
Christians, his death as atonement from Paul, the character of his
resurrection from Luke, his present role from Hebrews and the hope
of his parousia from the earlier decades' (*Unity and Diversity in the
New Testament*, 2nd edn, London: SCM, 1990, pp. 226–27).

20. With Eng. trans. and commentary by J. A. Fitzmyer, New York: Paulist, 1986.

21. Cf Raymond E. Brown, *The Gospel According to John I–XII* (Anchor Bible 29), Garden City: Doubleday, 1966, p. cx.

22. Cf Brown, *op.cit.*, 146, on the significance of the verb *hypsoun*, 'to lift up', used by John of the crucifixion of Jesus.

23. Cf R. E. Brown, 'Wisdom motifs,' *The Gospel According to John I-XIII* (Anchor Bible 29), New York: Doubleday, 1966, p. cxxii: 'One aspect that immediately sets the Fourth Gospel apart from the other Gospels and gives it peculiar force is its presentation of Jesus as incarnate revelation descended from on high to offer men light and truth. In discourses of quasi-poetic solemnity, Jesus proclaims himself with the famous "I am" formula, and his divine and celestial origins are apparent both in what he says and in the way he says it. His otherworldliness is visible in the way that he can treat with majestic disdain the plots against him and the attempts to arrest him. He is best described in his own words: "In the world but not of it." '

24. *Mt* 11.25–30, citing Wisdom passages like the *Wisdom of Solomon* 9.17; 2.13; *Sir* 24.19. Cf *Lk* 10.21–22. Cf Brown, *op.cit.*, p. cxxv.

25. Commentators note the discrepancy and find difficulty in accounting for it. Cf B. J. Hubbard, *The Matthean Redaction of a Primitive Apostolic Commissioning*, Missoula: Scholars Press, 1974.

26. Sean Freyne, *Galilee, Jesus and the Gospels. Literary Approaches and Historical Investigations*, Philadelphia: Fortress, 1988, p. 2.

27. J. Hick, *op.cit.*, p. ix.

28. Cf J. Macquarrie, *op.cit.*, 51: 'If Wrede had been correct, one might have expected Paul's christology to have been decidedly docetic, and indeed the whole history of Christian theology would probably have been different. But such is simply not the case. Paul certainly believed that Jesus Christ was a definite historical and human personage.'

29. *Contra Celsum* 2,9 (*SC* 132,304). Henry Chadwick in his edition of the *Contra Celsum* (Cambridge: CUP, 1965, p. 74) notes what he terms 'this difficulty of the particularity of the Incarnation'. Other theologians have, on the contrary, found it of great assistance in developing their Christology. Chadwick feels the need to defend the orthodoxy of Origen: 'It is a genuine question whether, or rather in what sense, Origen is an Origenist' (*Early Christian Thought and the Classical Tradition*, Oxford: Clarendon Press, 1966, p. 96). Henri Crouzel, the patriarch of Origen studies (Robert Daly), concurs: 'In brief, although statements that have given rise to Origenism are to be found in the works of Origen, all the arguments which serve for the

refutation of Origenism can likewise be found there' ('Origenism,' *New Catholic Encyclopedia* 10, New York: McGraw-Hill, 1967, p. 773).

30. 'Prosopological' in the language of French scholars; cf M.-J. Rondeau, *Les commentaires patristiques du psautier (IIIe-Ve siècles)* II *Exégèse prosopologique et théologie* (Orientalia Christiana Analecta 220), Roma: Pont. Inst. Stud. Or., 1985, on those passages in the Psalms that have been taken to refer to Jesus/Christ (Grk *prosopon*, person).

31. *Enarratio in Ps* 3.9 (*CCL* 38,11).

32. *Contra Faustum* 22,94 (*PL* 42,463).

33. R. M. Grant, *op.cit.*

34. Art.cit., 112,130.

35. Cf his *Contra Gentes* pp. 40–41.

36. I am following the usual reference in these terms, as expressed for example by Raymond E. Brown, *The Churches the Apostles Left Behind*, New York: Paulist, 1985, p. 15: 'I suggest, therefore, that the term "Apostolic Age" should be confined to that second one-third of the first century, and that the last one-third of the century should be designated as the 'Sub-Apostolic' period.'

37. For text and commentatry, see B. Layton (ed.), *The Gnostic Scriptures*.

38. 'Does christology rest on a mistake?' in S. W. Sykes and J. P. Clayton (ed.), *Christ, Faith and History. Cambridge Studies in Christology*, Cambridge: CUP, 1978, p. 8.

39. J. N. D. Kelly, *Early Christian Doctrines*, New York: Harper and Row, 1978, 5th edn, p. 327.

40. The Greek text of the Chalcedon formula reads at this point: *asynchytos, atreptos, adiairetos, achoristos* (Denzinger-Schoenmetzer 302).

41. See note 4 above.

42. *Christ in Christian Tradition* I, pp. 446, 555. Karl Rahner, on the contrary, cites the Chalcedonian formula as an instance of the minimal impact biblical theology had (he is writing in 1954) on dogmatic theology ('Current problems in Christology,' pp. 154–55, 168).

43. 'One Jesus, many Christs?' in *Christ, Faith and History*, p. 132.

44. One wonders if Sunday Mass, with all its distractions, is the ideal locus for the celebration of the densely phrased Nicene-Constantinopolitan creed.

45. Sean Freyne suggests the early Council statements decultured Jesus: 'As long as the high, Chalcedonian Christology remained unchallenged, there was little interest in the social and cultural context of Jesus' earthly ministry' (*Galilee*, 2).

It should be noted that an accent on the mystery of Christ is not a return to such a high Christology lacking an interest in Jesus' life and ministry, as Paul's letters confirm. It simply provides a context for evaluating him, which conciliar Christology also forsook. The trees and the wood should go together.

46. *Jesus Christ in Modern Thought*, p. 166.

47. J. Kavunkal, 'Towards an Indian missiology,' *Indian Missiological Review* 14 (March 1992) p. 83.

48. Cf John Thornhill's survey of such Australian figures in his *Making Australia. Exploring our National Conversation*, Sydney: Dwyer, 1992.

49. Tom Collins (Joseph Furphy), *Such is Life* (1903), Melbourne: Lloyd O'Neil, 1970, pp. 111–12.

50. *Apology* xvii (*CCL* 1, 117).

51. *The Way of Jesus Christ*, pp. 43–44.

52. K. Rahner, 'The position of Christology in the Church between exegesis and dogmatics,' *Theological Investigations* 11, London: DLT, 1974, p. 198.

53. F. Young, 'A cloud of witnesses,' 35. Young calls for the kind of developing restatement of this mystery as has occurred in the case of Christian tradition about the Eucharist.

54. J. Ratzinger, 'A conversation with Joseph Ratzinger' in *Faith: Conversations with Contemporary Theologians*, ed. Teofilo Cabestrero, Eng. trans., Maryknoll: Orbis, 1981, p. 153.

55. K. Rahner, 'Current problems in Christology,' *Theological Investigations* I (1954), Eng. trans., London: DLT, 1961, p. 190.

56. 'Towards a fundamental theological interpretation of Vatican II,' 725. Cf J. Kavunkal, 'Towards an Indian missiology', 84: 'Historical Christianity cannot be equated with the transhistorical Reality, which we have presented as the Logos, the Christ.'

57. John Wijngaards, 'A double-edged appeal,' *The Tablet* 9 February 1991, pp. 180–81.

58. *Jesus God and Man* (1966, 2nd edn), Eng. trans., London: SCM, 1968, p. 48.

59. Cf John Hick, 'Jesus and the world religions,' *The Myth of God Incarnate*, p. 181: 'Should *our* revelation of the Logos, namely in the life of Jesus, be made available to all mankind? Yes, of course, and so also should other particular revelations of the Logos at work in human life — in the Hebrew prophets, in the Buddha, in the *Upanishads* and the *Bhagavad Gita*, in the *Koran*, and so on.'

60. *Trinity and World Religions*, Bangalore: CISRS, 1970, p. 43.

61. Jacques Dupuis, SJ, in his *Jésus Christ à la rencontre des religions* (Paris: Desclée, 1989, p. 317), says of the universal Christ: 'Il appartient à toutes les religions; plus exactement toutes lui appartiennent, parce qu'il est présent et actif en toutes, comme aussi en tous les hommes.'

62. *Global Responsibility*, pp. 94–95. Küng dismisses in a footnote approaches such as Panikkar's, without naming him (note 109, p. 155).

63. *Salvation in Christ*, Santa Barbara: privately published, 1972, p. 64 (quoted by P. F. Knitter, *No Other Name? A Critical Survey of Christian Attitudes Toward the World Religions*, London: SCM, 1985, p. 156).

64. 'The mystery of the Church in Orthodox tradition,' *One in Christ* 24 (1988) pp. 300–301.

5
Church, salvation, religions and Christianity

Our postmodern world's religious diversity, which we are only lately acknowledging, suggests adoption of a more comprehensive Christological perspective than has been usual in our closed community. Such a Christology and a theology of Church as mystery of life, appearing in Paul, the Fathers and the recent magisterium, can allow us to envisage the salvation of others in ways other than their becoming followers of Jesus, anonymous or explicit. The Fathers in their world recognised the Logos at work wherever God's values are evident, as Jesus had beatified them in his. We can thus admit the religious riches of other communities, engage them in conversation, and rethink our missionary purpose.

We have noted that a search for an adequate Christology — which is what this book is engaged in — brings us to a study of Church in the sense of community of salvation. The biblical picture of Jesus stresses his role as saviour, and Paul's thinking on the mystery of Christ homes in on its ecclesial dimension; for both perspectives the death and resurrection of Jesus and its saving effects are at the focal point of the divine plan, which brings us 'redemption through his blood (and) the forgiveness of our trespasses' (*Eph* 1.7). Such is a brief synopsis of the scriptural tradition *of* and *for* the Jesuan community of salvation, and we had to note that later doctrinal tradition in that community tended to drift from this ecclesial and soteriological accent to an ontological one. Much theologising within the Jesuan community since the patristic age, if not respecting fully the Pauline perspective, has tended to follow these elements of community tradition in predicating Jesus' role in relation to all other, non-Jesuan communities in some such way as this:

— all people and religions anticipate an absolute saviour;
— Jesuan tradition and scholastic reasoning (about causality) can demonstrate this absolute saviour to be Jesus; and
— so Jesus is absolute saviour of all people, and other 'saviours' only point to him.[1]

Removing the blinkers

It is therefore refreshing to find a theologian who, without much evidence of appreciation of the Pauline notion of the mystery of Christ and also without much living contact with other communities' religious traditions and contemporary practice, is prepared to entertain the possibility that the dimensions of the divine plan might be rather less clearly determined than the customary blinkered synopsis allows.

> The question suggests itself whether there might not be a formula for saving history as God's progressive taking possession of the world in history, as the manifestation, ever clearer and more hidden at once, of God in the world as his quasi-sacramental *mysterium*. The Christ would appear as the summit of this history and Christology as its sharpest formulation, just as inversely saving history would appear as the prelude to and the extension of Christ's own history. Perhaps the ancients had a better idea of all this than we usually have today, with our still very pale and vague idea of the time before Christ as the preparation for the fullness of times. The old speculation about the Logos, which ascribed to him an activity and history in creation 'before Christ but Christ-like' distinct from the invisible Father, would be well worth rethinking, after being purified of its subordinationist elements.[2]

Were we not so relieved to recognise a wider than usual perspective, we might suggest to the writer not to see saving history only in linear terms BC ... AD, to depth his reading of (Paul and) those apologists who thought also of the situation of contemporary non-Jesuans and not simply BC characters, and to distinguish in usage between Jesus and Christ. Still, we concede the difficulty we ourselves have, being raised within one faith community on its traditions, and constantly viewing the world and its history — and the God of all — from its viewpoint. Paul, as he confesses more than once, had the same difficulty in breaking out of a blinkered perspective, even with extraordinary encouragement; the theologian we have just quoted, drilled in the theological processes of (one school of) his tradition, would be slow to venture beyond them. Steadfastness in one's own tradition, as Hans Küng reminded us,[3] is commendable in surveying the religious pluralism of the postmodern world; myopia is another thing.

There is no doubt that for pondering God and his dealings with all peoples the prime requirement is breadth and openness to the revelation he gives us, from whatever source. What object of our meditation could be more profound and comprehensive? Rightly do we apply 'mystery' to this study, both in its transcendence of our normal categories and in its 'inexhaustible intelligibility', 'unlimited comprehensibility'.[4] Like Paul we cannot allow ourselves to be confined within the foreshortened, narrow, 'tribal' perspective of a group settling for one glimpse of the total reality in one particular situation, even if that glimpse comes to us through the light of the Sun of Justice; Father Faber once remarked that 'if we were not blinded by the light all around us, the so-called darkness of paganism would seem to us a real light illuminating every man coming into the world.'[5]

This is not to settle for some falsely egalitarian relativism, conceding that one religion is as good as another, and abjuring all the Christological positions of our own community. It is rather to appeal for that openness to mystery, a divine plan beyond our prejudices, and to protest against the narrow fixation of viewpoint evidenced in references to other communities than our Jesuan community as 'the opposition'[6] and in the unwillingness of a Jean Daniélou to 'placing Catholicism on the same level with all other religions, whereas the catholicity of Catholicism consists in the fact that it is the true religion and the religion of all men ... The essential difference between Catholicism and all other religions is that the others start with man.'[7] Yes, myopia — and hybris — are to be avoided.

This, then, is an area — Christ, Church, churches, religions, salvation — where we need to fall back on the wider biblical perspective, that of Paul the converted bigot and missionary. In the Gospels, as it happens, Jesus is not shown speaking much about Church, *ekklesia* occurring only twice in his mouth (*Mt* 16.18; 18.17);[8] his concern is all about the values of the *basileia* which he hoped would characterise his community of disciples and (in the Johannine material particularly) about the life he is and comes to share.[9] We are thus given no evangelical support for conceptualising Church as an exclusive inward-looking clique, but rather encouraged to look for the people of God wherever the *basileia* of God is to be found. For Paul, who supplies us with abundant documentation by contrast, to think of Church is to think of one dimension of the mystery of Christ, that divine design that from the foundation of the world has been gathering up all things on earth and in heaven.

Church a mystery of life

So the Church is primarily mystery,[10] wisdom, plan, will, purpose, the sacred reality underlying the scores of models and figures called upon in the Jesuan scriptures and other early literature to highlight one or other aspect of the divine design.[11] That ecclesial perspective was better grasped by ancients like Caesarius of Arles, who was happy to see the Church as that sheet let down from heaven (in Peter's vision in *Acts* 10) containing all kinds of animals and reptiles and birds of the air,[12] and Gregory the Great and Augustine, whom Vatican II quotes numbering within the Church all good people from (not Abraham, or even the Baptist, but) good man Abel in primeval history to the last of the elect,[13] than by moderns like Bellarmine, whose influential ecclesiology (p. 33) was much more niggardly, exclusive and societal.

Jesuans themselves, at least at the official level, have in our time abjured Bellarmine's pyramidal model of Church stressing only authority and external recognition, and have followed Paul and John in seeing Church as a mystery of shared life, *communio, koinonia*, fellowship.[14] Augustine's further statement, 'No commentator is required for the testimonies of the canonical Scriptures highlighting the fact that the Church consists in fellowship of the whole world (*in totius orbis communione*),' [15] has found echoes in *Lumen Gentium*, the Anglican–Roman Catholic International Commission's (ARCIC) *The Final Report* (1982) and *Church as Communion* (1991), the 1985 Synod's *Final Report* and the papal letter following the 1987 Synod, *Christifideles Laici*. This understanding of Church enables us to accept more appreciatively Origen's and Cyprian's dictum, Outside the Church no salvation. In a Church of *koinonia*, shared life, the saying is superfluous, indeed tautologous: outside of life there is no life.[16] In Pauline terms it reads: 'outside of the mystery of Christ there is no salvation'.

The churches of Jesuanity, therefore, may never be so divided as to rupture this communion, this shared life, what the Fathers also called *pax*, peace. Their existence is not a scandal: they have been recognised from earliest times. It is their division that is contradictory to *koinonia*: what should be common, *koinos*, is withheld. The

Fathers admitted the danger of insisting on conformity where there is legitimate diversity in the churches and even of terminating communion, ex-communicating, over minor differences. Eusebius quotes the advice of Irenaeus to Pope Victor about the year 190 to dissuade him from thus overreacting to the Quartodeciman Christians of Asia (so called for celebrating Easter on 14 Nisan and breaking their fast that day):

> Such a diversity of observances has not just arisen now, in our time, but dates from long ago, from our forebears ... They all nevertheless keep the 'peace', as do we, one with another; *the difference in the fast confirms the agreement in the faith.*[17]

Yves Congar quotes other such instances from patristic times in *Diversity and Communion.*[18] Paul VI gave new spirit to inter-church dialogue in addressing the heads of the Eastern churches, with whom the 'peace', *koinonia*, had been sundered for so long, in terms of 'sister churches': 'In each local church the mystery of divine love is at work. Is this not the reason for that fine traditional expression, "sister churches", which local churches love to use of one another?'[19] And Patriarch Athenagoras replied in similar terms. The contemporary ecumenical movement has promoted a lively dialogue as well between the Jesuan churches of the West, which we need not examine further here. The point has been sufficiently made that the mystery of Christ in its ecclesial dimension, a mystery of shared life, *koinonia*, can take its course without utter conformity; there *can* be diversity and communion, at least among Jesuan communities.

Salvation within Church

But what about the many other religious communities throughout the world, whose members far outnumber the followers of Jesus[20] and for whom Jesus is not their saviour (at least as far as they are aware) — have they a way to salvation? Where do they stand with respect to 'Outside the Church no salvation'? with respect to the mystery of Christ? They clearly do not measure up to Bellarmine's criteria for Church membership, while for Daniélou their religions are man-made, unlike Catholicism (did all those Roman liturgical procedures, dogmas, office-bearers, policy statements all come down from heaven on tablets of stone?). At least for Catholics Vatican II has had the effect of evaluating the great world religions positively for the first time,[21] and its documents on Church, the missions and the modern world proclaim a universal and salvific will of God which is limited only by the evil decision of human conscience.[22] Does that mean the other religions have their own way to salvation, outside of Christ, Church, Jesus?

Or does the tradition of our community insist that to find salvation they must join us, must become followers of Jesus? Is that what 'Outside the Church no salvation' means (as it has been defined even by an 'ecumenical' council[23])? They themselves do not feel the need of the Jesuan way to salvation; theirs is adequate, thank you. As Rabbi Hugo Gryn says to Jesuans, 'That takes nothing away from your Good News — but, please, have the sensitivity to understand that I have some Good News as well. What is it? One example. I think one of the spiritual strengths of Judaism is that many of the religious things that we do, we do in our homes. Christians tend to keep them confined to the church.' [24] The rabbi would probably concede (with J. Moingt) that 'Christianity is indeed a religion of the absolute, ... but it is not an absolute religion.' [25] One might go further and remind the rabbi and Jesuans both of those words of Amos:

> Are you not like the Ethiopians to me,
>   O people of Israel? says the Lord.
> Did I not bring Israel up from the land of Egypt,
>   and the Philistines from Caphtor
>   and the Arameans from Kir? (9.7; cf *Is* 19.24–25)

We can point to those statements in our tradition, biblical and dogmatic, that Jesus alone is the Way, the Truth and the Life, that mission involves going to all nations and baptising them in trinitarian formulas. Yet we have had to acknowledge in our survey of scriptural statement in the previous chapter that, particularly in *John* and very occasionally in the Synoptics, the Jesus who speaks is the pre-existent Logos rather than the Jesus of Galilee — the difference of perspective we noted in these scriptures (not the separation of persons of which the Pope warned us in *Redemptoris Missio*). Yet Paul, too, while conscious (to some extent)[26] of the dimensions of the divine plan, is in no doubt that Jesus died for him and for all others. Again we need to remind ourselves of the discrepancy between the big picture represented by 'the mystery of Christ', in which all people and all things in heaven and on earth find a place and are gathered up, and the smaller picture which is generally being addressed in our scriptures, the Jesuan world and those who were invited to join it — the kind of world that a

Daniélou or a Bellarmine envisaged, beyond which all were 'pagans'. As a Jesuan I am convinced by my faith that Jesus is my way to God, and in the Jesuan community I find that way. Should I expect the world's 917 million Muslims, 722 million Hindus, 338 million Confucians, 329 million Buddhists, 19 million Jews and 17 million Sikhs to join me in the Jesuan community? Should I and my fellow Jesuan missioners be working to that goal? Is that what *conversion* is really about — from one community to another, and not simply to the God of all?

There are those pastors who believe so, as we have seen, though a Buddhist response to the Decade of Evangelisation gives us little hope of success. 'As far as Buddhists, Hindus and Muslims are concerned I do not think that any of them will be converted. The people have for generations followed their particular religion and for them it is unshakeable. After five hundred years of evangelising in Sri Lanka 75 per cent of the people are still Buddhist. Apart from a fringe who have been touched, people there are quite happy with their religion. Why should they change? Despite the efforts of centuries Christianity has made little impact in a country like Sri Lanka.' [27] Perhaps that diminishing Jesuan third of the world's population can defy the odds and stage a turnaround — but is that the way to go? Is that what the mystery of Christ would suggest?

Anonymous Jesuans?

While that *pastoral* strategy is taking effect, we can devise a *theological* ploy for the interim, reasoning this way: salvation comes to all through Jesus; all those who are saved are Jesuans, whether they admit or even know it; those who do not are implicit or anonymous Jesuans, even if explicitly they adhere to another community. Perhaps the best known exponent of this theology, Karl Rahner, expresses it this way:

> Christianity understands itself as the absolute religion, intended for all men, which cannot recognize any other religion beside itself as of equal right. This proposition is self-evident and basic for Christianity's understanding of itself ...

> Normally the beginning of the objective obligation of the Christian message for all men — in other words, the abolition of the validity of the Mosaic religion *and* of all other religions which (as we shall see later) may also have a period of validity and of being-willed-by-God — is thought to occur in the apostolic age ...

> Christianity does not simply confront the member of an extra-Christian religion as a mere non-Christian but as someone who can and must already be regarded in this or that respect as an anonymous Christian.[28]

There is something breathtaking in the arrogance of this argumentation, not simply for its exclusiveness, but also for its lack of explicit dependence on Jesuan tradition: no reference to the considerable body of patristic debate on this delicate topic, no explicit reference to the Jesuan scriptures until the last line of a 20-page article, when (of all people) Paul is quoted briefly in support! It is abrasive theologising in a traditional vacuum — and yet it has been given credit for prompting Vatican II's change of heart in the decree on non-Christian religions! The only other comment appropriate at this stage is that the writer's perspective suggests that for Christian, Christianity we should read Jesuan, Jesuanity: his blinkered view is by no means that of Paul on the mystery of Christ.

We have quoted before Hans Küng's *Global Responsibility. In Search of a New World Ethic,* in which he makes a case that world peace depends on peace between the major world religions. Küng does not hold for the idea of anonymous Jesuans, dragging them willy-nilly into the Jesuan community: 'No theological sleight of hand will ever force them, against their will and against their desire, to become active or passive members of the Church.' [29] He himself thus makes the mistake of identifying the Jesuan community with the Christian Church; and so his only recourse is to conclude, 'In fact, then, there is salvation outside the Church' [30] — outside the Jesuan community, in his meaning, which is not the full sense of the dictum. So in the end he is as untraditional as his fellow — needlessly, for lack of an adequate Christological perspective.[31]

Küng exemplifies a further difficulty in making truth, norm, universality the primary criterion in estimating the validity of any religion;[32] and he highlights the limitations of other religions than his own, concluding,

> To this extent the world religions can be called ways of salvation only in a relative sense, not simply as a whole and in every case. However much truth they exhibit in certain respects, which Christians must affirm, they do not offer *the* truth for Christians.[33]

The shortcomings of these religions, as of Jesuanity for that matter, are not the point. What is at issue is whether we have an adequate Christology, providing an equally adequate ecclesiology, arising from the mystery of Christ that will allow us to see God's graces and gifts showered on all he has created, including all peoples and members of all religions — even if for Jesuans this is eminently realised in Jesus and the Jesuan community. We are not involved in a patronising comparative exercise, I submit, point-scoring in favour of one particular community;[34] it is just a question of whether we can conceive adequately of Church and call it Christian because representing that plan, that mystery that is Christ for all people, whatever particular community (Jesuan or not) provides them with a path to salvation.[35] The mystery, the wisdom is not monochrome but multicoloured, *polypoikilos*, manyfaceted; this is equally true of its ecclesial dimension, even if we are raised with black and white vision, as people like Dom Bede Griffiths returning periodically from his ashram remind us.

The grace of Christ for all

Our study of scriptural and patristic tradition has given us grounds for a Christology and ecclesiology moving in that direction. Rahner himself, whose 1961 article we quoted above and found to be short on reference to such helpful tradition, fifteen years later entertained briefly that possibility.

> If there can be a faith which is creative of salvation among non-Christians, and if it may be hoped that in fact it is found on a large scale, then it is to be taken for granted that this faith is made possible and is based upon the supernatural grace of the Spirit. And this is the Spirit who proceeds from the Father and the Son, so that as the Spirit of the eternal Logos he can and must be called at least in this sense the Spirit of Christ, the divine Word who has become man.[36]

But the possibility of speaking not immediately of Jesus but of Christ, the divine Word, in this context of the salvation of all people is felt by Rahner (again without reference to scriptural and patristic tradition) to 'contradict the fact that Jesus Christ is intended from the outset by God's salvific will as the redeemer of the world. We get out of these and similar, unmentioned difficulties only by saying that the Incarnation and the cross are, in scholastic terminology, the "final cause" of the universal self-communication of God to the world which we call the Holy Spirit.' [37] Rahner's implicit, uncritical dependence on a scriptural datum, lack of reference to further traditional comment, and preference for scholastic processes deprive him of an adequate approach to the topic to which he has returned so often.

What he was neglecting in the Fathers was a series of considerations on the question of the salvation of members of other faith communities; that he was aware of its existence is clear from his nod in its direction above on p. 104. In the first couple of centuries after Jesus there was interest shown in the religious situation of non-Jesuans, including Jews, by apologists and catechists like Justin, Theophilus, Clement of Alexandria, Tertullian and Origen, of whom the last was probably the most profound theologically. They had the advantage, not shared by all modern theologians, of being in living contact with their subject. They generally agreed that Providence has these peoples' welfare in mind as well, granting them revelation and grace. Theophilus, Tertullian and Clement speak of God enlightening peoples through spokespersons like Moses, biblical authors, even the Sibyl and pagan poets like Euripides. 'In olden times the Logos educated through Moses, and then through the prophets,' [38] says Clement, who credits Greek philosophers and Euripides with knowledge of a superior being;[39] the way of truth is one, but into it, as into a perennial river, streams flow from all sides.[40] Philosophy was like a schoolmaster leading the Greeks to Christ; it was a stepping stone to the philosophy which is according to Christ.[41] Theophilus, who can count on little in writing to his pagan friend Autolycus, refers him at great length to the Sibylline oracles as being 'true and useful and just and lovely' [42] and in the same vein to Aeschylus, Pindar, Euripides, Sophocles and other classical authors of pagan antiquity.[43] Even Augustine tells us in the *Confessions*[44] that his good Christian mother Monica believed an education in the pagan classics would make him a better Christian.

We have seen Origen (in the *Contra Celsum*) speaking of the Logos distinctly from Jesus, while insisting that he does not *separate* the Son of God from Jesus. In his commentary on *John* he spends much time explaining John's use of 'God', 'Word' and the force of the definite article in the prologue to the Gospel. He distinguishes people according as they accept 'the God', gods who participate in 'the God' (the sun and moon given to some people as gods), and those gods that are not gods at all, just man-made objects. Then he differentiates people according to their participation in the Word himself: those (like the prophets Hosea, Isaiah, Jeremiah) to whom the Word of the Lord has come; those who have known only Jesus, 'having supposed that the Word which became flesh was the totality of the Word' or 'those who have known nothing except

Jesus Christ and him crucified, who see the Word as flesh;' thirdly, 'those who have devoted themselves to words which participate in some way in the Word,' like Greek philosophers; and fourthly, those who have believed in words which are altogether corrupt and godless.[45]

For this notion of the Logos operating beyond the Jesuan community (not simply temporally prior) Origen is indebted to Justin, who like Origen is concerned to develop a soteriology that will accommodate not only Jesuans but also Jews (in the *Dialogue* particularly) and other citizens of the Roman empire (especially in the *Apology/ies*).[46] To this end he develops his notion of the Logos as a seed, *sperma*, sown among all people, the *Logos spermatikos*.

> I confess that I boast and with all my strength strive to be found a Christian, not because the teachings of Plato are different from those of Christ, but because they are not in all respects similar, as neither are those of the others, Stoics and poets and historians. For each one spoke well in proportion to the share he had of the divine *Logos spermatikos*, seeing what was related to it. But they who contradict themselves on the more important points appear not to have possessed the heavenly wisdom and the knowledge which cannot be spoken against. So whatever things were properly said among all people are the property of us Christians. For next to God we worship and love the Word, who is from the unbegotten and ineffable God, since he also became man for our sake so that, becoming a partaker of our sufferings, he might also bring us healing. For all the writers were able to see realities darkly through the sowing of the implanted Logos that was in them ...
>
> For whatever either philosophers or lawgivers uttered well, they did so according to their share in discovering and contemplating the Logos. But since they did not know everything of the Logos, who is Christ, they often contradicted themselves.[47]

We have noted that other ancient theologians (like Athanasius)[48] and modern (like Rahner) have had concerns about subordinationist overtones in other statements of the doctrine of the Logos.[49] We also observed that pastors unhappy about the possible abuse by heretics of a theological development have preferred to discourage that development, even (as in the case of Cyril and more recent examples) doing so by force and duress. What is relevant here is that a body of commentators (on the Jesuan scriptures, basically) in the early period of the community when it was appropriate to take a wide perspective for evaluating Jesus and his

Way found assistance for their missionary work in the notion of a provident God working through his Logos for the benefit of all people — a notion akin to the Pauline mystery of Christ. Theologians and missionaries in today's pluralist world have had recourse to this same theology in an attempt to look beyond their own Jesuan community.

God's *basileia* in all people

A second principal contribution to Christology, ecclesiology and soteriology by these Fathers beyond seeing the Logos at work in all people — a Johannine and Pauline idea — is the accent they place on the values of the *basileia* to be found among them — a more Synoptic accent. Theophilus of Antioch, we saw, presented Christianity without reference to Jesus, and showed its essence to be realised in faith, truth and other virtues which a man like Autolycus could adopt without proceeding to specifically Jesuan beliefs and practices. Clement too, who was convinced that (as his commentator Henry Chadwick remarks) 'God's interest in the Gentile races did not begin only after the Incarnation,' [50] saw a commonality in people from a moral viewpoint: 'Equal natural righteousness reached all ... Each one of us is a partaker of His beneficence as far as he wills.' [51] Origen endorses this commonality: 'All wise people, to the extent that they advance in wisdom, participate in Christ, insofar as he is Wisdom.' [52] Origen is aware that this catholicity in his approach may be thought heterodox by Jesuans,[53] as also his approval of philosophers' ideas of immortality; so he clarifies the conformity of his ideas with the Gospel:

> The blessed life to come will be only for those who have adopted a value system in accordance with Jesus and worship of the Creator of all things ... The blessed end in our view with God in Christ — Word, Wisdom, all Virtue — will be for those who lived pure and irreproachable lives.[54]

That is a way of salvation possible for all people, Jesuan or not: worship of the Creator and a way of life in accordance with virtues of his *basileia*.[55]

This book began by acknowledging religious pluralism as a feature of our postmodern world. There have been many attempts to develop an adequate theological stance to this religious pluralism. For the Jesuan theologians the talisman of orthodoxy and/or adequacy is, predictably, the figure of Jesus (usually referred to in these debates as Christ — an unnecessary confusion, as we have observed). Michael Barnes in his *Religions in Conversation*[56] has usefully summarised the major exclusivist and inclusivist positions about other religions developed by Jesuan theologians such as Karl Barth and Ernst Troeltsch and those offering a compromise position of 'anonymous Christians' such as Karl Rahner; in all these positions Jesus and Jesuanity are central.

As none of these positions has satisfied Jesuans or those in the other religious communities, there has naturally developed another solution to the 'problem', out of the conviction that 'christology [=Jesuology] turns out to be the final touchstone and limit for Christian [=Jesuan] attempts to understand religious pluralism,' as one exponent of a new approach, Paul F. Knitter, remarks.[57] This approach, which Küng refers to sarcastically as 'a "brand new" doctrine' [58] and rejects out of hand as he does Rahner's anonymous Christians, is 'a move away from insistence on the superiority or finality of Christ [=Jesus] and Christianity [=Jesuanity] toward a recognition of the independent validity of other ways.' [59] It takes form in a series of writings entitled variously *No Other Name?*, *The Myth of Christian Uniqueness*, *Many Paths. A Catholic Approach to Religious Pluralism*,[60] and so forth.

Our interest in these various approaches to religious pluralism is primarily Christological, endeavouring to relate Jesus to the mystery of Christ — the task of this book — even if ecclesiology is necessarily bound up with this. We recognise the area is littered with dilemmas, the waters fraught with perils more numerous than Scylla and Charybdis. We can lurch from the exclusivism of a Daniélou to indifferentism and syncretism in our attitude to Church and salvation. We can insist on the truth and normativeness of Jesus and Jesuanity, or highlight the validity of other paths, other names. We can allow non-Jesuan believers to be true Christians, or deny it and admit that outside the Church there is salvation.

One rule of thumb for not falling foul of extreme positions is to follow biblical perspectives and the Fathers in seeing a distinction (not separation) between Jesus, on the one hand, and Christ the mystery and Christ the Logos, on the other. There is no need to make Hindus and Moslems into anonymous Jesuans if they can be shown to be Christian.[61] There is no need to confute Cyprian by recognising ways to salvation outside the Jesuan community and concluding this occurs outside the Christian Church. There is no need to arrive at a denial of Jesus' divine status as scriptures and councils uphold it just because other religions point to a saviour under different names. This is not compromise by way of religious indifferentism, syncretism, relativism; it is simply precision arising from a close examination of Jesuan tradition.

Indian theologians on religious pluralism

An example of how such Christological precision would allow well-meaning religious dialogue to proceed further. In 1988 the Indian (Catholic) Theological Association at its twelfth annual meeting tried to arrive at a theology of religions that would do justice to their real experience that 'pluralism and multiplicity in their various forms characterize the Asian continent.' [62] These Indian theologians admit that 'various historical factors have brought us a clearer and profounder knowledge of the riches of the major religions, dispelling much of the ignorance which in the past littered fear, suspicion and hostility.' They see a tendency to inclusivism in the early Church, turning to an attitude of total rejection or exclusivism after the encounter with Islam. This brings them to ask themselves,

> Are the many religions part of God's design and provision for humankind? Does religious pluralism constitute a situation of grace? ...
>
> Is the faith-experience behind the different symbols really identical as the mystics seem to suggest, or is it different and specific in each religion? Are there one faith and many religions, or many faiths and many religions? ...
>
> Is it possible, then, to have a theology of religions acceptable to adherents of all religions without watering down some truths, undermining some convictions, compromising some principles, or imposing one's own conceptions and positions?
>
> Or, is the possibility already present in the universal openness of all human persons to the Ultimate Reality? Is it not implied in the first article of the christian creed, and in all faith in One Absolute Ground/Source [of] Reality?

It is a wonderfully open, respectful, repentant, informed approach to a lived reality — something not often true of discussion of the subject. These theologians on the subcontinent resume all their considerations under the three attitudes commonly taken to other religions — ecclesiocentrism, Christocentrism and theocentrism — and they look at their relative adequacy. It is here that the lack of access to available precision proves a handicap. Because they identify Christocentrism with Jesucentrism and thus speak of 'a narrow Christocentrism' that will not fit the Indian situation, they have to abandon the former two approaches to a solution and settle for a lowest-common-multiple approach.

> Already, at least in an incipient manner, inter-religious dialogue, common actions for the building of a better society and the inculturation process are taking place in India. It is out of this praxis that Indian theologians have been attempting to move away from a narrow christocentrism to a theocentrism, trying at the same time to be faithful to their commitment to God and to man in Christ. Assuredly christocentrism does not exclude theocentrism. But in the Indian context theocentrism implies the possibility of understanding other religions as ways offered by the common author of life and salvation, as his first self-gift. These theologians are aware that theocentrism by itself does not articulate a universal theology of religions, nor can it take into its orbit secular and atheistic ideologies.

It is such a pity that authentic experience, honesty and good will could not proceed to take advantage of biblical and patristic aids to seeing that Christology need not be narrow and intolerant of religious diversity if not confined to Jesuology, and that thus theology of Church need not be restricted to the Jesuan community.[63] These theologians could then have arrived at a Christocentric theology of religions in India, taking into its orbit as well 'secular and atheistic ideologies'.

Religions in search of *basileia*

Paul and the Fathers could have helped those Indian theologians; their statement, otherwise so impressive, is short on reference to the former, and only a nod is made in the direction of Justin and other unnamed Fathers. For one thing, they would have looked at Logos and the mystery of Christ, not simply at Jesus, and reviewed the religious diversity of India in that *polypoikilos* light. The second contribution we recognised in those patristic considerations would also have helped them. Beginning with the evangelical emphasis on God's *basileia* in the mouth of Jesus as his invitation to all good people, they could with Theophilus and Origen have seen the Christian characteristics of the lives of adherents of many non-Jesuan religions. Bernard Lonergan has listed them (relating them to

Judaism, Islam, Zoroastrian Mazdaism, Hinduism, Buddhism, Taoism) as the following shared beliefs:

> that there is a transcendent reality;
> that he is immanent in human hearts;
> that he is supreme beauty, truth, righteousness, goodness;
> that he is love, mercy, compassion;
> that the way to him is repentance, self-denial, prayer;
> that the way is love of one's neighbour, even of one's enemies;
> that the way is love of God, so that bliss is conceived as knowledge of
>   God, union with him, or dissolution into him.[64]

Certainly adherents of those religions see common ground in ob-servance of the evangelical values. 'We would like the other religions to accept Islam as a legitimate faith community which has a very valuable, sensible system of ethics and belief,' says Zaki Badawi. 'We believe in the same one God as you believe in. We have the same commandments as you and the same ethical system. Our community is developing its own western milieu, but we are from the same Abrahamite religion. We share so much. The real division is now between secularism and religion.' [65] A Hindu likewise observes: 'Hinduism teaches that all religions are of equal validity, that all religions lead to the same goal — whatever you call that goal. The means are different but the goal is the same. The basics of all religions are the same — love and honesty, the pursuit of truth, compassion towards our fellow human beings.' [66] It is not out of any egalitarianism (as perhaps the latter writer suggests) that we look for the *basileia* values in these religions;[67] nor is there any at-tempt to rate various religions on some normative scale, as Küng in-sists on doing. With scriptural and patristic backing, we are endeavouring to situate peoples and religions in the mystery of Christ and recognise the presence of the Logos, as we can place Jesus and the Jesuan community within that context as well; terms like 'pagans' and 'the opposition' (even 'instruments of the devil')[68] are clearly inappropriate. Michael Barnes, who prefers the term 'conversation' to 'dialogue', puts the practical dimension to this theological attitude well:

> When faith meets faith, truth does not confront falsity; rather, we are speaking of communities of men and women struggling to come to terms with ultimate reality. Christians [=Jesuans] share that struggle. Theology in a pluralist world begins and ends with the conversation, with learning over and over the meaning and implications of the act of faith.[69]

Such an open, accepting, non-judgmental attitude can, understandably, give rise to unease in pastors concerned both for numbers and for orthodoxy. In my own area of the Lower Blue Mountains outside Sydney, the ecumenical activities of our inter-church group are not participated in equally by all Jesuan groups; smaller, less open groups tend to see a threat posed by such participation, and of course there are often hidden factors built into this reluctance such as financial viability as well as doctrinal sensitivities. It is also a fact that we have yet to welcome any non-Jesuan groups to join us. We cannot all espouse the commendably disinterested attitude to the Jesuan Decade of Evangelisation voiced by a member of the Baha'i community: 'We would welcome a Muslim decade too, because for a Baha'i any effort that is made to spread God's word and to bring religion to people's lives must be a good thing.' [70]

That seems a commendable motto for religious missionary activity, 'to spread God's word and to bring religion to people's lives'. If, on the contrary, it strikes you as religious indifferentism, consider these words of the present Pope to a new Nigerian ambassador to the Holy See: 'As you know, the Church has a deep respect for Muslims since she believes that the plan of salvation encompasses all who acknowledge the Creator. This respect includes a readiness to cooperate with them for the betterment of humanity and a commitment to search together for true peace and justice. Dialogue is the gateway to such cooperation.' [71] Closer to home these words raise an echo with those struggling to develop a rationale for work among the Aborigines — the ancient people of the Australian continent possessed of their own ages-long spirituality. In an article, *The plight of Catholic missions in Australia,*[72] the distinguished archeologist and worker among the Aborigines, Eugene Stockton, cites the oft-repeated cry of missioners, 'What are we trying to do?' In lamenting that much effort to date has been assimilationist, Father Stockton suggests instead the way of *basileia*:

> We are empowering the poor/oppressed to go free — liberation in a holistic sense including salvation, self-determination, freedom from the fear, pressures, internal constraints, freedom to lead, to minister, to express, to make their own integration of Old and New Laws, to become fully Aboriginal in a sense not possible even under traditional ways.

Practising missioners in predominantly Muslim and Hindu countries, such as the Columbans, likewise give expression, not to

119

any opposition they meet in efforts to encourage people in these countries to forsake their own religious communities and become followers of Jesus, but to the appreciation they arrive at of the ideals espoused by these people. Terry Twohig, missioner in a Muslim area of the Philippines, concludes:

> In a situation of prejudice, dialogue means an abiding and genuine search for goodness, beauty and truth. This search is based on the conviction that no one person has a monopoly of these. For are not goodness, beauty and truth emanating from one and the same source, God? Who or what can monopolise Him? Thus each person must be open to the fact that he can be enriched by the goodness, truth and beauty in the other. Each must be ready to discover the face of God in the other's faith.[73]

Father Twohig, who showed no sign of being less a follower of Jesus for his admiration of the principles of Islam, and no less an admirer of Islam for the burgling of his house by locals, received a letter of solidarity from his friend Sultan Maguid Maruhom deploring this transgression of Muslim principles and concluding: 'You might be interested in how I define my religion, how I believe it to be. It is not far from your belief in your religion. Like you, four magnificent words come immediately to mind when describing my faith. Truth, Peace, Justice and Equality ... If I have the opportunity, I would work and be proud of working side by side with you in order to bring justice and peace to both our peoples.' [74]

An ecclesiology for mission

Another Columban, Richard Keelan (lately deceased), who worked with Hindus and Muslims in Fiji, also dialogued with them, including a Muslim scholar:

> While he was very happy to talk about Islam and have me listen, there was no interest on his part in my talking about Christianity while he listened. Strangely enough, I did not find all this depressing. It has taken me many years of working among the Hindus and Muslims of Fiji to accept that very few of them wished to become Christians no matter how hard I tried to bring this about. It took me longer to appreciate how important their beliefs were in their daily lives, that their religion led them to try to lead good lives even if, like us Christians, they sometimes failed in this. I had to accept that in some way that I could not comprehend, they too were being given the grace which enlightened their minds and touched their heart.

It has taken longer for me to begin to wrestle with the idea that all of this has something to do with 'the unsearchable riches of the mystery of Christ' and with the action of the Spirit who 'breathes' where He will.[75]

It is a pity that these insights came so slowly and so painfully to these ministers of the Word,[76] and that they could not have been given in their ministerial formation an adequate Christology and ecclesiology, the basis surely of an adequate missiology. Still, like them the early apologists and catechists we read forged their theology amidst living contact with non-Jesuan people and thus came to an appreciation of a mystery of Christ more comprehensive than the mystery of Jesus.[77] A pity, too, that recent magisterial statements like *Redemptoris Missio* show neither signs of any patristic inspiration nor of the wider biblical perspective. Missioners like Fathers Twohig and Keelan in difficult situations looked for such theological guidance in pastoral practice, and like John Wijngaards were disappointed not to find it.[78] By contrast, the editor of *The Far East* was delighted to include as an example of necessary guidance these words of John Paul II about religious dialogue:

> There is only one divine plan for every human being who comes into this world, one single origin and goal ... The differences are a less important element when confronted with the unity which is radical, fundamental and decisive.[79]

Doubtless the Pope believes that for me as for him the difference Jesus makes is radical, fundamental, decisive. But when he writes of 'every human being', it is the unity of the one divine plan that is basic and common. If our Christology extends beyond Jesus to consideration of the whole divine plan, our theology of Church as mystery can be sufficiently comprehensive to include as well those who never heard of him or placed any store by him. If our Church is thus truly Christian and not simply Jesuan, salvation in this Church reaches to all good people, who find it nowhere else. If our salvation comes in the mystery of Christ, not all need turn to Jesus to find it. We need have no recourse to theological 'sleight of hand' to class unwitting Jesuans as anonymous, since they can be formally (if not explicitly) Christian within the mystery of Christ.[80] We need place no impossible burdens on our missioners, since their task is not to multiply followers of Jesus but to nourish true children of the God from whom stems that 'one divine plan'.

Points for discussion

1.   Hans Küng asserts the need for steadfastness in one's own tradition as a requirement for entering religious dialogue. In your experience of such dialogue, have you found yourself comfortable in this regard? Do you need to prepare yourself better for this role in the contemporary Church?

2.   Is it clear to you that we can admit the religious riches of other (non-Christian) traditions without undermining our own? Are exclusivism or relativism the only options open to us? Relate the question to the mystery of Christ.

3.   What is the theology of Church out of which you think and live? Is it sufficient for theologising about the salvation of members of other religions? What is your position on 'Outside the Church no salvation'?

4.   When you contribute to 'the missions', what do you expect your money and missionary resources to be directed to achieving? Are 'the missions' still relevant? Consider also the phrase 'the propagation of the faith'.

Further reading

M. Barnes, *Religions in Conversation. Christian Identity and Religious Pluralism*, London: SPCK, 1989.

D. Bosch, *Transforming Mission. Paradigm Shifts in Theology of Mission*, Maryknoll: Orbis, 1991.

J. Hick, P. Knitter, *The Myth of Christian Uniqueness. Towards a Pluralistic Theology of Religions*, Maryknoll: Orbis, 1987.

H. Küng, *On Becoming a Christian* (1974), Eng. trans., New York: Doubleday, 1974.

K. Rahner, 'Christianity and the non-Christian religions,' *Theological Investigations* 5, London: DLT, 1966.

The Month 1991 September–October, on the Decade of Evangelisation.

Vatican Secretariat for non-Christians, 'The attitude of the Church towards the followers of other religions,' *Bulletin* 56 (1984) pp. 126–41.

Notes

1.   Cf Karl Rahner, 'Jesus Christ in non-Christian religions,' *Foundations of Christian Faith* (1976), Eng. trans., London: DLT, 1978, pp. 318–21.

2. K. Rahner, 'Current problems in Christology,' pp. 166–67.

3. *Global Responsibility*, pp. 94–102.

4. Edward Schillebeeckx in writing on Church is handicapped, perhaps through inadequate reference to biblical tradition, by his understanding of 'mystery' only as index of a dualistic tendency to seek 'immunity from scientific clarification, ideological criticism or theological hermeneutics' (*Church, The Human Story of God* [1989], Eng. trans., New York: Crossroad, 1990, p. 213). We have dealt fully with this (not uncommon) misunderstanding of the term above in ch. 2.

5. H. De Lubac, *Catholicism*, 4th edn, 1947, Eng. trans., London: Burns and Oates, 1962, p. 110.

6. K. Rahner, 'Christianity and the non-Christian religions,' *Theological Investigations* 5, London: DLT, 1966, pp. 133–34.

7. *The Salvation of the Nations* (1948), Notre Dame: University of Notre Dame Press, 1962, pp. 7–8.

8. Cf Raymond E. Brown: 'To state the facts simply, Jesus did not live in the framework of a Christian church, and only once in his recorded words did he ever speak about church in the larger sense' ('Communicating the divine and human in Scripture,' 6). Brown thus disallows the latter mention in *Mt* as referring only to the local assembly.

   Even with the single mention of church , *Mt* 16.18, 'On this rock I will build my church,' which does not occur in the Marcan pericope of Peter's confession, difficulties have been found. 'The reference to building *a church* fits in with the thesis of a post-resurrectional setting for the words of Jesus, for there are difficulties in assuming that the Jesus of the ministry planned for a church,' conclude the editors (Brown et al.) of *Peter in the New Testament* (London: Chapman, 1974, pp. 91–92) after careful examination.

9. Küng suggests we should not take as cynical Alfred Loisy's observation on this fact: 'Jesus proclaimed the kingdom of God, and what came was the Church' (*The Church*, Eng. trans., London: Search Press, 1968, p. 43).

10. J. M. R. Tillard, in asking 'What is the Church of God?' (*One in Christ* 20 [1984] pp. 226–42), sees it as 'fulfilment of the "mystery"' of the Pauline letters, as we have, and adds: 'An ecclesiology which wants to grasp the nature of the Church in its depth cannot easily seek its inspiration elsewhere than in the first chapters of the Letter to the Ephesians' (p. 227).

11. Paul Minear, *Images of the Church in the New Testament*, Philadelphia: Westminster, 1960, identifies 96 such images.

12. *Sermons* 176,4 (*CCL* pp. 104,715).

13. *Lumen Gentium* 2.

14. See my *Mystery of Life. A Theology of Church*, Melbourne: Collins Dove, 1991.

15. *De unitate ecclesiae* 1,20,56 (*PL* 43,434).

16. R. Panikkar agrees ('A Christophany for our times,' p. 19). At that place he also sees the wisdom in a medieval comment that 'the New Testament's *mysterion* was infinitely deeper and broader [a basis for ecclesiology] than the Latin *sacramentum*' (see my *Mystery of Life*, pp. 16–19, for detail on these terms).

17. *Historia Ecclesiastica* 5,24 (*SC* 41,70), emphasis added.

18. (1982), Eng. trans., Mystic: Twenty-Third Publications, 1985.

19. Quoted by Congar, *op.cit.*, p. 88.

20. According to the Vatican's 1991 *Annuario Pontificio*, Christians represent a diminishing third of the world's population of 5.2 billion people (*The Tablet* 28 September 1991, 1191); Muslims (917 million), Catholics (906), and Hindus (722) are the largest religious groups.

21. In the Decree on the relationship of the Church to Non-Christian religions, *Nostra Aetate*, promulgated 1965. Cyril Hally reminds me that even here the argument is not yet theological, but sociological, philosophical and pastoral, and that the magisterium has yet to endorse a particular theology of religion.

22. Cf K. Rahner, 'Towards a fundamental theological interpretation of Vatican II,' p. 720.

23. The Council of Florence-Ferrara, 1442: 'The Holy Roman Church firmly believes, professes and preaches that no one outside the Catholic Church — not just heathen but Jews, heretics and schismatics — cannot share in eternal life but will go into eternal fire 'prepared for the devil and his angels' unless before the end of their life they are joined to the Church' (DS 1351).

24. 'We have Good News too,' *The Month* 1991, p. 369.

25. Quoted by Augustin Dupré La Tour, 'Christology and non-Christian religions,' *Theology Digest* 35 (1988 Summer) p. 104.

26. Paul's worldview, of course, was incomparably more limited than ours; he had no idea of the racial diversity and religious pluralism that we have come to discover. The barbarians of his world were simply those who could not speak Greek, saying instead 'bar-bar'. He shows no awareness of the great religious breakthrough towards an awareness of divine transcendence in Asian religions in the first millennium BC, of which Bede Griffiths speaks.

27. Anil Goonewardene, 'Closeness to people of faith,' *The Month* 1991, p. 373.

28. K. Rahner, 'Christianity and the non-Christian religions,' pp. 118,119, 131. Cf Bishop Butler: 'A person who genuinely fears God and does what is right would obviously wish to become a Christian if they recognised this as God's will; it *is* God's will, and he/she wishes to do God's will, hence, he/she may be said to desire implicitly what they reject explicitly' (*Theology of Vatican II*, London: DLT, 1967, p. 113).

29. *On Becoming a Christian* (1974), Eng. trans., New York: Doubleday, 1974, p. 98.

30. *Op.cit.*, p. 91. Cf *Global Responsibility*, p. 78: 'For a long time that was the official Roman Catholic position (*Extra Ecclesiam nulla salus* — Outside the church there is no salvation!). As if the church were already the kingdom of God! As if God's Spirit were not also at work in all other religions, which indeed are all provisional!'

31. Instead, Küng could have been more rigorously logical (and religiously perceptive) in the manner of Raimundo Panikkar: 'The good and *bona fide* Hindu as well as the good and *bona fide* Christian are saved by Christ — not by Hinduism or Christianity *per se*, but through their sacraments and, ultimately, through the *mysterion* active within the two religions' (*The Unknown Christ of Hinduism*, rev. edn, pp. 85–86).

32. Cf *Global Responsibility*, pp. 77–88.

33. *On Being a Christian*, p. 104.

34. Again Panikkar, living (unlike Küng and most of us) in close contact with other traditions, could help in supplying a full range of criteria for dialogue: 'There seem to be three indispensable prerequisites for such an encounter: a deep human honesty in searching for the truth wherever it can be found; a great intellectual openness in this search, without conscious preconceptions or willingly entertained prejudices; and finally a profound loyalty towards one's own religious tradition' (*op.cit.*, p. 35).

35. John B. Cobb Jr agrees this is the way our theology should be moving: 'If all the great ways continue to the last day distinct from one another, each open to all, enriched by all, and transformed by all, I as a Christian see nothing lacking in that' ('Toward a Christocentric catholic theology' in L. Swidler [ed.], *Toward a Universal Theology of Religion*, Maryknoll: Orbis, 1987, pp. 99–100). He has difficulties with the notion of a 'universal theology of religion', and speaks rather of 'ways'. Because he does not distinguish the different perspectives, as we have, and generally intends a Jesucentric theology, he seems to fall short of the necessary Christocentric synthesis.

36.   'Jesus Christ in non-Christian religions,' p. 316.

37.   *Ibid.*, p. 317.

38.   *Paidagogos* 1,1,2 (*SC* 70,108). Tertullian, too, speaks of the use of litera-
       ture for recording good people's thoughts, and with pagan authors
       particularly in mind says, *'De vestris sumus: fiunt, non nascuntur
       Christiani'* (well turned again by the Fathers of the Church translator
       as 'We are from your own ranks: Christians are made, not born':
       Apology xviii [*CCL* 1,118]), reminiscent of his other remark about the
       soul being 'by natural instinct Christian'.

39.   *Protrepticus* 26, *Stromata* 5.133.8–9 (*GCS*).

40.   *Stromata* 1.37.2. Similar thinking and terminology can be found in
       some Vatican II statements about other religions: 'elements which
       are good and true,' 'precious things both religious and human,'
       'seeds of contemplation,' 'elements of grace and truth,' 'seeds of the
       Word,' 'rays of that Truth which enlightens all people' (collected in
       'The attitude of the Church towards the followers of other religions,'
       Secretariat for Non-Christians *Bulletin* 56 [1984] p. 135). Cf A. Push-
       parajan, 'Mission and dialogue: are they contradictory to each
       other?' *Indian Missiological Review* 13 (1991 No.2) p. 61.

41.   *Stromata* 1.28.3. Paul Tillich sees another side to this openness of the
       Fathers: 'This astonishing universalism, however, was always
       balanced by a criterion which was never questioned, either by the or-
       thodox or by the heretical groups: the image of Jesus as the Christ, as
       documented in the New, and prepared for in the Old Testament.
       Christian universalism was not syncretistic; it did not mix, but rather
       subjected whatever it received to an ultimate criterion. In the power
       of this polarity between universality and concreteness it entered the
       Medieval period, having to compete with no religion equal to it in
       either of these respects' (*Christianity and the Encounter of the World
       Religions*, New York: Columbia Uni Press, 1963, pp. 36–37). To be sure,
       there is no doubt of the Fathers' faith in Jesus: that is not at issue.

42.   II,92.

43.   II,37.

44.   II,3,8 (*CCL* 27,21).

45.   *Comm. on John*, 2. pp. 17–33 (Fathers of the Church translation).

46.   Patrologists suggest the second *Apology* may in fact be the conclusion
       of the former.

47.   *Apology* II, 13,10 (*PG* 6,465,459).

48.   Athanasius is not happy with identifying the Word with that word
       'which some are accustomed to call *spermatikos*' (*Contra Gentes* 40; ed.
       R. W. Thomson, Oxford: Clarendon, 1971).

49. Pannenberg, relatively well cognisant of patristic statement, gives a thorough evaluation of Logos theology, ancient and modern, though principally in relation to creation (*Jesus God and Man*, pp. 160–69, and 390–97).

50. *Early Christian Thought and the Classical Tradition*, p. 45.

51. *Stromata* 5,134 (*GCS* 417).

52. *Comm. on John* 1,246 (*SC* 120,182).

53. Karl Barth is quoted (by Michael Barnes, 'When faith meets faith,' *The Tablet* 4 January 1992, p. 12) as saying: 'He who does not believe in universal salvation is an ox, but he who dares to teach it is an ass.'

54. *Contra Celsum* 3,81 (*SC* 136,182). The translations of the *SC* edition and of Chadwick, *op.cit.*, p. 161, are deficient here.

55. A modern theologian concurs: 'The kingdom of God, the central term in Jesus' religious message, is broader and richer than Christianity [=Jesuanity] and the churches of Christ [Jesus]' (E. Schillebeeckx, *Church, The Human Face of God*, p. 102).

56. *Religions in Conversation. Christian Identity and Religious Pluralism*, London: SPCK, 1989.

57. *No Other Name? A Critical Survey of Christian Attitudes Toward the World Religions*, London: SCM, 1985, p. 134.

58. 'What is nowadays proclaimed as a "brand new" doctrine sometimes simply proves to be old doctrine from the spirit of Protestant liberalism, which certainly "also" really heard God speak through Jesus and his message, but abandoned the normativeness and "finality" of Jesus Christ — indeed had reduced him to the level of a prophet "along with others" and so had lost all the criteria for discerning the spirits. Karl Barth and "dialectical theology" (including Rudolf Bultmann and Paul Tillich) had rightly protested against such liberalism. A step back from that is hardly progress' (*Global Responsibility*, p. 98). Küng documents the new-old doctrine from Knitter and Hick; he does not go back beyond Protestant liberalism to patristic teaching, as Tillich does (see note 28 above). E. Schillebeeckx is not so dismissive of Knitter's approach because he avoids Küng's error of immediately invoking truth and universality in considering other religions (*Church, The Human Face of God*, p. 162).

59. P. F. Knitter in John Hick & Paul F. Knitter (ed.), *The Myth of Christian Uniqueness. Towards a Pluralistic Theology of Religions*, Maryknoll: Orbis, 1987, p. viii.

60. Eugene Hillman, Maryknoll: Orbis, 1989.

61. Because of his Christology, which is more comprehensive than Rahner's and Küng's, Panikkar can say: 'It is acceptable to Hindus to be "anonymous Christians", provided one also admits that Christians are "anonymous Hindus" (though this expression makes little sense in a tradition which takes polynomy for granted, ever since the famous *rgvedic* saying, "One is he whom the sages call by many names")' (*op.cit.*, p. 13).

62. 'Towards a theology of religions: an Indian Christian perspective,' *Kristu Jyoti* 5 (1989 No.1) pp. 51–63. Cf their 'Towards an Indian Christian theology of religious pluralism' the following year (*Kristu Jyoti* 5 [1989 No.4] pp. 64–74).

63. Four years later Asian theologians meeting in Thailand addressed (a little less comprehensively) the same challenge, only to fall at the same hurdle (reported in *Indian Missiological Review* 14 [1992 March] pp. 62–76).

64. *Method in Theology*, p. 109.

65. 'Presenting God for all to see,' *The Month* 1991, p. 370.

66. Niru Desai, 'All faiths are equal,' *The Month* 1991, p. 372.

67. The Secretariat for Non-Christians, in fact, speaks similarly in writing on 'dialogue for the reign of God': 'A further level of dialogue is that of deeds and collaboration with others for goals of a humanitarian, social, economic, or political nature which are directed towards the liberation of mankind' ('The attitude of the Church towards the followers of other religions,' p. 135).

68. 'Muslims are instruments of the devil, who is our arch-enemy. Anyone who knows Scripture will agree with me' — a remark of the secretary of the Christian Association of Nigeria, a group combining all strands of Christianity in that country and presided over by the Catholic Archbishop of Lagos, reported by an African commentator on the failure to achieve dialogue in that country (Paul Gifford, 'Christian crusaders,' *The Tablet* 22 June 1991, p. 761).

69. 'Faith meets faith,' *The Month* 1991, p. 367.

70. Hugh Adamson, 'Faith for this age,' *The Month* 1991, p. 375.

71. Quoted by Paul Gifford, 'Christian crusaders,' p. 760.

72. *Nelen Yubu* 27 (1986 Winter) 25. The Pope himself had rejected any assimilationist approach to missionary work among the Aborigines in addressing them in 1986 at Alice Springs: 'For thousands of years you have lived in this land and fashioned a culture that endures to this day. And during all this time the Spirit of God has been with you. Your "Dreaming", which influences your lives so strongly that, no matter what happens, you remain for ever people of your culture,

is your own way of touching the mystery of God's Spirit in you and in creation. You must keep your striving for God and hold on to it in your lives' (*The Pope in Australia*, Sydney: St Paul, 1986, p. 166).

73. 'Some reflections on dialogue,' *The Far East* 72 (1990 No.4) p. 12.

74. *Ibid.*, 9.

75. 'The limits of belief,' *The Far East* 72 (1990 No.7) p. 15.

76. Especially as Vatican II had been explicit on these matters in its advice to missioners: 'They ought to know well the religious and cultural traditions of others, happy to discover and ready to respect seeds of the Word which are hidden in them ... His disciples should know the people among whom they live and should establish contact with them, to learn by sincere and patient dialogue what treasures a bountiful God has distributed among the nations of the earth' (Decree on the missionary activity of the Church #11).

77. For an extensive (if theologically incomplete) survey of attitudes to mission from the beginning, see David J. Bosch, *Transforming Mission. Paradigm Shifts in Theology of Mission*, Maryknoll: Orbis, 1991.

78. 'The encyclical is ambivalent. It says all the right things about respect for what the Spirit does in other religions, about open-mindedness, frankness and humility. But it also reaffirms belief in Christ as the only "way, truth and life" and the Church as the ordinary means of salvation without leaving room for the tension this creates. The dialogue that is going on in many parts of the world is beset by much more heart-searching and theological probing than the encyclical seems to allow for. The Christ that it calls upon us to proclaim is not sufficiently linked to the cosmic Christ of all creation or the hidden Christ in other religions' ('A double-edged appeal,' *The Tablet* 9 February 1991, p. 181).

79. 'How the other half believes,' *The Far East* 72 (1990 No.4) p. 1.

80. Cf Panikkar: 'If christians have to speak of an unknown Christ, other religions will legitimately use other languages and not allow the christian language to become a universal language' ('A Christophany for our times,' p. 12).

6

Christ, creation and Jesus

A dualistic attitude to the world pre-dates the Church of Jesus, which has however retained elements of it, despite more integral accents in biblical, liturgical and patristic traditions; eastern Fathers in particular recognised the cosmic dimension of the mystery of Christ. Our contemporary western Church does not consistently recognise its responsibility towards a world that is being abused and awaits fulfilment of the Pauline promise of reconciliation. Can we relate to Jesus this process of cosmic reconciliation, or should we invoke again the wider perspective of the mystery of Christ in the manner of Paul, Wisdom and the Fathers?

Matthew's angel, we have seen, has much to account for. Is it fair to trace a line from his anthropocentric words, 'Call him Jesus, for he shall save his people from their sins,' to the polarised attitude of Thomas A'Kempis in the fourteenth century, 'This is the highest wisdom, by despising the world to make progress towards the kingdom of heaven' (*The Imitation of Christ*, Book 1, Chapters 1, 3)? That influential little book, which remained prescribed reading at least for religious in the Catholic community until effectively sidelined by Vatican II, and whose echoes could constantly be heard in pre-Vatican II homiletics, came to us via the two cities analogy of *Hebrews,* the *Epistle to Diognetus* and Augustine, who all spoke of a City of God which is to come and is preferable, presumably, to the City of Man here below. Their analogy even crept into a key passage of *Gaudium et Spes* directed at the abolition of the dualism lying behind it:

> This Council exhorts Christians, as citizens of two cities, to strive to discharge their earthly duties conscientiously and in response to the Gospel spirit. They are mistaken who, knowing that we have here no abiding city but seek one which is to come, think that they may therefore shirk their earthly responsibilities ...

Therefore, let there be no false opposition between professional and social activities on the one part, and religious life on the other. The Christian who neglects his temporal duties neglects his duties toward his
neighbour and even God, and jeopardizes his eternal salvation.[1]

The two cities and Christology

That analogy can do with a spell; it has caused enough dualism and
even schizophrenia in good people, far outweighing the sense of
balance of earthly and heavenly goods achieved in Christian thinking.
The imbalance stemming from the angel, Augustine and A'Kempis
(but not Francis of Assisi, of course) rests on an inadequate Christology, as we have seen throughout this work; only one biblical
perspective is presented for people's consideration, and the stabilising context of the wider perspective is obscured. That defect allows
ancient imbalances to permeate Christian thinking, affecting (in the
Council's view) one's attitude to faith, vocation, duties, neighbour
and even God. As Johannes Metz says, 'It could be shown that it
was an unchristian conception of the world that was chiefly behind
the Christological heresies of the early Church.'[2] That makes sense:
unless one grasps the dimensions of the revealed divine plan for all
things that is the mystery of Christ, one is going to get an unsound
idea of the world, Jesus, the Church and other incarnational
realities, as pre-Jesuan times and literature illustrated. The lack of
integrity that the Council laments did not begin with Jesus and his
followers; dualistic aberrations go back much further as an in-
herently human tendency that continues to surface, not needing
dualistic analogies to foster it.

We shall never lay that tendency to rest, coming to us as it does
with our mother's milk, but we can at least dispose of some its
manifestations (especially if our Christology is sound). That
longtime antipathy between the (Jesuan) Church and science, for instance, rests on a misunderstanding of the mystery of Christ, encouraging the Church to see empirical sciences as enemies of the
spiritual. These days scientists like Australian biologist and
Templeton prize winner Charles Birch acknowledge the wider
vision that escapes the limitations of Matthew's angel:

The ecological model of the universe helps us to overcome the
dichotomy between the individual and its relations to its environment,
between the living and the non-living, between freedom and deter-
minism and between nature and God. And it provides a basis for a non-
anthropocentric ethic that includes nature as a whole ...

God is involved with the cosmos but is not identified with it. God is both within the system and independent of it.[3]

A Jesuan cosmology?

Theology, too, has thrown off its neglect and suspicion of the material universe and this-worldy realities; it has 'gone green,' says one commentator,[4] recognising the interest of many contemporary theologians in ecological issues. Matthew Fox has highlighted the relation of these issues to Christology, and calls for the Christian Church to develop a cosmology like that of older religions of native peoples of the Americas, Africa, Asia, Australia and Polynesia. 'Christianity has been out of touch with its "core", its center, its sense of mystical practice and cosmic awareness.'[5] As a result, he says, 'Mother Church is dying.'[6] These writers and others, unlike a theologian equally conscious of the cosmic dimension of the mystery of Christ, Jürgen Moltmann, tend to suggest a necessary association of such Christology with mysticism and also an esoteric quality, which are not of the essence. But at least the perspective of theology becomes more comprehensive and more integral, less dualistic.

It would not be correct to say, as Fox implies, that the Church of Jesus has not had a cosmology, that its faith does not embrace all of God's creation as its proper object, even if this dimension was not always highlighted. The liturgy prays on the feast of Christ the King:

> Almighty, ever-living God, it is your will to unite the entire universe under your beloved Son, Jesus Christ, the king of heaven and earth. Grant freedom to the whole of creation, and let it praise and serve your majesty for ever.

That reminds us that faith and experience are one thing, tradition of the community's faith and experience another. The liturgy has transmitted the cosmic dimension of the mystery of Christ more soundly[7] than, say, the homiletic tradition, some aspects of doctrinal tradition, and even the community's appreciation of the whole of biblical tradition. From these latter you might be inclined to assume, like Fox, that our community never enjoyed an understanding of the totality of the divine plan.

The Biblical tradition

We surveyed the biblical tradition of Judaism and Jesuanity in Chapter 3, and found there a diversity of perspective that might encourage, and in fact has encouraged, some of the faithful to let this-worldly realities slip from their theological and pastoral horizon. Matthew's angel is not completely at fault. Like all communities' literature, composed from their own (self-centred) viewpoint, the Old Testament generally concentrates on the people as beneficiaries of divine care.[8] From cultic credos of *Deuteronomy* to the victory celebrations of *Maccabees*, the focus is the same:

> In your steadfast love you led the people whom you redeemed;
> you guided them by your strength to your holy abode (*Ex* 15.13).

The accent, we saw, falls thus in Torah and Prophets (Former and Latter), and biblical scholarship from similar prejudice long gave preference to this material as more estimable. Yet it is in the Writings, and specifically in psalms and Wisdom, that the more comprehensive view of God's action is taken, extending to all of creation and not merely the human. Above on p. 53 we saw salvation history psalms like 136, 135, 104 and 93 beginning a litany of praise of God not with the customary mention of the marvels of the Exodus but with creation of heaven and earth, sun and moon and stars. We saw also and most conspicuously the remarkable catholicity of the Wisdom literature in its acceptance of all people and things into its purview. For Wisdom, all people good and evil (not categorised simply as Jew and Gentile) and all created realities are worth study under Providence (not the God of the patriarchs) — a perspective shocking for some Old Testament composers and later scholars unable to appreciate this redimensioning.

Those composers, too, responsible for the two different creation stories in the primeval history in *Genesis*, and particularly the Yahwist who built an extended narrative with this story as integral element (despite omission of it from some traditions), showed a theological conviction that an account of God's dealings with his world would not be complete without treatment of material creation and some mention of other peoples. This is a sapiential viewpoint, and the sages have been credited with a part in the composition of the Priestly story in Chapter 1. What is important for us to recognise here in particular is the repeated emphasis on the goodness of all created things, and human beings' responsibility for the rest of creation because they are made in God's image and *likeness* (Heb. *demuth*) — a connection that remained obscure until Ugaritic scholars like Mitchell Dahood found a clue in tablets found at Ebla composed in a more ancient semitic language than biblical Hebrew.

These tablets make mention of a *dimutu* in lists of deities, suggesting that the Priestly composer in using the word thus portrayed human beings not as despots, empowered to waste and destroy, but as deputy deities responsible like the creator for prudent management of other things.

Wisdom on creation

We have developed above on p. 58 the remarkable and theologically enlightening perspective of Old Testament Wisdom.[9] Happily, it is something that has latterly come to be appreciated better by scholars (even to the extent of an extreme 'pan-sapiential' movement, as often happens in scholarly reaction). Theologians concerned to bring created realities within the compass of theology have exulted to discover this sapiential perspective, without always grasping it fully. What Wisdom has to offer is not simply the figure of hypostatised wisdom, Lady Wisdom, appearing in *Proverbs*, *Sirach* and *Wisdom of Solomon* as an agent in creation, significant as this is.[10] It is principally a perspective on reality, recognisable and distinct from a prophetic, historical or apocalyptic perspective,[11] and composed of aspects, accents, characteristics — anthropological, social, cosmic, epistemological and moral, religious and theological, traditional and thematic (not to mention literary). We need to appreciate the sages' serious acceptance of, and closeness of touch with, material creation as integral to the whole of God's work if we are to be helped by them to a comprehensive theology, see Jesus as a Wisdom figure on the model of Solomon, and particularly respond to Paul's canvas for the mystery of Christ and his use of Wisdom motifs and of 'wisdom' as a synonym for that mystery, plan, purpose.

For similar reasons to Old Testament composers — that emphasis on human salvation — the New Testament generally, and not simply Matthew's angel, excludes the welfare of the material universe from its scope; Jesus as *our* saviour is at the focus. John does talk, ambiguously, of 'the world', which Jesus comes to save, but we saw this has the sense of the (evil) people in it — from which A'Kempis and many others took their cue. While the Jesus of the Synoptics is at ease living and teaching in the real world, in the manner of Solomon, nevertheless it falls to Paul to take on the mantle of the sages fully and push out the perspective, not only expanding the boundaries of the people of God but also acknowledging the cosmic dimensions of the whole divine plan, the mystery of Christ. So (under 'the mystery and the cosmos' in Chapter 3) we saw Paul speaking of Christ (not simply Jesus of Nazareth but a figure inheriting all the roles of divine, hypostatised wisdom)[12] gathering up and reconciling 'all things, things in heaven and things on earth'. The world, 'all creation', like us human beings is in process of transformation from its imperfect state,[13] a process which we assist by our detachment. No doubt of a cosmic viewpoint here.

Fathers East and West

Still, there is some excuse for those who have not found such a viewpoint in our sources, largely because they have concentrated on historical material in one testament and on the Synoptic Jesus in the other. Closer to the Scriptures than ourselves, the Fathers, particularly in the East, had little difficulty accommodating the cosmos into their theology. Theophilus of Antioch accounts for creation of all things by reference to a *Logos prophorikos*;[14] he would normally have moved from that point to the Incarnation except that his pagan friend Autolycus could not follow him there. The Cappadocians spoke at length likewise of the creative role of the Logos in respect of all created nature. Irenaeus, in the West but not of it, demonstrated true Pauline integrity of vision with his notion of 'recapitulation', coming to him straight from *Ephesians* accent on all things 'gathered up' in the mystery of Christ, under the pressure of polemic against gnostic dualism and anti-material creation myths. The same notion in original Greek dress, *anakephalaiosis,* appears later in Maximus the Confessor, the father of Byzantine theology.[15]

Jaroslav Pelikan in his chapter on 'The Cosmic Christ'[16] can document his theme readily from the East, while commenting on the relative reserve of Fathers of the West, an observation made earlier by Marie Dominique Chenu: 'It is a fact that every time this oriental theology filters westward it is at once received with reserve, sometimes with open hostility. Its cosmic and Christological optimism is rather shocking to the mind of the west, dominated as it is by the Augustinian view of the universe and of sinful humanity.'[17] Accent on the Fall, sin, atonement and the Cross did not encourage integrity and optimism regarding material realities. Even the beautiful *Epistle to Diognetus* on Christian life in the world, possibly the work of Hippolytus of Rome in the early third century, has picked up the two cities analogy and betrays its dualism (see Appendix for text). It was left to medieval mystics to restore to the

West some of that 'cosmic optimism'; Matthew Fox has made the names and writings of Hildegard of Bingen, Mechtild of Magdeburg, Meister Eckhart, Julian of Norwich, Nicholas of Cusa familiar to modern readers for their celebration of material creation, and reminded us that a medieval systematic theologian of the stature of Thomas Aquinas was prepared to build a Christian cosmology on a pre-Christian model of Aristotle (and suffered for it).[18]

Christology and creeds

If, in responding to the complaint that the Jesuan community does not have a cosmology like other religions, we have to concede that biblical and patristic tradition has been ambiguous about the world, we can at least point to a series of dogmatic credal statements from the beginning that are unequivocal about its origins, and initially Christological as well. Oscar Cullmann has refuted 'the erroneous belief that according to early Christianity the work of Christ is related only to salvation, but not to creation.' [19] Taking an early confession like 1 Cor 8.6 — 'For us there is one God, the Father, from whom are all things and for whom we exist, and one Lord, Jesus Christ, through whom are all things and through whom we exist' — he points out that the separation of God and Christ in later creeds does not yet exist and that both are involved in creation. He concludes that 'early Christian theology is in reality almost exclusively Christological,' observing as well (as we have noted from our survey of the Scriptures) that, unlike later controversies, 'the New Testament hardly ever speaks of the person of Christ without at the same time speaking of his work.' [20]

The fact of divine creation of the world our community creeds, consistently expressed, in the face of contrary philosophical and religious systems and myths, from the one known as the Apostles Creed and stemming from the first couple of centuries in Rome — 'I believe in God, the Father almighty, creator of heaven and earth' — through Nicea and Constantinople (we observe the separation of creation from Christ noted by Cullmann) to the Fourth Lateran Council in 1215 — 'We firmly believe that there is one God, creator of all visible and invisible things, spiritual and corporeal' — and Vatican I's attempt to be exhaustive and also distinguishing spiritual and material creation:

> This one true God, by his goodness and omnipotent power — not for the sake of acquiring or increasing his happiness but in order to manifest his

perfection by the goods which he bestows on creatures — by his most free counsel created together, out of nothing, from the beginning of time, both the spiritual and the corporeal creature, namely, the angelic and the earthly, and afterwards the human creature as composed of spirit and body.[21]

Can we detect in this laboured distinction of spirit and body, spiritual and corporeal, angelic and earthly a hangover from an earlier dualism in place of the monistic integrity of Irenaeus and Maximus, something typical of a medieval and modern Western worldview?[22] That would be consistent with a magisterium, theology and pastoral practice that have tended to weigh in more heavily on the side of the spiritual, other-worldly, religious, sacred, eternal as against the material, this-worldly, secular, profane, temporal, with the encouragement of a two-cities analogy and (a selective reading of) Scriptures and Fathers. The bishops at Vatican II with their statement on the Church in the modern world attempted again to lay that dualism to rest, as we saw; but two decades later at the 1985 Synod the attempt was not endorsed, bishops suggesting the Council had been too heady and not alert enough to the evils of secularism and immanentism:

> The signs of our times do not exactly coincide, in some points, with those of the time of the Council. From among these special attention must be paid to the phenomenon of secularism. The Council certainly did affirm the legitimate autonomy of temporal realities (cf *Gaudium et Spes* 36 and elsewhere). In this sense a correctly understood secularisation must be admitted. But totally different is that secularism that consists of an autonomous vision of man and the world, one which leaves aside the dimension of mystery, indeed neglects and denies it. This immanentism is a reduction of the integral vision of man, a reduction which does not lead to his true liberation but to a new idolatry, to the slavery of ideologies, to a life in the narrow and often oppressive structures of this world.[23]

Retaining a balance

That viewpoint, if predictable, certainly represents a step back from a more positive attitude to the world taken by Vatican II [24] and Pope Paul VI in his statements such as *Populorum Progressio* on the development of peoples and *Evangelii Nuntiandi* on evangelisation in the modern world. It is also, as we have seen, a travesty of the biblical notion of mystery, light years away from Paul's vision of the mystery of Christ gathering up all things in heaven and on earth — in fact, the divorce of the world from Christology noted by Cullmann is now complete. In place of Paul VI's deliberate and balanced distinction of secularism and secularisation, commending the latter as 'the effort, in itself just and legitimate and in no way incompatible with faith or religion, to discover in creation, in each thing or happening in the universe, the laws which regulate them with a certain autonomy, of culture and particularly of the sciences (GS 59),' [25] the Synod dismisses it in the manner of other recent magisterial statements where it is frowned on as equivalent to an atheistic secularism, thus encouraging the creeping spiritualism observable in the medievals and Vatican I creed. There is likewise in the synodal jeremiad no attempt to balance immanence with transcendence and helpfully distinguish the former from the feared immanentism. Pastoral concern can, as we have noted before, blur necessary distinctions.

Thank God, therefore, for a pastor like Paul VI who had the serenity to preserve them and in *Populorum Progressio* could write positively also of humanism, aware no doubt that this too would upset the dualists:

> In the design of God, every person is called upon to develop and fulfil themselves, for every life is a vocation. At birth, everyone is granted, in germ, a set of aptitudes and qualities for him to bring to fruition. Their coming to maturity, which will be the result of education received from the environment and personal efforts, will allow each man to direct himself toward the destiny intended for him by his creator. Endowed with intelligence and freedom, he is responsible for his fulfilment as he is for his salvation ...

> What must be aimed at is *complete humanism*. And what is that if not the fully-rounded development of the whole man and of all men? [26]

So, to the question, 'Does the Jesuan community have a cosmology, an adequate doctrine on the world', the answer if not categorically negative is hardly consistently positive. (If we ask further if that doctrine is soundly tied to an adequate Christology, the response is still weaker.) Orthodox statements from the East would continue to include the cosmos in the question of salvation. The World Council of Churches saw the need to adopt as the theme for its 1991 Assembly in Canberra, 'Come, Holy Spirit, renew the whole of creation'; one of its lead speakers from Asia, Chung Hyun-Kyung, and a constant litany of Aboriginal interventions admitted longtime disregard of this theme. The Catholic community has lurched from forward to reverse gears in its statements on the human, the secular.

Development and liberation

Underlying the positive and negative statements by the community, of course, are its *theologies* of the world, humanity and material creation (hopefully stemming from a comprehensive Christology). We saw Paul VI pleading for rounded development of peoples, more human conditions of life and a complete humanism. Theologians particularly in underdeveloped countries were heartened by this call, while seeing some inadequacy in the term 'development', which to them did not express adequately the radical change from economic, social, political and cultural dependence of some peoples if they were to attain a minimally human way of life, for which 'liberation' is more appropriate and richer in human content.[27] During an address in Sydney, Juan Luis Segundo, having explained the futility of concentrating on spiritual development of people if they still had to achieve basic humanisation of living conditions, was moved from his habitually phlegmatic delivery when a questioner enquired, what is the meaning of humanisation? 'How could you ask what it is to be human?' he burst out. 'If you've never been in love, no point in asking about the meaning of love.'

For followers of Jesus, his self-definition as liberator from oppression and deprivation in Isaiah's terms at the beginning of his ministry in *Luke* 4 is programmatic and paradigmatic; Paul VI, in another exercise of real magisterium, explains to the community in *Evangelii Nuntiandi* the significance of liberation true and false (##29–39).[28] Aloysius Pieris sees the full Christological as distinct from simply Jesuological significance of such liberation theology and praxis in writing on the proper attitude of the Church in Buddhist countries: 'Christian ashrams that follow *Jesus* by their "struggle to be poor," but do not serve *Christ* through a "struggle for the poor," fail to proclaim Jesus of Nazareth as the Christ and the Lord of history.'[29] In other words, human liberation is (not simply imitation of Jesus but) part of that process of reconciliation, gathering up, bringing to completion of all things that Paul (and Irenaeus and Maximus ...) saw that the *oikonomia* of the mystery of Christ involves; spiritual, religious, other-worldly, eternal values cannot be properly promoted independently of that.

So it is the reconciliation of 'all things', 'all creation', that God's

plan in the mystery of Christ involves, not simply human liberation; Paul is explicit about that, suggesting also (in *1 Cor 7*, as we
saw) that the two are related to the extent of human responsibility
for the former (endorsed as well by up-to-date exegesis of *Gn* 1.26).
The scope of that plan, as of universal history, is vast. If we shed
our inherent dualism, we realise that intuitively; but our awareness
is reinforced by acquaintance with the work of cosmologists, mathe-
maticians, astrophysicists and other empirical scientists.[30] Of
course, a paleontologist, theologian and student of Paul like Teilhard de Chardin can reach a particular depth of insight:

> In the consciousness of this progression and synthesis of all things in
> *Xristo Jesu*, I have found an extraordinarily rich and inexhaustible
> source of clarity and interior strength, and an atmosphere outside
> which it is now physically impossible for me to breathe, to worship, to
> *believe.*[31]

A world in need of reconciliation

Yet a biologist like Charles Birch can also conclude: 'For many
people in his time the world was a dualism. Not so for Paul. God is
the God of "all things". Nature as well as human history is the theatre
of grace.' [32] The work of theoreticians and scientists on the origin
and fate of the Universe as we know it (as distinct from the unknown universe) depths our appreciation of the vastness of the
mystery, if not achieving a Christological interpretation in the manner
of Teilhard. They present evidence[33] for its origin in a big bang 15
(or 30?)[34] billion years ago and ponder its fate either as eternal expansion or eventual contraction in a 'big crunch'. From them we appreciate that our Galaxy containing trillions of stars is just one
among many millions of galaxies scattered across a vast sea of
space, and that even these constitute only 10 per cent or as little as
one per cent of the Universe compared with the unknown 'dark
matter'. The extent of 'all creation' is enormous, the degree to which
its reconciliation at our hands has been assisted is depressing, as the
Earth Summit in Rio and our contemporaries increasingly remind us:

> Is our Mother Earth dying? Consider Bhopal; Chernobyl; ... [35]
>
> Christianly, Lake Michigan must be regarded as groaning in travail,
> waiting to be set free from its bondage of decay.[36]
>
> The key words are repeated every day in the media: scarcity of re-
> sources, traffic problems, environmental pollution, destruction of the
> forests, acid rain, greenhouse effect, gap in the ozone layer, climatic

141

change, waste dumping, population explosion, mass unemployment, breakdown of government, international debt crisis, Third World problems, excessive armaments, nuclear winter ... The greatest triumphs and greatest catastrophes lie closely together.[37]

While politicians and businessmen continue to be enraptured by prospects of economic growth, the environment deteriorates apace: forests shrink, deserts expand, croplands lose topsoil, greenhouse gases accumulate, plant and animal species vanish.[38]

We in the West are talking of the final triumph of our civilisation as though it was now proved that there was no other way ahead but ours. But our civilisation has still to show that it can provide for the poor of the world.[39]

Yes, the canvas is immense, this mystery of Christ and its goal of universal reconciliation and redemption. We followers of Jesus cannot be content to ponder the progress of our own community under God's guidance, just as Israel's sages suggested to their community to widen their perspective. Nor is it sufficient to look beyond the Jesuan community to other human communities on the way to salvation. 'Salvation history cannot be reduced to the history of religions or to the history of Judaism and Christianity. For the whole of secular history is itself already under the guidance of the liberating God of creation.' [40] No, as Paul and his commentators suggest, the salvation, redemption, reconciliation, *recapitulatio*, *anakephalaiosis* that the mystery of Christ requires includes the whole world, 'all creation', and as God's *demuth* we are responsible for it.

Conservationists and liberationists of all kinds are today constantly reminding us of this, without perhaps a solid Pauline basis for their position and wanting us only to trust their intuitions. My wife was recently challenged by an advocate of 'Cruelty-free shopping', reminded that 'every time we visit the grocery store, the pharmacy, or go shopping for clothes or shoes, we vote with our consumer dollars *for* or *against* animal suffering,' and urged to avoid buying not only furs and ivory but also suede, leather goods and down and feather doonas; eggs, cheese and meat products were also listed on the sensitive list. Should she listen to these crusaders? Do they have right on their side when they challenge our lifestyle in close detail? Was Professor M. Swaminanthan, president of the Indian National Academy of Science, right to tell a meeting of UNESCO some years ago, 'If we work for the poor and the penguins simultaneously, we can hope for a better present and future'? [41] Does Jesus have anything to say on this subject, or the mystery of Christ? The possibilities are endless and alarming; we are bound to hear more about them, and should know our position not only on these crusaders and the 'Greenies' but on our proper stewardship.

We can begin with Paul on the gathering up of *all* things in the mystery of Christ, on the destiny of *all* creation (if obscure) being intertwined with ours and dependent on our cooperation, respect and detachment. Details on the practical implications of these insights, as on our role as God's *demuth*, will require — as always in theology, 'faith in search of understanding' — our good sense, the use of reason. One clear implication is a monistic attitude to the world, marked not by dualism but integrity. Spiritual and material, religious and secular, and the rest are binomials, not antitheses: distinction, yes, not opposition. Teilhard, for all the impatience he generates in those looking to him for a consistent system, is surely in line with Paul's thinking in telling us (in his less philosophical, more pastoral writings): 'By virtue of the creation and, still more, of the Incarnation, *nothing* here below is *profane* for those who know how to see. On the contrary, everything is sacred to those who can distinguish that portion of chosen being which is subject to Christ's drawing power in the process of consummation.' [42]

The world and the mystery

With the encouragement of Paul's modern namesake, we need to distinguish secularity and a necessary secularisation (if we are not to lapse into superstition, a creeping sacralisation evident in primitive societies, where medical problems, for example, are referred to religious persons for treatment) from a faithless secularism, recently discredited in communist regimes. Delineating and esteeming the secular, this-worldly alongside the religious has not always been characteristic of magisterial statement in the Jesuan community;[43] yet it is required for sound theology and good pastoral practice on the basis of *Genesis* and Paul, as we have seen, as well as from consideration of the Incarnation. Johannes Metz in his *Theology of the World* (how often do we see and read books with such a title?) makes the case forcefully, even if he might support it further from Paul:

> In Jesus Christ, man and his world were accepted by the eternal Word, finally and irrevocably — in hypostatic union, as the Church and theology state. But what is true of this nature that Christ accepted is also fundamentally true of the acceptance of man and his world by God ...

143

Hence we may say that 'to Christianise the world' means fundamental-
ly 'to secularise it' — to bring it into its own, bestowing on it the scarcely conceived heights or depths of its own worldly being, made possible
by grace, but destroyed or buried in sin. Sin has something violent
about it, it forces on the world something other than its own worldly
being. Sin (and in it the 'father of sin') does not tolerate and let things
be themselves. It itself is not freedom, but slavery, it enslaves everything. It overpaints, distorts, forces, destroys things. But grace is
freedom ... Grace perfects the true worldliness of the world. And that
is why the Church or the historically tangible sign and the institution of
this grace within the world is not the opponent but the guarantor of the
world. The Church exists for the sake of the world.[44]

We shall go further into the relation of Incarnation and world shortly; the Church's role in respect of the world we have developed
elsewhere.[45] For the moment it is worth pondering to what extent
the world and secularity appear in theological curricula, religious
education programs and pastoral preaching by comparison with
spiritual themes. 'Worldly' will remain a pejorative term while we
fail to grasp the dimensions of the mystery of Christ.

To break out of our (hereditary?) dualism about created things,
people have moved in different directions over the ages. Pantheism
has been one option. Teilhard, composer of *A Hymn to Matter* and a
work on *The Spiritual Power of Matter*, has been thought guilty of it
with such remarks as these: 'You who have grasped that the world
— the world beloved of God — has, even more than individuals, a
soul to be redeemed, ... ;'[46] 'Christ has a cosmic body that extends
throughout the whole universe.'[47] So he takes care to distinguish
his position from pantheism.[48] Sallie McFague, in departing from a
monarchical notion of God's dealings with the world and choosing
instead the model of the world as God's body so as to show that
'the body includes more than just Christians and more than just
human beings,' also has to mount that defence: 'It does not totally
identify God with the world any more than we totally identify ourselves with our bodies.'[49] For Charles Birch this ecological model of
God is not pantheism, let alone classical theism, but panentheism,
and is thoroughly incarnational.[50] Birch, John B. Cobb[51] and others,
to avoid an instrumental view of nature — its value for us — and
allow it intrinsic value, have moved to a biocentrism, where all
living things have value; 'deep ecology' goes further in rejecting
human transcendence over the rest of nature and appealing for
'ecocentric egalitarianism'.[52]

Only living beings?

While we can have no quarrel with working for both the penguins and the poor, we could not do justice to Paul if in our responsibility for assisting in the reconciliation of 'all creation' we drew the line at non-living things (ignoring, for instance, the unequal distribution of resources and the inanimate environment, *le milieu divin*),[53] nor on the other hand would we be faithful to biblical teaching on creation if we treated all creatures as of equal value with equal responsibilities. To the human being falls the task of bringing the divine design to completion. 'We may, perhaps, imagine that the creation was finished,' says Teilhard. 'But that would be quite wrong. It continues still more magnificently, … and we serve to complete it, even by the humblest work of our hands.'[54] Discharge of that task in the context of the mystery of Christ brings great dignity to human labour at whatever level and in whatever form. In advocating a change from Anthropocentrism to Life centrism at the WCC Assembly at Canberra, Chung Hyun-Kyung took an interpretation of life, possible for Asian and Aboriginal people, that does not draw the line at 'inanimate' nature:

> One of the most crucial agendas for our generation is to learn how to live with the earth, promoting harmony, sustainability and diversity. Traditional Christian creation theology and Western thinking puts the human, especially men, at the centre of the created world and men have had the power to control and dominate the creation. Modern science and development models are based on this assumption. We should remember, however, that this kind of thinking is alien to many Asian people and the indigenous people of the world. For us the earth is the source of life and nature is 'sacred, purposeful and full of meaning'.[55]

Orthodox theology is more comfortable with this thinking than the West. 'The Church is not a community of human beings unrelated to the non-personal cosmos,' says John Zizioulas. 'Salvation is for the entire creation which is subject to the yoke of death, and until death is eliminated from the entire cosmos there can be no salvation for the human being.'[56]

We in the West must acquire such a holistic theology if we are to make sense of our expanding knowledge of and sensitivity to our universe and planetary environment, and accommodate it better within our experience of rapid change and deeper grasp of our traditions. We need the theological matrix that served Paul for mis-

145

sion in his time of totally redimensioned horizons, as the Priestly author of *Genesis* 1 devised one for his age of turmoil and transition. Less adequate theological models, handicapped by dualistic and less comprehensive viewpoints, will not suffice; contemporary movements will show up their deficiencies. Jürgen Moltmann appeals for 'a cosmic theology which completes and perfects the existential and the historical christology ... The End-time condition of world history today requires us to see the real misery of human beings as one with the growing universal misery of the earth.' [57] If that sounds lugubrious, let us think instead of the joy, realism and acceptance of the whole of creation manifested by those holistic theologians, the sages.

Jesus or Christ?

The greatest of the sages in our tradition, and our saviour, is Jesus, a greater than Solomon and a man at home in the real world. Is it to him we turn for the key to the problem of the reconciliation of all creation? Or do we, as we have done consistently to this point, retain the wider perspective of the mystery of Christ, 'the Christ event' (in the words of Bultmann, Knox, Macquarrie), 'the greater Christ' (Moltmann)? The solution to this dilemma is, as we have noted previously, fraught with difficulties. There is need to be faithful to traditions — biblical, patristic, dogmatic; we must recognise diversity of perspectives while not *separating* historical Jesus from pre-existent Logos or 'Cosmic Christ' — though a *distinction* in concept and terminology would help towards clarification, as tradition suggests. Dorothy Sölle's bald statement, 'Christology is the attempt to grasp the mystery of Jesus,' [58] strange in one who had earlier written a theology of creation, is a simplistic option for one perspective, with consequences we have pondered before.

That definition of Christology and its consequences have, of course, a more eminent exemplar in German theology in Karl Rahner, who addressed our question with his customary rigour repeatedly during his long career. We have noted in him, however, in connection with the question of religions and salvation in Chapter 5, a reluctance to invoke the assistance of biblical and patristic traditions in their diversity and comprehensiveness, with the result that Christianity (=Jesuanity) is seen 'as the absolute religion, intended for all men, which cannot recognise any other religion beside itself as of equal right' and that the validity of other religions is judged to have expired with the apostolic age.[59] A Pauline perspective to theologising — in fact, any explicit scriptural contextualising — is missing from Rahner's ecclesiology and Christology; there is likewise no advantage taken of the great patristic theologians of East and West whom we have found so helpful for developing a relevant theological matrix. Rahner's base for his Christology is the datum of the Incarnation as elaborated in dogmatic tradition, particularly Chalcedon, and developed with the aid of scholastic categories, such as causality. In place of the multidimensional, *polypoikilos*, mystery of Christ, Rahner thinks of the divine plan in linear terms, with Jesus appearing at a critical midpoint, effectively cancelling the continuing religious validity of what preceded him and establishing the only acceptable model of salvation for the future.[60]

Though strangely giving credit to his confrere Teilhard on the question of evolution, his dismissal of creation in place of the Incarnation as 'the beginning of the divinisation of the world' and the absence of a cosmic Christ from his theology create quite a different climate in his work. 'In his major systematic works,' admits one of his commentators, 'Rahner does not explore the relationship between the risen Christ and the cosmos. There is no systematic equivalent to Teilhard's concept of Christ as the Omega point. There is no real statement of the Cosmic Christ.' [61] Those theologians calling for a more comprehensive Christology in the light of a wide biblical perspective and in dialogue with the contemporary world, like Macquarrie and Moltmann, are in for a disappointment.

In his essay, 'Christology within an evolutionary view of the world,' bereft of any exegesis or patristic reference (despite the availability of such illuminating material to be found in Wisdom, Paul, Origen, Irenaeus, other Greek Fathers), Rahner explains what he thinks of God's plan for the world. He accepts evolution as an implication of God's creation of a universe in which the spiritual element in the human being is moving towards self-transcendence granted by God in grace and then glory. This design, because of Rahner's limited window on tradition, he does not recognise as Christological until the Incarnation:

> In a history which, through the free grace of God, has its goal in an absolute and irrevocable self-communication of God to the spiritual creature — in a self-communication which is finally established through its goal and climax, i.e., through the Incarnation — the redeeming power which ovecomes sin is necessarily found precisely in this climax of the Incarnation and in the realization of this divine-human reality. The world and its history are from the outset based on the absolute will of

God to communicate himself radically to the world. In this self-communication and in its climax (i.e., in the Incarnation), the world becomes the history of God himself.[62]

It does not matter so much that this is not the language of Scriptures or Fathers, nor that it does not employ terminology and even categories to which our age can relate. What does matter is that this rigorous (but blinkered) theologising is conducted in a traditional and existential vacuum; concentration on the Jesus of the Incarnation to the exclusion of Logos, Pauline mystery, risen Lord of the cosmos forces Rahner into unnecessary rationalising[63] in place of an openness to the community's full tradition required for sound theology.

Keeping the perspective wide

Those theologians that take a wider perspective, on the basis of a more adequate review of tradition, for envisaging the reconciliation of all creation rather than this anthropocentric view of human history climaxing in the Incarnation of Jesus as the goal of divine self-communication are predictably disappointed in Rahner's theology of evolution,[64] as we are. When elsewhere he makes statements such as this, 'Christ is already at the heart and centre of all the poor things of this earth, which we cannot do without because the earth is our mother,'[65] there is no underpinning from his habitual anthropocentric model. It is not enough for his sympathetic commentators, endeavouring to relate his theology to contemporary concern to gather the cosmos into an adequate theological scheme, to state as a conclusion from Rahner's theology, 'This human being, Jesus of Nazareth, who is truly of the Earth, truly part of the biological evolution of the universe, has become, in his humanity, the very centre of creation. Jesus Christ in his life and death, in his grace-filled human reality, has become a power shaping the whole cosmos;'[66] that remains to be demonstrated.

Developing a theology of all created realities requires a perspective that includes from the outset all things, human and non-human, animate and inanimate, spiritual and material, and that sees their reconciliation being achieved within a comprehensive divine design that Paul calls the mystery of Christ, the Fathers refer to in similar terms, and modern theologians describe variously as Christ-event, the Greater Christ, etc.;[67] members of other religious communities doubtless have their names for it. It is a scheme which

from the outset, in all its dimensions (not solely linear), is Christological in the sense of Christ as mystery and in light of our belief in
the universal creative presence of the Word.[68] Within this scheme,
this developing design for all things and people operating from
before the foundation of the world, Jesus comes at a particular moment within a particular people, and his followers (like me) among
various peoples in the Jesuan community recognise that moment as
a focal point of the scheme of reconciliation, salvation, liberation for
them. Particularly by implementation of the divine value system
which Jesus preaches as God's *basileia* (and others in other communities proclaim as their vision of God's will for his universe), he
urges us to work with him in 'gathering up' all things in Christ.
Sölle (and Rahner) to the contrary, Christology is not simply an attempt to grasp the mystery of Jesus; ask the poor and the penguins,
not to mention the Buddhists and Hindus. Moltmann is right to set
its dimensions wide: 'Christ existent as Jesus of Nazareth — Christ
existent as "the community of his people" — Christ existent as cosmos.' A *polypoikilos* mystery, Paul would say.

Points for discussion

1. Do you detect in your own life and attitudes the dualism of
   the two cities analogy? How helpful is that biblical and patristic analogy for right living?

2. Has pastoral care in our community come to grips with the
   worldly dimension of the mystery of Christ? Think of preaching, religious education programs, Church involvement in contemporary problems and causes, magisterial statement, etc.

3. The Church prays on the feast of Christ the King that God may
   'grant freedom to the whole of creation'. What does that mean
   in practice? Do we have a responsibility here?

4. Do words like 'humanism', 'secular', 'secularisation', 'worldly'
   still carry a pejorative meaning for some people? Should they?
   Are you aware of Church teaching that clarifies the issues?

Further reading

B. Byrne, *Inheriting the Earth. The Pauline Basis of a Spirituality for our
Time*, Sydney: St Paul Publications, 1990.

D. Edwards, *Jesus and the Cosmos*, Sydney: St Paul Publications, 1991.

M. Fox, *The Coming of the Cosmic Christ*, Melbourne: Collins Dove, 1989.

J. Metz, *Theology of the World*, Eng. trans., New York: Herder and Herder, 1969.

Paul VI, *Populorum Progressio*, Eng. trans., London: CTS, 1967.

Vatican II, *Gaudium et Spes* (Constitution on the Church in the Modern World), Eng. trans., W. Abbott, *The Documents of Vatican II*, London: Chapman, 1966.

Notes

1. *Gaudium et Spes* 43 (Abbott trans.); cf 57.

2. *Theology of the World* (1968), Eng. trans., New York: Herder and Herder, 1969, p. 35.

3. *On Purpose*, Sydney: NSW Uni Press, 1990, pp. 84, 90.

4. Margaret Hebblethwaite, 'Theology goes green' *The Tablet* 19 May 1990, pp. 625–26.

5. *The Coming of the Cosmic Christ*, Melbourne: Collins Dove, 1989, p. 7.

6. *Ibid.*, pp. 27.

7. There are those who would quarrel with the soundness of the figure of God in his relationship with the world involved in this prayer for the feast of Christ the King; cf Sallie McFague on the monarchical model by comparison with a metaphor of the world as God's body (*Models of God. Theology for an Ecological Nuclear Age*, London: SCM, 1987, pp. 59–78).

8. Dorothy Soelle makes a distinction between this 'Liberation Tradition' and a 'Creation Tradition' (*To Work and To Love. A Theology of Creation*, Philadelphia: Fortress, 1984, p. 10).

9. See my 'The perspective of Wisdom,' *Scripture Bulletin* 21 (1991 No.2) pp. 16–20.

10. Matthew Fox, for instance, is inclined to settle for this aspect of Wisdom in his (brief) examination of OT Wisdom in *The Coming of the Cosmic Christ*, pp. 83–85, thus forfeiting a more adequate account of 'Biblical sources for belief in the Cosmic Christ'.

11. It also seems a mistake on Fox's part to see references in the Latter Prophets to created realities as a serious interest in them as part of the divine plan rather than simply as illustrative of the general biblical message of *human* fidelity/infidelity to divine initiative or as apocalyptic furniture (*op.cit.*, pp. 85–86).

Likewise his enthusiasm for OT apocalyptic seems misplaced (*ibid.*, pp. 4–5,7,86–87). These composers differ markedly from the sages in their attitude to this-worldly realities, employing them only like surrealist painters as a backdrop to their portrait of divine manoeuvres.

12. James Dunn, in making a detailed analysis of the hymn in *Colossians* 1.15–20 ('Christ as Wisdom in Paul' in *Christology in the Making. An Inquiry into the Origins of the Doctrine of the Incarnation*, London: SCM, 1980, pp. 187–96), is at pains to downplay reference in the hymn to a pre-existent Christ in the conviction that 'Paul, equally firm in his monotheism [as OT composers],' could not think this way, and so he prefers to see reference to the risen and exalted Lord. (The *NJBC* commentator has no such qualms, probably because stressing more than Dunn independent authorship of the hymn.) Dunn, whose commentary would be assisted by distinguishing between Jesus and Christ in the way followed above, does at least highlight Paul's inconsistency or at least movement between the two referents, as we have noted before.

13. Cf B. Byrne, 'Hope for the world' in *Inheriting the Earth*, Sydney: St Paul Publications, 1990, pp. 83–94.

14. *Ad Autolycum* II, pp. 10, 13, 22.

15. Irenaeus's text we now have only in Latin translation — hence *recapitulatio* for Maximus's Greek, both terms corresponding to the verb in *Eph* 1.10 for all things being gathered up, capped off, united (see my *Mystery of Life*, p. 51, for fuller explication).
     John Macquarrie, who finds Maximus especially illuminating on the theology of creation, is struck also by the later words of John Damascene during the iconoclastic controversy: 'Of old, God, the incorporeal and uncircumscribed, was not depicted at all. But now that God has appeared in the flesh and lived among men, I make an image of the God who can be seen. I do not worship matter, but I worship the creator of matter, who for my sake became material and deigned to dwell in matter, who through matter effected my salvation. I will not cease from worshiping the matter through which my salvation has been effected' (*Jesus Christ in Modern Thought*, pp. 167–69).

16. *Jesus Through the Centuries*, pp. 57–70.

17. *Is Theology a Science?*, Eng. trans., London: Burns & Oates, 1959, p. 107.

18. *The Coming of the Cosmic Christ*, pp. 109–127.

19. *The Christology of the New Testament* (1957), Eng. trans., 2nd edn, London: SCM, 1963, pp. 1–2.

20. *Ibid.*, p. 3.

21. DS 3002.

22. For all his Aristotelian cosmology, St Thomas can still devote greater attention to angels in Part I of the *Summa* (fourteen questions) than he does to the Paschal Mystery — in Part III! Paul would hardly concur.

23. *Final Report*, Sydney: St Paul Publications, 1985, II A1.

24. It is interesting that Karl Rahner, in his estimation of the theological significance of Vatican II, does not rate this attitude relevant ('Towards a fundamental theological interpretation of Vatican II'); the 'actualization of the essence of the Church as a world Church' which the Council achieved has no reference, for Rahner, to the world as the whole created universe. His perspective here is all of a piece with his Christological viewpoint elsewhere, as we shall see.

25. *Evangelii Nuntiandi*, Sydney: St Paul Publications, 1975, #55.

26. *Populorum Progressio*, London: CTS, 1967, ##15, 42 (emphasis added).

27. Cf Gustavo Gutierrez, *A Theology of Liberation* (1971), Eng. trans., London: SCM, 1974, pp. 26–27.

28. Hence the crassness of Rome's first response to liberation theology, *Instruction on Certain Aspects of the Theology of Liberation* from the Sacred Congregation for the Doctrine of the Faith (1984), which perversely makes no reference to that key Lucan passage and also omits mention of Pope Paul's treatment of liberation and base communities in *EN*. The second attempt, following the visit of the Brazilian bishops to the Pope, *Instruction on Christian Freedom and Liberation* (1986), is somewhat more nuanced, but those passages are still not gone into, whereas the two cities analogy and two orders of reality are harped on. Needless to say, a Christological approach is not taken, nor is there shown appreciation of the mystery of Christ!

29. *Love Meets Wisdom. A Christian Experience of Buddhism*, Maryknoll: Orbis, 1988, pp. 87–88.

30. Dermot Lane is surely speaking *a priori* when he concludes, 'It would be theologically naive to expect contemporary cosmologies to be able to add new light to our understanding of christology' (*Christ at the Centre. Selected Issues in Christology*, Dublin: Veritas, 1990, p. 146). Happily, he proceeds to give the lie to this presumption.

31. *Le Milieu Divin. An Essay on the Interior Life* (1957), Eng. trans., London: Fontana, 1964, p. 38.

32. *On Purpose*, p. 97.

33. Cf John Gribbin, *The Omega Point. The Search for the Missing Mass and the Ultimate Fate of the Universe*, London: Corgi, 1988.

34. Suggested by two German astronomers, Josef Hoell and Wolfgang Priester (John Gribbin, 'Astronomers double the age of the Universe,' *New Scientist* No. 1802, 4 January 1992, p. 12).

35. M. Fox, *op.cit.*, p. 13.

36. Lutheran theologian Joseph Sittler to the World Council of Churches in Geneva in 1970 on the poisoning of Lake Michigan (quoted by C. Birch, 'The liberation of nature,' *Colloquium* 22 [1989 No.1] p. 2).

37. H. Küng, *Global Responsibility*, p. 13.

38. George McRobie reviewing *State of the World 1991*, ed. Lester Brown, Earthscan (*The Tablet* 2 November 1991, p. 1348).

39. Mark Tully, *No Full Stops in India*, Viking, in a review by Kevin Rafferty (*The Tablet* 4 January 1992, pp. 16–17).

40. E. Schillebeeckx, *Church*, p. 11.

41. Quoted by C. Birch, 'The liberation of nature,' p. 2.

42. *Op.cit.*, p. 66.

43. Hence our indebtedness to statements from Vatican II like *Gaudium et Spes* and the Decree on the Apostolate of the Laity, *Apostolicam Actuositatem*, esp. #7 where an explanation is given of the 'elements that make up the temporal order' (an unfortunate 'Churchy' term!) and its various levels of goodness.

44. *Theology of the World*, pp. 26, 49–50.

45. See my *Mystery of Life* on the various positions, Church versus world, Church and world, Church for world (pp. 53–63).

46. 'The spiritual power of matter' in *The Heart of the Matter* (1976), Eng. trans., London: Collins, 1978, p. 69.

47. 'The Cosmic Christ' in *The Prayer of the Universe* (1965), Eng. trans., London: Collins, 1977, p. 90.

48. *Le Milieu Divin*, p. 119.

49. *Models of God*, p. 71.

50. *On Purpose*, pp. 90–91.

51. 'The new Christianity must substitute a vision of a healthy biotic pyramid with man at its apex for the absoluteness of man,' *Is It Too Late? A Theology of Creation*, Beverly Hills: Bruce, 1972, p. 55.

52. C. Birch, 'The liberation of nature'.

53. John Carmody likewise 'would have a new theology of nature lay great stress on existence … At the center of any theology of creation I would find adequate is God's endowment of being. All that exists, inanimate and animate, non-human and human, depends directly on God, only exists or is real because of the divine largesse' (*Ecology and Religion. Toward a New Christian Theology of Nature*, New York: Paulist, 1983, pp. 120, 118).

54. *Le Milieu Divin*, 62. Cf D. Soelle, *To Work and To Love*, p. 37.

55. 'Come Holy Spirit, renew the whole of creation,' 5, quoting Kwok Pui Lan. For Charles Birch, on the contrary, 'ecosystems and valleys and mountains … are not subjects for moral consideration' because not possessing intrinsic value ('The liberation of nature,' p. 9).

56. 'The mystery of the Church in Orthodox tradition,' p. 296.

57. *The Way of Jesus Christ*, pp. 256, 44.

58. *Thinking About God. An Introduction to Theology* (1990), Eng. trans., London: SCM, 1990, pp. 106, 111.

59. Cf ch. 5, note 19.

60. 'Christianity and the non-Christian religions,' p. 119.

61. Denis Edwards, *Jesus and the Cosmos*, p. 122.

62. 'Christology within an evolutionary view of the world,' *Theological Investigations* 5, Eng. trans., London: DLT, 1966, p. 186. Cf 'History of the world and salvation history,' *TI* 5, p. 114. There is obviously a relationship between Rahner's exclusivist attitude to religions and his unwillingness to move from Jesus to Christ in theologising on the place of the cosmos in the divine plan.

63. A not uncommon remark on Rahner's theologising; cf N. Ormerod, *Introducing Contemporary Theologies*, Sydney: Dwyer, 1990, p. 98.

64. J. Moltmann, in reviewing Rahner's theology of self-transcendence, says, 'If modern "anthropocentrism" really means that the world is turned into material for human beings, then it no longer preserves ancient, pre-modern "cosmocentrism" within itself, nor does it permanently embrace the lower orders of nature … It is hard to see what redemption this Christ can bring to the graveyards of nature and human history' (*The Way of Jesus Christ*, p. 300).

65. 'Hidden victory,' *Theological Investigations* 7, New York: Seabury, 1977, p. 157.

66. D. Edwards, *op.cit.*, p. 123. Cf his *Made from Stardust. Exploring the place of human beings within creation*, Melbourne: Collins Dove, 1992.

67. 'Christ existent as Jesus of Nazareth — Christ existent as 'the community of his people' — Christ existent as cosmos: *Christus semper maior*, Christ, always more and more …
   It is only the cosmic dimension which gives the human, historical experiences of Christ their all-embracing meaning. We can only think of Christ *inclusively*. Anyone who thinks of Christ *exclusively*, not for other people but against them, has not understood the Reconciler of the world. And yet a narrow, personally-centred and church-centred Christianity does exist, with its tragic incapacity to discover

Christ in the cosmos — an incapacity which has made it guilty of destroying nature through its refusal to give help where help was needed' (J. Moltmann, *op.cit.*, pp. 275–76).

68. John Carmody, in developing his new Christian theology of nature, takes a Christological approach with the encouragement of a Logos theology in the Fathers (*op.cit.*, p. 121ff).

7

Living the mystery

Do dogma, devotion, theology equip us for life in the postmodern world? Salvation is its fundamental problem: we are called to respond to it in a more comprehensive way than before, and require a more comprehensive Christology. What are the implications of other communities' ways to salvation for traditional doctrines of sin, grace and redemption? What is our practical stance towards issues of cosmic survival, New Agers, technological advances, bioethical choices? The mystery of Christ supplies a needed synthesis, plan, pattern for life; the mystery is to be lived.

It was the usual cosy scene on the eve of Christmas. There we all were, seated on the grass in Glenbrook Park as the dusk gathered and we lit our tapers, nodding politely to our Uniting Church friends, smug in our sense of ecumenical togetherness and after-dinner well being. The district band struck up, a little uncertainly after its more customary marches, the opening bars of the first carol, and we launched into it.

> O holy Child of Bethlehem, descend to us, we pray,
>   Cast out our sin, and enter in; be born in us today.

We went on for a while undisturbed, carol after carol, easily warming to our task in the summer evening in the bush. There was something too cosy about it. Not just the fact that we were an atypically select group of Aussies, not cosmopolitan or multicultural at all (the 'new Australian' migrants not venturing so far from the big city), all comfortably off, with no vestige of a slum in our village a few kilometres up the mountain from the Nepean River that terminates the sprawling metropolis of Sydney.

Diminishing the mystery

The carols themselves didn't help: predictably sentimental and, I thought, nourishing in these good people the impression that Christmas is what it is all about (we never get together ecumenically at Easter). The gushing comment in the Christmas number of *The Tablet* also hadn't helped: 'This effortless, unfused acceptance of mystery is what the best poetry is about: carols illumine faith, they do not try to explain it and they certainly do not try to explain it away.' [1] That's where the difficulty lies, I concluded: the mystery is too effortlessly accepted, even diminished, confined to the birth of Jesus. The context of the whole mystery of Christ is missing: where are the poor and the penguins, the non-Jesuan billions, the universe and its history?

Just then things began to improve. The band struck up 'Hark! the herald angels sing,' which put paid to some of my concerns.

> Late in time behold him come, offspring of the virgin's womb;
>   Veiled in flesh the Godhead see, hail, the incarnate deity!
> Mild he lays his glory by, born that man no more may die,
>   born to raise the sons of earth, born to give them second birth.

At least those Aborigines lighting their fires 47,000 years ago on the banks of the Nepean a mile or two away from us could do with the acknowledgement of an Incarnation 'late in time'; we Jesuans are mere recent arrivals on this scene, not to speak of a mystery of Christ at work 'from before the foundation of the world'. Does the Aboriginal Dreamtime count for nothing? How does these peoples' experience of God relate to the coming of Jesus?

> How silently, how silently, thy wondrous gift is given!
>   So God imparts to human hearts the blessings of his heaven.

Someone gave a brief reflection after some more carols. O, that we could have heard words like those of Paul VI to members of Hindu, Moslem and Parsee faiths in India on one occasion:

> Your land is the house of ancient cultures, the cradle of great religions, the seat of a people which has searched for God with untiring zeal, in deep silence and awe, in hymns of intimate prayer. Seldom is such a holy longing for God marked with words so full of the spirit of the coming of the Lord, as in the words of your holy scriptures, which centuries before Christ beseeched: 'Lead me from falsehood to truth; lead me from darkness to light; lead me from death to eternal life.' It is a prayer

which belongs to our era too. Today more than ever before, this prayer could be uttered from our very own hearts.[2]

We needed that night to have our cosy, insular devotion challenged and extended.

All of a sudden our complacency was really punctured. Members of the band sprang up as if stung, and scattered in all directions. Our piety was suspended as we beheld musicians and instruments in disarray. It seems that, since last year, the band's position on the ancient clay bank had become the home of a nest of bull ants, who by the fifth hymn had begun to make their presence felt. I thought of that line from Thomas Berry, 'We need to go to the earth, as the source whence we came, and ask for its guidance.'[3] We waited until the band settled down once more, this time on the grass, and moved into 'Once in royal David's city stood a lowly cattle shed.' It was a sweet irony, and a salutary reminder to us on this ancient spot in the 'Southern Land of the Holy Spirit' that we were not alone, that creator God had long endowed this sacred site with life forms and natural beauty that our narrow, human, Jesuan piety does not always take account of in times of celebration and recall.

We soldiered on with our carolling, paused for a collection for the needy, before concluding — more fittingly — with 'Joy to the world':

> Joy to the world! The Lord is come; let earth receive her king;
>   let every heart prepare him room, and heaven and nature sing,
>   and heaven and nature sing, and heaven, and heaven and nature sing.

Devotion, dogma and theology

I suppose I went home that night feeling pleased with myself like everybody else, having participated in a ritual celebrating the birth of Jesus in a public place in our district in the mountains; we had done the Jesuan thing for all to see. Still, the ritual raised those niggling doubts about the adequacy of the devotional exercise in terms of our awareness today of earlier inhabitants of our land, the land itself, multicultural and multifaith Australia: we hardly did justice to them in celebrating Jesus — we hardly related Jesus to the whole mystery of Christ, in other words.

Devotion, of course, follows dogma rather than theology; we can scarcely expect it to be nudging the frontiers of more exploratory (if ancient, well-grounded) theologising. It is theology, not faith's devotional expression, that must face up to the uncomfortable questions and not shrink from them on the falsely humble (but really

159

lazy) appeal to 'mystery' in Agatha Christie's sense. From the Scriptures through Augustine to Anselm and our day, our tradition insists that the understanding that theology brings to faith comes from hard work and study; uninformed faith is a soft option. How many Jesuans, for instance, lack a thorough understanding of their Jesuan faith and religion because of ignorance of the Jewish scriptures due to lack of opportunity or inclination? I meet that all the time amongst Catholics; no use lamenting, 'it's all a mystery' — get out there and learn about the Old Testament (not to mention the scriptures of other religions, ...).

So theology must come up with an adequate statement of the relationship of Jesus to the mystery of Christ if we want our carols, our prayers and other devotional forms also to be more adequate. That is what this book is about. And this is the time for theology to be asking this particular question. The Gulf War, for instance, heightened tensions between Israel and Arabs, both Christian and Moslem, and religious conflicts in former Communist states have brought the religious situation of other peoples more into our ken; theologians like Hans Küng have given up taunting the Vatican about infallibility and the existence of God to devote themselves to the question of world peace depending on peace between world religions. Greenies and ecologists have filled the vacuum left by the vanishing threat of nuclear disaster in our concerns about the planet's future to keep us worried about global survival; Matthew Fox and Thomas Berry, not to mention New Agers, are trendy reading. Our religious and this-worldly perspectives are being pushed out willy nilly.

So the question theologians need to pose is: how is Jesus to be related to this postmodern world of ours, and in particular to the many non-Jesuan religions followed by the increasing majority of its population, and to the ecological concerns for the world's survival? We have endeavoured to show in earlier chapters that these questions have an answer in the mystery of Christ, God's design for all peoples and all things; even ancient traditions could see as much and provide clues for our accommodating these features of our contemporary scene. Simple restatements of older attitudes may not suffice.[4]

Theology's hard questions

On the former question we Jesuans begin with the statement that *for us* Jesus is the Way, the Truth and the Life; there can be no quibble about that, nor does this book represent one. Today, however, the harsh things John said about 'the Jews' who did not accept him we admit to be tinged with anti-semitism, like Jesus' polemic with Pharisees in Matthew's version. We may not today simply repeat that attitude, coloured as it is with the concerns of authors of the time writing for particular situations.[5] Also as exegetes, we must submit to closer scutiny those New Testament passages like *John* 14.6 above to see which perspective is being adopted, widely Christological or narrowly Jesuological: is it Jesus speaking in the name of the heavenly King, or (as usual in *John*) the King himself?

Likewise, the recipe given during the 1991 special Synod of bishops on the evangelisation of post-Cold War Europe was found by some to be simplistic in recommending simply preaching the person of Jesus to a multifaith continent. We have noted similar reserve on the part of some practising missioners to a like recipe in *Redemptoris Missio* for missionary work everywhere. Likewise, it seems strange that a body as open to the dimensions of this question as ARCIC II could produce a lengthy, considered statement on *Salvation and the Church* and speak only of salvation through Jesus, admitting that 'a question not discussed by the Commission, though of great contemporary importance, is that of the salvation of those who have no explicit faith in Christ [=Jesus]' [6] — which is rather like speaking of the salvation of the world and not mentioning the cosmos. Paul, one feels, would have had some strong words to say to ARCIC.

Questions 'of great contemporary importance' like this, you see — and there could hardly be anything of greater importance than the salvation of the bulk of the human race — cannot be dodged by theology, if theologians are to preserve integrity. We may, with Karl Rahner, begin all Christological considerations with a statement that the Incarnation is unique in human history, irrevocable and irre-versible,[7] but we cannot bracket out of consideration those for whom it, Jesus and the Jesuan way of life are irrelevant. Edward Schil-lebeeckx begins his study of Church by setting himself this challenge: 'We have to be able to explain why Jesus, confessed as the Christ, is the only way of life *for us*, though God leaves other ways open for others.' [8] That gets to the heart of the problem, and we must face it, little as we may like to contemplate a conclusion that Jesus and Jesuanity are contingent and limited, not equally necessary and nor-mative for all; all our life we have read *our* community's texts that resist that conclusion.[9] Schillebeeckx concludes:

The revelation of God in Jesus, as the Christian gospel preaches this to us, in no way means that God absolutizes a historical particularity (even Jesus of Nazareth). We learn from the revelation of God in Jesus that no individual historical particularity can be said to be absolute, and that therefore through the relativity present in Jesus anyone can encounter God even outside Jesus, especially in our worldly history and in the many religions which have arisen in it. The risen Jesus of Nazareth also continues to point to God beyond himself. One could say: God points via Jesus Christ in the Spirit to himself as creator and redeemer, as a God of men and women, of *all* men and women. God is absolute, but no single religion is absolute.[10]

To this Paul would add that the question is a Christological one because God's action as creator and redeemer of all occurs, as does the historical particularity of Jesus, within the plan that is the mystery of Christ. We saw in Chapter 5 the Indian theologians, through failure to realise this Pauline insight, having to fall back like Schillebeeckx here on a theocentric rather than Christocentric approach to religious diversity in their country. (Such theological precision has implications even for worship and devotion — hence my unease during the carols at Christmas.)

Salvation the crucial problem

For all of us salvation is a vital question; for all people with right values the salvation of (some) others has always been of concern. As a theological issue, though, only in our time has salvation become 'a fundamental, central and even crucial problem ... the great stimulus within our whole existence, ... the great motive force within our present history, not just in religious and theological but also in secular terms.'[11] It is an issue with clearly ecclesiological and cosmological dimensions. It is also clearly related to the question of the significance of Jesus:[12] is Jesus the saviour of all? are there other ways to salvation? if there is a historical particularity about Jesus, is this true also of the salvation he achieves for us? Is it good enough to say with Schillebeeckx that 'the God of Jesus is the redeemer of all men and in this sense is the exclusive redeemer'?[13]

Vatican II, on the basis of such statements in the Jesuan scriptures as *Rom* 8.32 ('He who did not withhold his own Son, but gave him up for all of us'), is less evasive, though still healthily agnostic: 'Since Christ [sic] died for everyone, and since the ultimate vocation of the human being is in fact one, and divine, we must believe

162

that the Holy Spirit offers to everyone the possibility of being associated, in a manner known only to God, with this paschal mystery.' [14] John Paul II makes this conciliar statement basic to his argument in *Redemptoris Missio* that preaching Jesus and the Paschal Mystery is the staple of missionary effort in all situations.[15] The Council at least admits the practical difficulty of such a principle, and has recourse to other principles for its implementation in the case of non-Jesuans, about whose fate this conciliar document remains optimistic. So the argument is positive rather than speculative: Scripture says it is true. The Fathers could also have been invoked for the argument that we are in need of healing because of Adam's fall, and Jesus' assumption of our humanity achieves that healing. So Gregory of Nazianzus:

> What he has not assumed, he has not healed;[16] but what is united to his Godhead is also saved. If only half Adam fell, then what is assumed and saved must be half also; but if the whole fell, it must be united to the whole of him who was begotten, and so be saved as a whole. Let them not then begrudge us our complete salvation, or clothe the saviour only with bones and nerves and the mere appearance of humanity.[17]

So that 'fundamental, central and even crucial problem' of the salvation of all human beings, from the Aborigines so many millennia before Jesus to the non-Jesuan bulk of today's inhabitants of the Earth, lands us right back in the middle of dogma and theology about sin and the Fall, grace and redemption, from Paul on the plight of all people to Augustine's opposition to Pelagius, from the 'Augustinian' Councils of Carthage and Orange in the fifth and sixth centuries to Trent in the sixteenth and Vatican II in our day, and to contemporary situationist and personalist theologies of sinfulness and redemption. While Western theology has tended to take the model of criminal and judge for this vast mystery, the East — less legalistic — has spoken of disease and healing. Gabriel Daly suggests we think in terms of the latter. 'It is the process of healing which is primarily revealed: we know of the disease partly from human experience but mainly, and salvifically, from what Jesus Christ has done for us by his life, teaching, death and resurrection.'[18]

He contrasts the approaches to redemption of Irenaeus, for whom all the human race and indeed the world is transformed in Christ by *recapitulatio* (p. 163 above), and Augustine seeing Jesus as the bait to snare the devil locked in combat with God and holding human beings to ransom.[19] He also suggests we could emerge from the theological morass if we could relate creation to redemption, nature to culture, and both to Christ; Matthew's angel tricked us into ignoring the redemption of the universe. For those like Raimundo Panikkar, with his notion of the universal Christ, there is little problem about the ways to salvation for all people:

> Christ is the universal redeemer. There is no redemption apart from him. Where there is no redemption, there is no salvation. Therefore any human person who is saved — and we know by reason and by faith that God provides everybody with the necessary means of salvation — is saved by Christ, the only redeemer. This amounts to saying that Christ is present in one form or another in every human being as he journeys toward God.[20]

Certainly Paul sees this process of salvation occurring within the mystery of Christ; treatment of justification outside that context has come to be acknowledged as a Lutheran misreading of him, we noted in Chapter 3. Reconciliation of us all in our sinfulness (what Karl Rahner calls our lack of God's sanctifying Pneuma) and of all creation in its struggle for deliverance is achieved through the *oikonomia* of that plan. Equally certainly Paul sees the healing 'of all *of us*' (*Rom* 8.32) achieved through the Father's gift of the Son in Jesus; all of the Jesuan community's tradition is unanimous on that, and, as Daly says, we Jesuans come to know of the disease partly through the healing Jesus has brought us.[21] The mystery of Christ, however, extends beyond that community and beyond humankind, despite the angel — hence the problem, or at least the mystery we have not always been encouraged to view in its wholeness.

Sin and salvation

So when the carol writer had us sing,

> Light and life to all he brings, risen with healing in his wings,

it is likely he did not share our preoccupations with the welfare of all peoples and their ecosystems. Our responsibility as Church is envisioned much more comprehensively today. Paul's view of the need of cosmic reconciliation, we saw, was visionary and apocalyptic, short on detail; 'Apocalypse Now' is today's catchcry, the disaster is upon us. 'The commitment to justice, peace and the integrity of creation extends to the foundations of the church's identity. "No heaven without earth!" So church life is inseparably bound up with the process of this earthly life.' [22] The dimensions of the problem and its solution have changed: '*Extra mundum nulla salus*, outside the world there is no salvation. Ordinary, everyday history is the sphere of God's liberating action.' [23]

In our lives within the mystery of Christ today, sin and salvation have to be grasped and dealt with under these different aspects. Our response, the response of all people, is still required to the challenge of God's will and reign, the *basileia* that Jesus (and other religious leaders) preached, if personal and cosmic reconciliation is to occur. An ancient codification of Jewish law as Ten Commandments will hardly do justice to the abuses of people and things calling for our response.[24] One postmodern pastor, the Cardinal Archbishop of Naples, has issued a list of such abuses relevant to the situation of his flock; it includes belonging to the Mafia, belief in astrology, extortion, illegal possession of arms, usury, taking a salary without working, bribery, wildcat strikes, alcohol and drug dependence, wizardry, vandalising historical and other monuments, dangerous driving, pollution of nature.[25] Where does sin show itself in our particular situation?

As that catalogue of sins is drawn from all humanity, Jesuan and non-Jesuan, so its remedy, the process of human and this-wordly reconciliation, is the responsibility of all people and not simply the followers of Jesus. It will be achieved by carrying out the will of the divine king, as Jesus instructed his disciples, and as have other spiritual guides. That kingly will, that *basileia*, in respect of all creation can be known by all human, rational beings. We do not need reminding that 'the kingdom of God, the central term in Jesus' religious message, is broader and richer than Christianity [=Jesuanity] and the churches of Christ.' [26] In this sense Jesuan morality is human morality. The great advantage that the followers of Jesus enjoy in access to the rich tradition about him is that they are thus brought into living contact both with the kingly teaching and the king himself. It should follow, of course, that we Jesuans are to the fore in the defence of human rights and the welfare of *le milieu divin*. Can we say that is conspicuously true in our postmodern world?

All religions for the world

It should follow also that all people serving the divine king in all areas of his kingdom should work together to discharge their common responsibility. Churches and religions of the world have not always thrown off an innate dualism and exclusive option for the

City of God to the extent of conceiving their common mission to include the City of Man and all creation; and yet the mystery of
Christ requires them to do so. Edward Schillebeeckx puts it well:

> Religions and churches are the *anamnesis*, i.e. the living recollection
> among us, of this universal, 'tacit' but effective will to salvation and the
> absolute saving presence of God in our world history. By their religious
> word, their sacrament or ritual and living praxis, religions —
> synagogues and pagodas, mosques and churches — prevent the univer-
> sal presence of salvation from being forgotten ... The churches live by
> the salvation that God brings about in the world. Religions — Hin-
> duism, Buddhism, Israel, Jesus, Islam and so on — are a segment of our
> human history and are incomprehensible without this 'secular' his-
> tory.[27]

Schillebeeckx would have done well not to stop at this sign value
of churches and religions; their role is one of action as well. Johannes Metz, whom we recall defining the Church as 'the historically
tangible sign and the institution of this [liberating] grace within the
world,' and who sees it existing for the sake of the world, goes this
further step: 'The Church itself is in the service of the universal will
of God for the world.'[28] Is that how people today perceive the
Jesuan churches, working for the world — or ignoring it?

The work of universal, cosmic reconciliation will require the concerted effort of all religions, and will obviously be dissipated by
inter-religious rivalry through lack of appreciation of the dimensions of the mystery of Christ; it is a Christological concern in the
widest sense, and thus also ecclesiological. Our conception of the
unity of the whole inhabited postmodern world, the *oikoumene*,
must extend to all religions in all countries, on theological grounds
as well as on the basis of the urgency of the task. Ecumenism cannot be restricted to the followers of Jesus; what is needed is 'deep
ecumenism' (in Matthew Fox's words)[29] or 'ecumenical ecumenism,
catholic ecumenism' (Panikkar),[30] inviting all religions, as John Paul
II did at Assisi in 1986, to pray and work together for the salvation
of our world. Our postmodern world is fast becoming, if painfully,
a post-protectionism world, where free trade replaces tariff barriers, if for no other reason than that the alternative is too damaging
to contemplate. The same might be said of ecumenism, deep
ecumenism, between all the world's religions. Dialogue is commendable between religions that concede God's saving plan for all his
children, the 1991 Synod pointed out, and need not amount to mere

relativism.[31] We recall Augustine's universal perspective: 'The Church consists in fellowship of the whole world (*in totius orbis communione*).'[32]

Deep ecumenism

An admirable example of the *koinonia*, communion, sharing between the world religions in the cause of peace and reconciliation is provided by the declaration made by the World Conference of the Religions for Peace held at Kyoto in 1970, described by Hans Küng as 'a world ethic of the world religions in the service of world society':

> Bahai, Buddhist, Confucian, Christian, Hindu, Jain, Jew, Muslim, Shintoist, Sikh, Zoroastrian and others — we have come together in peace out of a common concern for peace.
>
> As we sat down together facing the overriding issues of peace, we discovered that the things which unite us are more important than the things which divide us. We found that we share
>
> A conviction of the fundamental unity of the human family, of the equality and dignity of all human beings;
>
> A sense of the sacredness of the individual person and his conscience;
>
> A sense of the value of the human community;
>
> A recognition that might is not right, that human power is not self-sufficient and absolute;
>
> A belief that love, compassion, unselfishness and the force of inner truthfulness and of the spirit have ultimately greater power than hate, enmity and self-interest;
>
> A sense of obligation to stand on the side of the poor and the oppressed as against the rich and the oppressors;
>
> A profound hope that good will finally prevail.[33]

There can be (understanding but) no patience with the ignorant bigotry of those signatories of the open letter to the *Church of England Newspaper* in 1991 deploring acts of inter-faith prayer on the grounds that these acts 'imply that salvation is offered by God not only through Jesus Christ but by other means, and thus deny his uniqueness and finality as the only Saviour.'[34] Small wonder that shortly afterwards in Britain the Chief Rabbi was lamenting 'a disturbing insensitivity to Jewish concerns and a failure to come to terms with the existence of non-Christian paths to religious truth' and, on the other hand, the Muslim Parliament there was proclaiming, 'Islam alone is the antidote to a morally bankrupt and sick world.' [35] Such hostility and fragmentation of effort, arising from a misunderstanding of (Church in) the mystery of Christ, cannot be allowed to handicap the process of universal reconciliation. I find unnecessarily restrictive even John Carmody's call to arms:

> The sufferings revealed in the current state of the earth make a strong claim on the prophetic responsibilities of *people of biblical faith*. If they know their sacred texts, Jews, Christians and Muslims can all read the current global signs of the times as a call for repentance, restitution and radical change. The 'poor of the Lord' now needing defence are not only the widows and orphans abandoned by a careless, affluent society. They are also the very systems of the natural world, from tide pools to rye grasses. Unless *people of faith*, people of unearthly commitments and loves, step forth to defend the most voiceless of God's creatures, great numbers of such creatures are going to perish, and much of the beauty of creation with them.[36]

We hardly need a biblical tradition for our faith to detect the groaning in travail of all creation (though reading each other's scriptures is good ecumenical practice, of course). Even the carol tells us that 'fields and floods, rocks, hills and plains' await redemption, as heaven and nature sing.

It is in this spirit of deep ecumenism that we may plan our pastoral and missionary strategies for the third millennium, confident that they rest on a sound Christology, cosmology and appreciation of Church. John Paul II's message for the 25th World Day of Peace, January 1, 1992 made no bones about it: 'Inter-religious contacts, together with ecumenical dialogue, now seem to be obligatory paths ... We (Catholics) must respond to the great challenges of the contemporary world by joining forces with all those who share with us certain basic values, beginning with religious and moral ones.' Jesus on the Mount required no other basis for acceptance of the divine king and his kingly rule, *basileia*; why should we? To be sure, acquaintance with the person of Jesus and life in his community bring particular riches, but at this point in human history the possibility of this further commitment is, in the workings of Providence, beyond the growing majority of the human race.

God's reign the priority

It is not always possible for a pastor, feeling responsible for the spiritual welfare of the whole human community, to be as detached and farsighted as the Pope in his words above; numerical comparisons can induce panic in place of a serene theology. Early apologists like Justin and Theophilus and modern missioners like the Columbans, Wijngaards and Bühlmann achieve this conviction by lengthy experience in non-Jesuan countries. From his wide experience Bühlmann regrets the despairing and inappropriate efforts of missionaries over the years struggling to 'keep their baptismal statistics abreast of the population explosion' in their 'thirst for souls'.[37] Today he sees the task of missionaries as 'reaching out to believers of other religions for the sake of a better world.'

> Now the church — the church that is ourselves! — must enter the service of the Reign of God, see its identity in a context of that Reign, and for Jesus' sake take over the function of vanguard, of special escort, of inspiration, in this endless caravan of humanity on its journey through history.[38]

The theological basis of this pastoral strategy for Bühlmann is the conviction that people in all religions worship one Transcendence under a thousand different names. Some acquaintance with Pauline theology of the mystery of Christ would also suggest to him that the missionary is not thus helping a Hindu be made a better Hindu,[39] or making Jesuans of good Hindus, but making Hindus into better Christians — not Rahner's 'anonymous Christians [=Jesuans]', followers of Jesus without knowing it, but formally beneficiaries of that plan of the divine king we call the mystery of Christ on the basis of their acceptance of his kingly rule, which in fact Jesus preached as *malkuth* and the New Testament calls *basileia*, but which other religions know under other titles.[40] There is thus good Christological basis for missionaries in Islamic countries working with the Muslims for the betterment of the people, as we saw Columbans doing in Chapter 5, in the cause of basileic values without concern about lack of response of these people by way of acceptance of Jesus. If we find it hard to track divine Providence in this, we are in no worse situation than Paul at the close of his study of Jew and Gentile together in salvation history:

> O the depth of the riches and wisdom and knowledge of God!
>   How unsearchable are his judgments and how inscrutable his ways!
> For from him and through him and to him are all things.
>   To him be the glory forever. Amen (*Rom* 11.33,35).

The divine plan for all peoples and things, the mystery of Christ, is not resistant to comprehension in the light of Jesuan revelation —

not a 'mystery' in that inadequate sense; but it is breath-taking all the same. We can only admit our awe and gratitude.[41]

Creation continuing

If we do not adopt this concerted approach in the churches and religions to our task of reconciliation of all creation, of all peoples and things, it will in this age of cosmic awareness be taken over by others with less healthy attitudes and less well grounded principles. We have noted even in those with a sense of the need for cosmic redemption, like Matthew Fox, a tendency to assign this task to the area of mysticism, with the effect perhaps of putting it out of the reach of ordinary men and women. Theological works entitled *Mysticism and the New Age. Christic Consciousness in the New Creation*[42] or some such, demonstrating an esoteric vocabulary and impatience of traditional theological categories, and combining arcane lore and oriental spirituality with a utopian dream for the future, further this impression, giving that sense of 'mystery' that Paul wanted to eschew in speaking of the mystery of Christ and our role in it, that we spoke of in Chapter 3.

Paul saw the work of reconciliation as common to us all and very much part of living and weeping and buying and marrying (cf *1 Cor* 7.29–31) — not the preserve of cults and their initiates, much less fringe fanatics. Teilhard, who has been transformed by some such groups into a cult figure (fostered admittedly by his own jargon), was very much concerned about the living of daily life in ordinary circumstances. For him creation is continuing, 'and we serve to complete it, even by the humblest work of our hands ... ; that is to say, we bring to Christ a little fulfilment.' [43]

> Within the Church we observe all sorts of groups whose members are vowed to the perfect practice of this or that particular virtue: mercy, detachment, the splendour of the liturgy, the missions, contemplation. Why should there not be people vowed to the task of exemplifying, by their lives, the general sanctification of human endeavour — people whose common religious ideal would be to give a full and conscious explanation of the divine possibilities or demands which any worldly occupation implies — people, in a word, who would devote themselves, in the fields of thought, art, industry, commerce and politics, etc., to carrying out in the sublime spirit these demands — the basic tasks which form the very bonework of human society? [44]

That accent on the place of the mundane in the divine scheme of things, in the spirit of *Genesis* and Paul, quite likely inspired the helpful treatment of this theme at Vatican II in places of documents on the modern world and the apostolate of the laity. It is an accent the churches and religions ought be repeating constantly for the benefit of us all involved in working for the reign of God and universal reconciliation. Its ecological implications have been well developed by a range of theologians and scientists, like Birch, Cobb, Carmody, Moltmann, Metz, de Tavernier. They help us develop a balanced, responsible mentality that will enable us to keep at arm's length the fringe fanatics peddling their fads on the strength of their intuitions and personal preferences. We are going to have to make up our own minds on ecological and even dietary issues, whether pro- or anti-development, logging and mining, pro- or anti-animal liberation, cruelty-free shopping, and so many other postmodern concerns.

The mystery of life

Basically, what we require for life in the postmodern world is a comprehensive Christology (not to say a spirituality), based on an awareness of the mystery of Christ. The questions that challenge our beliefs and theology are so much more wide-ranging than before. There is also the sense of so many developments within the compass of that mystery in the course of our own lifetime. Development, of course, is not necessarily progress; but there can be little doubt that we in many countries have become much more sensitive to human rights, including religious liberty and freedom of conscience, and to environmental responsibilities, while realising as well the danger of excess and defect in these as in all human matters.[45] We can point to the great series of technological and medical discoveries that have eliminated some, though clearly not all, the physical scourges of humanity, and we can claim to have moved out into space beyond the limits of our planet, if leaving behind unsolved problems of massive proportions, like famine and global warming, Third World debt and illiteracy. The process of gathering up, capping off, bringing to completion all things in the mystery of Christ is observable. We may subscribe to the postmodern worldview of David Griffin and Charles Birch:

> As contrasted with the *modern worldview* which is sustained more by habit than conviction and which has promoted ecological despoliation, militarism, antifeminism and disciplinary fragmentation, the *postmodern*

worldview is postmechanistic and ecological in its view of nature, postreductionist in its view of science, postanthropocentric in its view of ethics and economics, postdiscipline in its relation to knowledge and postpatriarchal and postsexist in relation to society.[46]

At the opening of this book we asked, is all of life — my life — a mystery? It is. Not a puzzling 'mystery' to be solved, but a saving mystery to be lived. There will always be questions to be answered and problems to be dealt with — about life's injustices and the inequality of reward and punishment, about famine and war, fire and flood and other 'acts of God', about dying and death, the past and the future, about this world and the next world, body and soul, spiritual and material concerns; about the sacred and the secular, what is God's and what is Caesar's, about religion and religions, Church and churches. Christmas carols will not unravel all of this. Until my dying day I will have those lingering concerns. Has it all been worthwhile? Is my life significant? Have I made a difference? Or, like the sage of old, am I left to conclude that it's all futility, a chasing after the wind?[47]

A pity if that's what we are left to conclude; for there *is* a pattern, there is that plan Chaim Potok's character was desperately looking for (we saw it in Chapter 1). Paul knew it as the mystery of Christ, God's plan from before the foundation of the world to gather up all things and bring them back to him. Our individual lives occur within that plan, as do the fate and salvation of those teeming billions of human beings from the beginning, from the Aborigines on the banks of the Nepean to the teeming Asian peoples worshipping God in rituals and belief systems you and I have never known.[48] It is a plan that for most of human history was more the object of hope than of clear knowledge. For you and for me the coming of Jesus shed light on its meaning; others have found different ways of enlightenment and followed the royal way of the divine king. To all of us Paul gives the assurance he gave the pagan converts of Colossae: great among us are the riches of the glory of this mystery, which is Christ in each of us, the hope of glory (*Col* 1.27). We enjoy now, he is saying, a place in that bountiful design of God, whose very own life and glory we are destined to share. Every reason for gratitude and confidence as we accept the opportunity to live the mystery of Christ.

Points for discussion

1. Do devotional forms tend to imprison us in a worldview that is out of keeping both with postmodern concerns and with proper theological perspectives? Consider prayer forms, carols and other hymns, styles of pilgrimage, etc.

2. What are some of the challenging theological questions of this postmodern age? Are they being addressed? Can the theological perspective of the mystery of Christ offer a solution?

3. How have recent world developments brought you into closer touch with other religions (Islam, Judaism, Asian religions)? What response is expected of you personally to 'the fundamental, central, even crucial problem' of the salvation of all people?

4. In practice, how can God's reign, the values Jesus preached (and other religions profess), be brought into effect in our world? Take one ecological issue (e.g., use of resources, global warming) and show theological principles and practical steps involved.

Further reading

T. Berry, *The Dream of the Earth*, San Francisco: Sierra Club Books, 1988.

D. J. Bosch, *Transforming Mission. Paradigm Shifts in Theology of Mission*, Maryknoll: Orbis, 1991.

W. Bühlmann, *The Search for God*, Maryknoll: Orbis, 1980.

Concilium 1991/4, *No Heaven Without Earth*.

P. Potter, 'God's economy and the world's economy,' *Colloquium* 23 (1990 No.1) pp. 1–11.

M. Thomas, *Risking Christ for Christ's Sake. Towards an Ecumenical Theology of Pluralism*, Geneva: WCC, 1987.

E. Schillebeeckx, *Church. The Human Face of God* (1990), Eng. trans., New York: Crossroad, 1990.

Notes

1. Melanie McDonagh, 'Merrily on high,' *The Tablet* 21/28 December 1991, p. 1577.

2. Quoted by M. M. Thomas, *Risking Christ for Christ's Sake. Towards an Ecumenical Theology of Pluralism*, Geneva: WCC, 1987, p. 28.

3. *The Dream of the Earth*, San Francisco: Sierra Club Books, 1988, p. 195.

4. Theologians in Central and Eastern Europe are providing a model here in posing the questions that will develop a 'Theology after the Gulag' (title of an article by Zbigniew Nosowski in *The Tablet* 30 May 1992, pp. 670–71) akin to Jewish soul searching after the Holocaust.

5. Cf *Notes on the Correct Way to Present the Jews and Judaism in the Preaching and Catechesis of the Roman Catholic Church* IV, 21A (*Word in Life* 37 [1989 No.3] p. 19).

6. *One in Christ* 23 (1987) p. 158.

7. Cf 'Christology within an evolutionary view of the world'.

8. *Church. The Human Face of God*, p. 43. Cf p. 161: 'The real theme of this problem, how men can 'be blessed' if they have never learned to know Jesus Christ, began above all in modern times, and only in our time is it becoming a fundamental, central and even crucial theological problem.'

9. Of course, equally all our life (until a feminist hermeneutic reminded us of our myopia) we accepted the patriarchal viewpoint of these texts bracketing out that of half the human race. As a character, Sonia, remarks sardonically in Lloyd C. Douglas' 1935 novel *Green Light* (which itself incorporates an understanding of the mystery of Christ as 'the Long Parade'), 'The Bible was written by men — for men' (London: Pan Books, 1966, p. 249) — a startling insight in those days.

10. *Op.cit.*, pp. 165–66.

11. E. Schillebeeckx, *op.cit.*, pp. 161, 232. That seems a more adequate recognition of ecclesial urgency than the later statement in a Vatican document that the current shortage of priests and religious represents 'the fundamental problem of the Church, and therefore the fundamental problem of every particular church' (*Developments in the Vocational Pastoral Ministry in the particular churches*, from the Congregations for Catholic Education and for Institutes of Consecrated Life and Societies of Apostolic Life, 1992 [Sydney: St Paul Publications], #2).

12. In launching the Australian Bishops' *Guidelines for Catholic–Jewish Relations* in Sydney on November 2, 1992, before an audience of Jews and Christians, Bishop Bede Heather admitted: 'Between Judaism and Christianity there stand many barriers. The greatest of these is the mountain of Jesus of Nazareth ... It will long stand. But I believe some valuable inroads have been made into it in recent times.'

13. *Op.cit.*, p. 167. Our Scriptures, New and Old, support this stance in presenting God as the prime mover of salvation; even the Gospels are loath to use the title 'saviour' of Jesus, for various reasons.

14. *Gaudium et Spes*, p. 22.

15. #10, which strangely replaces 'divine' in its quotation of *GS* 22 with 'universal'.

16. Pannenberg (*Jesus God and Man*, p. 40) reminds us the phrase had already occurred in Origen's *Dialogue with Heracleides*.

17. *Ep* 101, opposing Apollinarius' denial of a human mind or soul to Jesus (*PG* pp. 37, 181–83).

18. 'Original sin' in Joseph A. Komonchak et al., *The New Dictionary of Theology*, Dublin: Gill and Macmillan, 1987, pp. 727–31.

19. *De Trinitate* pp. 13, 19 (*CCL* 50A, p. 408).

20. *The Unknown Christ of Hinduism*, p. 67.

21. A more recent student of original sin, who notes that Trent's statements share the dependence of Aquinas and especially Augustine on a literal reading of *Genesis* and an acceptance of the hypothesis of monogenism, has like Daly to settle for a definition of it as 'what Jesus saves us from' (Neil Ormerod, *Grace and Disgrace*, Sydney: Dwyer, 1992, p. 140).

22. Johannes Metz, Editorial, *No Heaven Without Earth* (Concilium 1991/4), p. vi.

23. John de Tavernier, 'Human or "secular" history as a medium for the history of salvation of its opposite: "Outside the world there is no salvation",' (*Concilium* 1991/4), p. 3.

24. It was one of the disappointments of the draft *Catechism for the Universal Church* that while only eight pars were devoted to the Beatitudes, the Ten Commandments received eight hundred! (See my 'On first looking into the *Catechism for the Universal Church*,' *Word in Life* 38 [1990 No.3] pp. 24–26.) The revised text is yet to appear.

25. *The Tablet* 21/28 December 1991, p. 1605.

26. E. Schillebeeckx, *op.cit.*, p. 102.

27. *Ibid.*, pp. 13–14.

28. *Theology of the World*, p. 50.

29. *The Coming of the Cosmic Christ*, p. 7,228. Cf E. Schillebeeckx, *op.cit.*, 189: 'Not least because of all kinds of cultural and social circumstances, the standpoint "from which" we, as Christians — or to put it perhaps more modestly, at least I as a Christian — begin to think is increasingly the ecumene of the world religions and the ecumene of humankind, to which agnostics and atheists also belong.'

30. *The Unknown Christ of Hinduism*, rev. edn, 1981, pp. 65–66.

31. *The Tablet* 21/28 December 1991, p. 1602. Not all Roman attitudes to ecumenical endeavour are so positive. The eventual response in 1991 of the Congregation for the Doctrine of the Faith to the 1981 *Final Report* of ARCIC I was so heavy on qualification as to lead many Anglicans to suggest abandoning the dialogue and to raise basic questions about ecumenical method (cf the article on it by Canon Christopher Hill, *The Tablet* 7 December 1991, pp. 1525–27). Edward Yarnold SJ, a member of ARCIC I, observed: 'The search for perfectly unambiguous formulas is a wild-goose chase' (*ibid*.); Rome and the Oriental Orthodox have been able to come to terms without requiring adherence to the formula of Chalcedon.

32. *De unitate ecclesiae* pp. 1, 20, 56 (*PL* 43, 434).

33. Quoted by H. Küng, *Global Responsibility. In Search of a New World Ethic*, p. 63.

34. *The Tablet* 14 December 1991, p. 1556. Not that Catholics have a clear record in this regard. We recall Pope Pius XI's vigorous condemnation of the ecumenical movement in 1928 in *Mortalium Animos,* which said among other things: 'Thus it is clear, Venerable Brethren, why this Apostolic See has never allowed its subjects to take part in the assemblies of non-Catholics. There is only one way in which the unity of Christians may be fostered, and that is by promoting the return to the one true Church of Christ of those who are separated from it; for from that one true Church they have in the past fallen away' (*AAS* 20 [1928] p. 14).

35. *The Tablet* 11 January 1992, pp. 54, 53.

36. '"Ecological wisdom" and the tendency towards a remythologization of life,' *Concilium* 1991/4, 102, emphasis added.

37. *With Eyes to See. Church and World in the Third Millennium* (1989), Eng. trans., Middlegreen: St Paul, pp. 96–97.

38. *Ibid.*, pp. 100–101. David Bosch, after his lengthy survey of mission theologies and strategies over the centuries, addresses the question, 'Whither mission?', and concludes: 'Mission is, quite simply, the participation of Christians in the liberating mission of Jesus ... It is the good news of God's love, incarnated in the witness of a community, for the sake of the world' (*Transforming Mission*, p. 519).

39. W. Bühlmann, *The Search for God*, Maryknoll: Orbis, 1980, p. 167.

40. 'When a religious truth is recognized by both parties and thus belongs to both traditions, it will be called in each case by the vocabulary proper to the particular tradition recognizing it. If Christians, believing in the truth of their own religion, recognize truth outside it, they will be inclined to say that a 'Christian' truth has been discovered there ... The Christ we are speaking of is by no means the

monopoly of Christians, or *merely* Jesus of Nazareth' (Panikkar, *The Unknown Christ of Hinduism*, rev. edn, pp. 7, 49).

41. Cf the Secretariat for Non-Christians: 'The Church goes out to meet individuals, peoples, and their cultures, aware that in every human community are found the seeds of goodness and truth, and conscious that God has a loving plan for every nation (*Acts* 17.26–27)' ('The attitude of the Church towards the followers of other religions,' p. 140).

42. George A. Maloney, New York: Alba House, 1991. See my review, *Word in Life* 39 (1991 No.3) pp. 25–26.

43. *Le milieu divin*, p. 62.

44. *Ibid.*, p. 66.

45. Cf the list of 'tendencias' discernible in the world today given by Gustavo Martinez, 'La evangelización de la cultura en y desde la iglesia particular,' *Medellín* 17 (1991 No.66) pp. 182–184.

46. C. Birch, *On Purpose*, p. xvi.

47. *Eccl* 1.14.

48. 'The Church wants to work together with all to fulfil this plan and by doing so recognise the value of the infinite and varied wisdom of God and contribute to the evangelisation of cultures' (Secretariat for Non-Christians, 'The attitude of the Church toward the followers of other religions,' p. 140).

Appendix I

The Epistle to Diognetus

The Epistle to Diognetus, an anonymous work possibly of the third century, Johannes Quasten says 'deserves to rank among the most brilliant and beautiful works of Christian Greek literature. The writer is a master of rhetoric ... The content reveals a man of fervent faith and wide knowledge, a mind thoroughly imbued with the principles of Christianity' (*Patrology* I, Westminster MD: Newman, 1950, pp. 251–52). Hippolytus of Rome has been suggested as author.

It is that correspondence to the true principles of Christianity claimed for the Epistle that is questionable; the author's rhetorical skills are obvious. In the compelling presentation of a 'Christian' worldview in sections 5 and 6 (*SC* 33, 62–66), traces of the dualism of the period obtrude, aggravated in fact by the rhetorical style. Augustine will imbibe this neoplatonic otherworldliness enthusiastically from Latin translations of Plotinus while a young man in Milan, his biographer tells us (P. Brown, *Augustine of Hippo. A Biography*, pp. 91ff); from Augustine all of us in the West have imbibed it, unfortunately.

> Christians are not distinguished from other people by either country, speech or customs. They do not dwell in cities of their own; they use no peculiar language; they develop no unusual lifestyle. To be sure, this teaching of theirs is no discovery due to imagination or speculation of inquisitive people; nor do they, as some others do, propound any doctrine of human origin. Yet while they settle in both Greek and non-Greek cities, as each one's lot is cast, and conform to local customs in dress, diet and lifestyle generally, they give evidence of a pattern of living that is remarkable and quite paradoxical.

They reside in their respective countries, but as aliens; they take part in everything as citizens, and put up with everything as foreigners; every foreign land is their home, and every home a foreign land. They marry like everyone else, and have families; but they do not expose their children. They keep a common table, not a common bed. They find themselves in the flesh, but do not live according to the flesh. They spend their days on earth, but their citizenship is in heaven. They obey the laws set down, but in their own lives surpass the laws. They love all people, and are persecuted by all. They are unknown, but are condemned; they are put to death, and yet enjoy life. They are poor, and enrich many; destitute of everything, they abound in everything. They are dishonoured, and in their dishonour achieve glory. They are calumniated, and are vindicated. They are reviled, and they bless; they are insulted, and render honour. They do good, yet are penalised as evildoers; when penalised, they rejoice because they are restored to life. The Jews make war upon them as foreigners; the Greeks persecute them; and those who hate them have no reason to cite for their enmity.

To say it briefly: what the soul is in the body, that Christians are in the world. The soul is spread through all the members of the body, and the Christians through the cities of the world. The soul dwells in the body, but is not part of the body; so Christians dwell in the world, but are not of the world. Itself invisible, the soul is kept a prisoner in the visible body; so Christians are recognised as living in the world, but their religion remains invisible. The flesh, though suffering no injury from the soul, yet hates and makes war on it, because it is hindered from indulging its inclinations; so too the world, though suffering no injury from Christians, hates them because they oppose its inclinations. The soul loves the flesh that hates it, and its limbs; so, too, Christians love those that hate them. The soul is enclosed within the body, yet it is it that holds the body together; so, too, Christians are shut up in the world as in a prison, yet are the very ones that hold the world together. Immortal, the soul dwells in a mortal abode; so, too, Christians, though residing as strangers among corruptible things, look forward to incorruptibility in heaven. The soul, when starved of food and drink, prospers; so, too, Christians, when punished, prosper daily more and more.

Such is the important post to which God has assigned them, and they are not free to desert it.

Appendix II

Composition of the Old Testament:
A timeline of key figures, events, authors

PATRIARCHS

Fall of Troy

Rome

Homer

MOSES

JUDGES   SAUL
         DAVID
         SOLOMON

ALEXANDER

EZRA   MACCABEES

ROMANS

Destruction
of Temple

Exodus

Monarchy

Northern | Fall of
          Samaria

Southern | Babylonian
           Exile

| 1900 | 1800 | 1700 | 1600 | 1500 | 1400 | 1300 | 1200 | 1100 | 1000 | 900 | 800 | 700 | 600 | 500 | 400 | 300 | 200 | 100 | | 100 | 200 |

O L D

c o m p o s i t i o n   o f   T o r a h

Former Prophets (Deuteronomist)

Chronicler

T E S T A M E N T

Amos
Hosea
Micah
I Isaiah

Jeremiah
Habakkuk
Ezekiel

Zephaniah
Nahum

II Isaiah III

Other prophets

N E W

T E S T A M E N T

P r o v e r b s

P s a l m s

Job

Sirach

Ecclesiastes

Wisdom

Appendix III

Composition of the New Testament: A timeline of key figures, events, authors

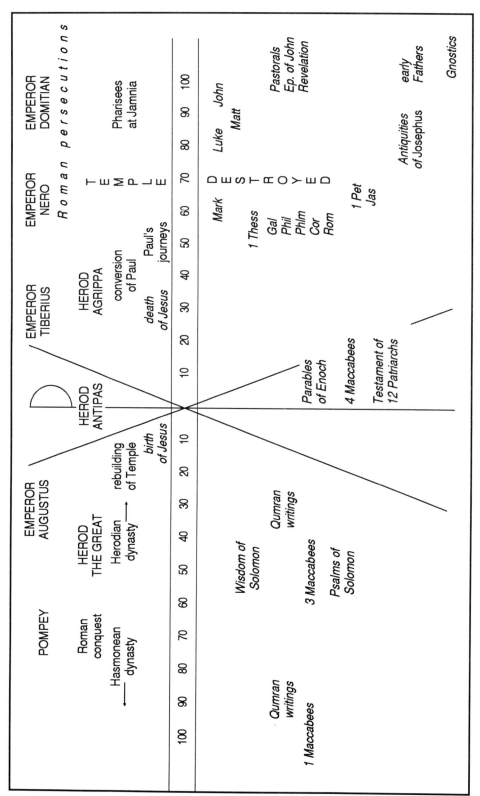

Glossary

APOCALYPTIC literature (in the Bible, for instance) endeavours to provide special access to revelation (Grk *apocalypsis*) through a series of visions, dreams, exotic imagery dealing especially with the world's end.

The APOPHATIC tradition in theology stresses what cannot be known (about God, for example), thus proceeding rather by way of negatives than by demonstration of positives.

ARCIC (Anglican-Roman Catholic International Commission), established in 1966 by Pope Paul VI and Archbishop Michael Ramsey of Canterbury, produced a series of joint statements collected in *The Final Report* (1981). ARCIC II has continued to meet.

BASILEIA is the word that appears constantly on Jesus' lips in the Greek New Testament (usually, but often unhappily, translated 'kingdom') for God's reign and value system that he comes to inaugurate.

BIOCENTRIC means life-centred, concerned for all living things, as opposed to concentrating on the human being alone, ANTHROPOCENTRIC.

CANON, a Greek word for yardstick or norm (cf Canon Law), is applied to that group of scriptural works found normative for a particular community, e.g., Jews, Orthodox, Catholics, Protestants.

CHRISTOLOGY is the branch of theology that studies the life, ministry, person and significance of Jesus as well as the broader dimensions of the mystery of Christ.

COMMUNION is from the Latin for sharing, fellowship, participation (Grk *koinonia*). It is used in a particular sense for sharing in the body and blood of the Lord.

COSMOS, a Greek word for the whole universe, is also used in the New Testament for this world and/or the people in it. Philosophers devise a COSMOLOGY to account for the makeup of the universe.

DEMYTHOLOGISING is the process of distinguishing the myth, or figurative overlay, that in the course of time or literary composition has been applied to a person or event highlighting its significance.

DOMINICAL, an adjective from Lat. *dominus*, 'lord', is applied to sayings of the Lord Jesus in the New Testament to distinguish them from others.

DUALISM, from Lat. *duo*, 'two', is a philosophical approach that tends to separate and even oppose what should rather be integrated, e.g., spirit and matter, soul and body.

ECCLESIA is a Greek (and then Latin) word for Church. ECCLESIOLOGY studies the Church or ECCLESIAL matters.

ECUMENICAL, an adjective from Grk *oikoumene*, 'the inhabited (lit. 'housed') part of the world' (Grk *oikos*, 'house'), has the meaning universal (when applied to Church Councils) or embracing all religious groups and not simply one's own.

ESCHATOLOGICAL, an adjective from Grk *eschaton*, 'last thing, end, goal', has the sense of looking towards or moving to the goal instead of remaining static.

EXEGESIS is the Greek term for explanation, applied especially to the Scriptures, a process by which the EXEGETE brings linguistic, historical and literary skills to bear on the text.

FATHERS (of the Church) were the great spokesmen and teachers in the first eight centuries of Christianity, East and West, whose theological works are extant. Few women's works have been preserved.

GAUDIUM ET SPES, lit. 'Joy and Hope', is the title of Vatican II's Constitution on the Church in the modern world, which is thus optimistic in tone.

HYPOSTASIS is a Greek word which can mean person; so we speak of the HYPOSTATIC union by which in the person of Jesus divine and human natures are united. HYPOSTATISATION (e.g., of the figure of Wisdom in biblical works) would therefore be more than personification, a mere figure of speech.

IMMANENCE, from the Latin for remaining within, is one of the divine attributes by which God is present within his world and not simply superior to it. Denying the latter and emphasising only the former is known as IMMANENTISM.

INCARNATIONAL theology stresses God's sacramental way of dealing with us so that spiritual goods come to us through tangible realities (Jesus, the Church, the Bible, the Eucharist, daily events, etc.).

JOHANNINE, the adjective from John, is applied to the New Testament works bearing that name.

KINGDOM, the usual (if inadequate) translation of *basileia* in the New Testament, is there less a geographical or political entity than the reign of God and his will and values that Jesus comes to inaugurate, in keeping with the Old Testament's picture of Yahweh as king.

KOINONIA, Greek for sharing, fellowship, participation, communion. The New Testament uses it of God's sharing life with us, and our sharing with others.

LUMEN GENTIUM (Lat. for 'light of the nations') is the title of Vatican II's Constitution on the Church, where Christ and by implication the Church are said to attract all peoples (a phrase used by the prophet Second Isaiah [42.6] of the Suffering Servant).

MAGISTERIUM, Lat. for the office of teacher (*magister*), is applied to those who teach by right of office in the Church, especially (but not exclusively) pope and bishops.

MINISTRY, from the Latin for service (Grk *diakonia*), is spoken of in the New Testament in reference to Jesus' life and the contribution of Christians in the areas of faith, life and worship as a result of gifts given to them for the benefit of the community. In the course of time some MINISTERS were ordained and vested with authority.

A MODEL in theology, as in other sciences, is an image or analogy that has the capacity to assist in explanation of the whole reality (such as the servant model of Church, the model of Jesus as liberator).

MODERNISM is a term applied to the teaching of some Catholic scholars a century ago who wanted the Church to come to terms with scientific, critical and historical developments in the world following the Enlightenment. Their particular approach was condemned by Pius X.

MONISM, as distinct from DUALISM, is the tendency to avoid unnecessary dichotomies and oppositions.

MYTH, in theological language, is a figurative overlay applied to persons or events in an effort to make their significance clearer. The term does not, therefore, denote falsity or fiction, though a myth may be stronger on truth than on fact.

ORTHODOX (lit. 'having correct beliefs') is the name applied to Eastern Christians who are not in union with the patriarch of the Western, Roman see.

PASCHAL is the adjective for the celebration of Easter, the Christian Passover (Heb. *Pesach*). The Paschal Mystery is therefore the great saving reality which is Jesus' death, resurrection, exaltation.

PATRIARCHAL: dealing with the founding fathers, the PATRIARCHS, and the biblical narratives that record their lives.

PATRISTIC theology and literature come from the Fathers (Lat. *pater*), those great spokesmen in the first eight centuries of the Christian Church, East and West.

PAULINE literature is that attributed to the apostle Paul; those letters that can be more closely associated with his own literary activity are called PROTO-PAULINE, others less closely associated DEUTERO-PAULINE.

PLURALISM in cultures and religions admits the existence of diversity, resisting acceptance of only one valid form (exclusivism) while not necessarily allowing all forms equal value (relativism).

POSTMODERN is the term applied by some to developments and trends — in history, philosophy, science, the arts, etc. — occurring since about the First World War, suggesting the modern period expired then.

SAPIENTIAL is the adjective for the Wisdom (Lat. *sapientia*) literature (of the Bible, for example).

SECULARISATION is the process of recognising the true character of secular, this-worldly realities, as distinct from SECULARISM, which denies the existence of any supernatural realities at all.

SUBORDINATIONIST tendencies in Christology over the ages have represented the Son as inferior to the Father.

SYNOD (Grk 'coming together, meeting') is an assembly of a diocese or the whole Church. Since Vatican II there has been a Synod of Bishops in Rome about every three years.

SYNOPTIC (Grk 'looking together') is the name applied to the Gospels of Matthew, Mark and Luke, who have a similar viewpoint on the life and ministry of Jesus by comparison with John.

TEMPORAL, of this time (Lat. *tempus*), as distinct from eternal, is a word applied to this-worldly realities.

TRADITION (Lat. *tradere*, 'hand on') is the process by which the community hands on — through scripture, in worship, by teaching, in catechesis, etc. — its basic experiences.

TRANSCENDENCE, as distinct from immanence, is that divine attribute by which God surpasses all human categories.

TYPOLOGY is an approach to interpreting the Old Testament, for example, by which some person or event is seen as a type (Grk *typos*, 'imprint, outline') of some future reality (anti-type).

WISDOM is a perspective that characterises certain books of the Bible, for example. One such book is actually called *Wisdom (of Solomon)*.

General index

Abel, 38,106
Aborigine, 3,10,13,15,21,92,119,128, 139,145
Abraham, 9,19,60,106,118
Achior, 55
AD, 13,14,40,60,70,71,104
Adam, 163
Adamson, H., 128
Aeschylus, 112
Africa, 6,13,93,128,133
AIDS, 3
A'Kempis, T., 131,132,135
Alexandria, 51,87
Alice Springs, 128
Americas, 133
Ammonite, 55
anakephalaiosis, 136,142
anamnesis, 166
angel, 16,18,30,50,62,67,131,135,164
Anselm, 39,160
anthropocentrism, 145,148,154,183
antidocetic, 88
Antioch, 32,86,89
anti-semitism, 161
apocalyptic, 27,32,50,68,75,135,151, 164,183
apocrypha, 74
Apollinarius, 175
Apologists, 32,77,82,85,97,104,112,121
apophatic, 39,183
Apostolicam Actuositatem, 153,171
Arab, 4,160
Arameans, 52,108
Aristotle, 137,152
Asia, 2,33,74,82,93,107,116,124,128, 133,139,145

assimilationist, 119,128
Assisi, 2,166
astrology, 10
astrophysics, 141
Athanasius, 36,87,113,127
atheism, 117
Athenagoras, 4,107
atonement, 136
Augustine, 10,36,38,39,86,106,112, 131,160,163,167,175,179
Australia, 3,49,91,119,132,133,157, 159,174
Autolycus, 32,43,86,112,114,136,151
Ayatullah Khomeini, 77
Aztec, 91,92

Badawi, Z., 118
Baha'i, 119,167
baptism, 80
Barclay, W., 31,43
Barnes, M., 115,118,122,127
Barr, J., 71,73
Barrett, C. K., 30
Barth, K., 115,127
Barth, M., 38
basileus, 83
Beatitudes, 82,90
BC, 13,14,70,71,104
Bellarmine, R., 33,106,107,109
Bentivegna, J., 98
berith, 72
Berry, T., 159,160,173
Bethlehem, 157
Bhagavad Gita, 101
Bhopal, 141
Big Bang, 141

Index of biblical citations